Planning for Children's Play and Learning

Praise for 3rd Edition:

'Experienced practitioners and students will find a host of new ideas to help them create interesting environments and starting points to promote young children's learning.' – *Early Years Update, April 2009*

'*Planning for Children's Play and Learning* includes practical guidance and ideas on creating stimulating learning environments indoors and outdoors, planning exciting learning experiences.' – *Early Years Update, September 2009.*

This new edition of *Planning for Children's Play and Learning* has been fully updated to reflect the revised Early Years Foundation Stage and in line with current policy and practice. It recognises the importance of play as a context for teaching, learning and assessment and links theory with practical examples to show practitioners how they can best support the children in their care.

With new material on learning stories, language development, ICT and the home learning environment, the book includes practical guidance and ideas on:

- creating stimulating learning environments indoors and out
- planning exciting focus activities and experiences
- responding to children's individual interests and supporting personalised learning
- sound observational practice and how to assess children's learning and development within the EYFS framework
- developing genuine partnerships with parents and learning links with home.

Incorporating 'Key Points for Good Practice' within each chapter, and direct links to the EYFS, this is a key text for all practitioners working with children in the later stages of the EYFS. It is also ideal for students pursuing Qualified Teacher Status in the Early Years and EYT Status, and for those enrolled in courses in Early Childhood Studies and Foundation Degrees in Early Years.

Jane Drake is an experienced nursery teacher with Early Years Professional Status who has worked for many years in schools and has supported settings across the private, voluntary and independent sectors. She is currently working as an Early Years Consultant and as a Lead Children's Centre teacher in Leeds. Jane has been a writer within the field of Early Years Foundation Stage practice for over ten years.

Planning for Children's Play and Learning

Meeting children's needs in the later stages of the EYFS

Fourth Edition

Jane Drake

Routledge
Taylor & Francis Group

LONDON AND NEW YORK

This edition published 2014
by Routledge
2 Park Square, Milton Park, Abingdon, Oxon OX14 4RN

and by Routledge
711 Third Avenue, New York, NY 10017

Routledge is an imprint of the Taylor & Francis Group, an informa business

First edition published 2001 by Routledge
Third edition published 2009 by Routledge

British Library Cataloguing in Publication Data
A catalogue record for this book is available from the British Library

Library of Congress Cataloging in Publication Data
Drake, Jane, 1959–
   Planning for children's play and learning : meeting children's needs in
   the later stages of the EYFS / Jane Drake. -- Fourth edition.
      pages cm
   Includes bibliographical references and index.
   ISBN 978-0-415-63275-1 (hb) — ISBN 978-0-415-63276-8 (pb) —
   ISBN 978-0-203-76208-0 (eb) 1. Play. 2. Child development.
   3. Early childhood education. I. Title.
   LB1137.D73 2013
   372.21—dc23

                                                      2013008577

ISBN: 978–0–415–63275–1 (hbk)
ISBN: 978–0–415–63276–8 (pbk)
ISBN: 978–0–203–76208–0 (ebk)

Typeset in Celeste
by RefineCatch Limited, Bungay, Suffolk

Printed and bound in Great Britain by
TJ International Ltd, Padstow, Cornwall

To Katy and Josh Drake

Contents

Acknowledgements

Crown copyright is reproduced with the permission of the controller of Her Majesty's Stationery Office.

I wish to thank

Working in Leeds, a child-friendly city where the voices, needs and priorities of children and young people are heard and inform the way decisions are made and actions are taken.

The Leeds Early Years and Childcare Consultants team, and the Early Years Improvement manager, for the wealth of knowledge and expertise that they have shared generously and enthusiastically to support me in my current role.

Children, parents and practitioners across the city of Leeds, particularly those who have allowed me to use photographs and examples of their work in this book. All the children, families, managers and staff at Chapeltown Children's Centre with whom it has been a privilege and an inspiration to work.

The Elisabeth Svendsen Trust for Children and Donkeys for granting permission to use their name, and a photograph of their staff and one of their donkeys, in Chapter 4.

The following colleagues, family and friends for their professional and moral support during the writing of the first, second and third editions of this book: Jane Barnfield, Chris Barnfield, Mona Fairholme, Jo Kurasinski, Susan Buxey, Claire Clements, Helen Sefton, Sarah Grossick, Helen Price, Linda Walker, Caroline Hennigan and Jane Donnelly.

My immediate family, Fred, Katy and Josh, for their continuing and unwavering support of, and interest in, my work.

Preface

In September 2008, the Early Years Foundation Stage (EYFS) became mandatory for all schools and early years providers in Ofsted-registered settings attended by young children. In the EYFS, we have had a framework for use by practitioners working with children from birth through to the end of the school year in which the child has their fifth birthday, and a clear message about the importance of continuity throughout this stage. More recently, and since the publication of the third edition of this book, the EYFS framework has been revised by the Department for Education (following a review by Dame Clare Tickell) with statutory effect from September 2012.

As I put pen to paper to update this book in line with the revised EYFS framework, I reflect on my own learning journey since writing the first edition in 2001. After many years as a nursery teacher in school nurseries, I was privileged to work as a Partnership Advisory teacher in Leeds. This role offered me an insight into the issues facing practitioners working in a range of sessional and full day-care settings and an opportunity to work alongside a team of exemplary early years teachers. Our team meetings always provided a forum for lively debate around current issues, policy and practice, and a passage through to a deeper, and more conscious, understanding of what is right for very young children.

Equipped with this valuable experience, I took up the position of teacher in a large, purpose-built Children's Centre in Leeds early in 2006. Here, working with children from zero to four years old, and with managers and practitioners from a variety of early years backgrounds, I began to more clearly understand the world of the very young child in full day care, and our unquestionable responsibility towards children in terms of ensuring and safeguarding their emotional well-being.

Throughout my time at the Children's Centre, the role of the teacher evolved and developed to encompass a number of aspects. I continued to work with schools and other settings within the reach of the Children's Centre developing practice towards smoother transitions for our children. My role within the centre involves me in supporting practitioners and management in ensuring that children have access to the best possible opportunities for learning and development within a context of high-quality care and genuine partnerships with parents.

The Children's Centre, with a staff team comprising many different professionals, offers rich opportunities for reflecting on my own developing role, and also for discovering how roles complement each other and enhance the team as a whole. In my experience, uncertainty about a new or changed role is sometimes an uncomfortable place to be but, when explored within a culture of mutual and professional respect, the outcome is usually increased clarity around responsibilities and a sharper vision of effective practice.

More recently, I have taken up the position of Early Years Consultant and now work as part of an innovative team with a passion for, and unwavering commitment to, quality in early years settings across Leeds. It is very motivating to work with like-minded colleagues, and to have daily access to a wealth of experience and knowledge within the team, but it is children that continue to be the ultimate inspiration. Their creativity and insatiable thirst for learning, if recognised and nurtured, will be the most powerful force available to any of us in securing positive outcomes in the early years and in establishing a blueprint for effective learning in the long term.

Since this book was first published, the role of the Early Years Professional (EYP) has emerged and EYPs have been appointed in a variety of settings to act as change agents, leading and improving practice across the EYFS. My own study towards achieving Early Years Professional Status has given me an insight into the nature and diverse demands of this role. The qualifications of early years practitioners have continued to be under scrutiny but the importance of passionate and knowledgeable leaders is not in question. The development of sound guidance from the government, and high-quality training at all levels, is an ongoing journey towards shaping a professional early years workforce that is both respected and valued.

I always welcome the opportunity to revisit and revise the material in this book in the light of my own developing practice. Although the practice suggested is based on broad principles which have not changed since the first edition, there is a need to update the text in line with the recently published statutory EYFS framework and non-statutory guidance materials, and to recognise changes in the revisions. The 'Principles into Practice' cards, published with the 2007 framework, will again be referenced in this edition as they continue to underpin a sound pedagogy.

This fourth edition focuses on supporting children towards the end of the EYFS, most of whom will be three, four or five years old. However, the EYFS recognises the continuum of learning from zero until the end of the reception year in school and emphasises the importance of viewing children's learning and development in terms of stage, not age. This book is offered as guidance and the developmental needs, and motivating interests, of the individual child and groups of children should be the driving force behind any decisions around planning.

> 'Every child is a unique child, who is constantly learning and can be resilient, capable, confident and self assured.'
>
> (Department for Education 2012)

The responsibility to 'get it right' for our youngest children is enormous and, as professionals working in the early years, we all have a serious duty to equip ourselves with the knowledge and skills necessary to fulfil our role. But we must also remember the importance of having fun with children and never lose sight of their right to a playful childhood. Success at this early age, and an excitement for learning, will enable the children in our care to embrace the next stage with confidence and self-esteem, ready to take another step on their lifelong learning journey.

Jane Drake
February 2013

Introduction

Adults who criticise teachers for allowing children to play are unaware that play is the principal means of learning in early childhood. It is the way through which children reconcile their inner lives with external reality. In play, children gradually develop concepts of causal relationships, the power to discriminate, to make judgements, to analyse and synthesise, to imagine and to formulate. Children become absorbed in their play and the satisfaction of bringing it to a satisfactory conclusion fixes habits of concentration which can be transferred to other learning.

(Department of Education and Science 1967, para 523)

This quote it still as true today as it was at the time of writing, over 40 years ago. In 1967, the Plowden Committee (Department of Education of Science 1967) acknowledged the importance of play, and defined its role, in the learning process. As we scrutinise the detail of the revised Early Years Foundation Stage framework we should remember that the fundamental principles of how children learn do not change from generation to generation. Although during the last four decades initiatives in education have been many and debates over the content and delivery of the curriculum vociferous, play is still valued, and continues to be promoted in the 2012 Statutory Framework as a powerful vehicle for learning. Frameworks, strategies, policies and guidance come and go but children's need to play, explore and 'find out' is constant.

The greatest resource available to a child as a learner is an adult who understands their learning and development journey, and how to support it. The effective documents and frameworks are those that guide and support practitioners in becoming, and being, that great resource.

With the introduction of the EYFS framework in 2008, we saw the bringing together of Birth to Three Matters and the Foundation Stage to offer a principled, and continuous, approach to practice with our very young children, from birth through to the end of the reception class. We now have a revised EYFS framework that recognises, and builds on, the successes of the 2008 framework in setting the standards for early years providers. This book reflects the principles of the EYFS and links practice clearly to the guidance material

Introduction

(Development Matters in the Early Years Foundation Stage, 2012) in order to support practitioners in implementing the statutory learning and development requirements.

The revised statutory framework for the EYFS defines seven areas of learning, three prime and four specific areas. The prime areas are:

- Communication and language
- Physical development
- Personal, social and emotional development.

The specific areas are:

- Literacy
- Mathematics
- Understanding of the world
- Expressive arts and design.

With the designation 'prime areas' comes a recognition of the significance of these particular areas in providing children with the foundations for learning. The prime areas are described as being 'particularly crucial for igniting children's curiosity and enthusiasm for learning, and for building their capacity to learn, form relationships and thrive' (Department for Education, 2012).

'Development Matters in the EYFS' provides guidance to practitioners in understanding children's learning and development in the prime and specific areas of learning. The grids are organised under the seven areas of learning from birth and include statutory Early Learning Goals which establish expectations for most children to reach by the end of their reception year. They are intended as a guide only, are not exhaustive and should not be used as a checklist. Guidance in each aspect is organised under the EYFS themes 'A Unique Child', 'Positive Relationships' and 'Enabling Environments', and these columns recognise the close relationship between assessment and planning.

The three 'characteristics of effective learning', as stated in the statutory learning and development requirements, are also further defined in the guidance. This clarification about the ways in which young children learn, and the emphasis on *how* as well as *what* they learn, is an important message to practitioners. It is the understanding of the interplay between the *how* and the *what* that is so crucial when planning appropriate and effective learning experiences for young children. In reflecting on 'school readiness', a notion which is prominent in the 2012 statutory framework, the characteristics of effective learning provide a good starting point for discussions. With positive attitudes and approaches to learning, children are well equipped to embrace, and take advantage of, all curricular opportunities offered to them throughout their school career. Without them, the effectiveness and impact of the school system will be limited. The three characteristics are as follows:

- Playing and exploring – engagement
- Active learning – motivation
- Creating and thinking critically – thinking.

How young children learn is a complex issue and precise definitions have sometimes been elusive so this clarification, with its high status in the guidance, is welcome. Of course, this knowledge is not new and information about how children learn is included in the Principles into Practice cards published in 2007. These cards have not been revised or included in the updated guidance but are still widely recognised as a sound foundation for good early years practice and are reflected in the 2012 Statutory Framework and the guidance materials. The cards will therefore continue to be referenced in this book to highlight principles underpinning practice.

Other previous definitions of how children learn include Fisher (1996) suggesting that young children learn by 'being active', 'organising their own learning experiences', 'using language' and 'interacting with others'. These four significant aspects of learning are evident in the other reports and studies; for example, the Rumbold Committee (Department of Education and Science 1990) recognised that:

- Learning should be primarily first hand, experiential and active. Young children need opportunities and space to explore and discover.
- Children's independence and autonomy needs to be promoted. Children should be encouraged to take responsibility for their learning.
- Talk is central to the learning process. It should be reciprocal and often initiated and led by the child.
- Young children are social beings and learning should take place in a social context.

> Play is essential for children's development, building their confidence as they learn to explore, to think about problems and relate to others.
>
> (Department for Education 2012)

Recognising the importance of being able to think creatively and imaginatively is key in understanding how young children begin to make sense of the world around them and links into their learning. As adults, we use our creative and imaginative skills every day to solve practical problems or to empathise with the feelings of others, and these skills and attitudes are developed through playful experiences throughout life. In all our planning for young children we should be offering opportunities for open-ended learning and celebrating individuality.

Introduction

Learning is a process not a product, a journey of discovery with endless outcome possibilities. Summing up creativity and imagination is a difficult task but as Duffy (1998) says:

> *Creativity* is about connecting the previously unconnected in ways that are new and meaningful to the individual; *imagination* is about internalising perceptions and ascribing objects and events with new meanings. Creativity and imagination may be hard to define but they are part of what makes us uniquely human.

In planning to support young children on their learning journeys, it is important to remember that play and work are indistinguishable to them. This, again, is not a new concept. Isaacs (1929), in the book *The Nursery Years*, stated that: 'Play is indeed the child's work, and the means whereby he grows and develops.' So, play should not be seen by the adult as a separate activity. For children, it is an integral and necessary part of their lives in the setting, and at home. Through play and first-hand experiences, children are motivated to learn and their learning needs can be identified and met.

However, it is not enough to simply subscribe to the 'learning through play' philosophy. Free play in an ill-equipped environment with little thought given to the opportunities and support offered is not guaranteed, or even likely, to lead to appropriately challenging learning experiences for all children. For experiences of the highest quality to take place, children's play and learning needs to be carefully planned. This does not necessarily mean that the practitioner will directly plan the content, or specific outcome, of play, although a more focused approach to activities is sometimes appropriate. Rather, he or she will create a fertile environment (including quality provision and adult support) that enables children to flourish as active learners through play. An inclusive approach will recognise and address the needs of all children within the provision, taking account of individual starting points for learning. Children should have opportunities for indoor and outdoor play and be able to make choices about where their learning takes place. They should be able to become deeply involved in their learning without unnecessary disruption and to return to ideas and experiences over time to ensure that knowledge and understanding becomes firmly embedded.

'Planning' is a very familiar word to all of us working in early years settings and 'planning' is widely understood to be an integral aspect of good practice. But what does this word mean to practitioners in the wide range of settings now established nationally? It is essential that teams have a shared understanding of how to support children's learning and a rationale for their practice. Of course plans need to be recorded in order to organise thoughts and ideas, and to provide a point of reference and reflection for all involved adults. However, although important, the more formal side of planning – the frameworks, systems and formats – should not eclipse those considered actions taken 'in the moment', by parents and practitioners, to enable children to take the next step in their play and learning.

Where such actions are never recorded they can be perceived as less important than the written 'plans' but it should never be forgotten that the most valuable resource available to a child is an adult who understands their development and who is excited by their learning. 'Planning' is not something that only happens at meetings and well in advance; it can also be the thought behind the responses of the interested adult to the child's explorations and evolving learning.

In conclusion to this chapter, and as an introduction to the main content of the book, the following summary is offered. The aim of the EYFS educator is to provide broad and balanced experiences, and opportunities that will enable all children to develop knowledge, concepts, skills and positive attitudes. This learning will often take place in the context of purposeful play, and always in a meaningful situation, and will be supported by knowledgeable adults. Children will access learning through a well-planned and appropriately resourced environment that takes account of the characteristics of young children as learners and the developmental course they take, and is responsive to individual interests and preoccupations both at home and in the setting.

Remaining chapters focus on the challenging task facing practitioners in fulfilling this aim.

To truly support children in their early years to reach their potential, it is fundamentally crucial for the adults who care for and work with children to understand how children learn, and the key role which they play in fostering children's lasting ability to be effective learners and doers across all areas.

(Stewart 2011)

Planning the learning environment and quality areas of provision

Children learn and develop well in enabling environments, in which their experiences respond to their individual needs and there is a strong partnership between practitioners and parents and/or carers.

(Department for Education 2012)

The content of this chapter is organised as follows:

Provision in the learning environment

The environment that is created in the early years setting should be exciting to children, inspiring in them an eagerness to explore and a zest for learning. Quality provision serves to support and challenge young children in their development across all areas of learning. Through the learning environment, and supported by the practitioner, all children can access a broad and balanced curriculum and make progress from their own starting point towards the early learning goals and beyond. The planned environment also provides the context for children's self-initiated learning. It should enable each child to pursue their own interests, allowing them to determine the direction of their learning and giving them licence to explore and experiment outside of any focus that is planned by the adult.

'Children need plenty of space and time to play, both indoors and outdoors.'

'Play comes naturally and spontaneously to most children, though some need adult support.'

Principles into Practice card 4.1. Learning and Development: Play and Exploration

(DfES Publications 2007)

When planning the environment, the practitioner needs to give consideration to which 'areas' should be included in the basic provision. The physical character-istics of the setting will influence decisions in terms of facilities and equipment available, and it may be that restricted space does not allow practitioners to offer the range of provision on a daily basis that they would choose in an ideal world. In the case of limited space, practitioners will need to plan carefully to ensure that the permanent provision (i.e. the provision offered to children every day) covers the basic curriculum and that the learning environment is enhanced regularly through the addition of extra resources (perhaps on a rotational basis) and the planning of focus activities (see Chapter 2) in order to further develop and extend children's learning in certain areas. The environment that is planned, and the curriculum that is offered, should be inclusive for all children. Of course every child is unique and it is the responsibility of the practitioner to identify and assess each individual's strengths and needs and to plan appropriately for these. However, within the group there may be children who require additional support in accessing the curriculum and the nature of their needs may have practical implications on the planning of the environment. For example, children with visual impairment need to be familiar with the layout of provision, they need to know that furniture and equipment will be in the same place every day and, if anything is changed, they should be involved in the rearrangements. All children need opportunities to learn through sensory exploration but for those with sensory impairment it is particularly important that they have access to appropriate equipment and experiences. For example, provision may include balls with different surfaces and containing bells or beads, books with large print or Braille, tactile clues such as using sandpaper 'labels' to identify a child's possessions, visual props such as puppets for use during story-telling in the book corner and scented water in the water tray.

Any information that is available before a child with special needs enters the setting should be used to support staff in preparing the environment appropri-ately (see also Chapters 4 and 6). Such preparation may include the provision of ramps or handrails for a child with physical or motor disabilities, white tape stuck on the edge of steps for a visually impaired child or the ordering of cotton gloves for a child with eczema to use in the sand tray.

The following areas of provision are recommended:

- Role-play area
- Construction area
- Mark-making/office area
- Maths area
- Water area
- Sand areas (wet and dry sand)
- Workshop area
- Malleable materials area (clay, dough, etc.)
- Music area (making and listening to music)
- Painting area
- Book corner
- IT area
- Movement play area.

There should also be regular opportunities planned and appropriate equipment available, for baking and various other food-preparation activities. Equipment for practising and developing physical skills such as climbing and balancing should be part of the permanent provision, and a list of suggested resources is included later in this chapter (under the heading 'The outdoor environment').

Rest and relaxation

Particularly for children in full day care spending long periods of time in the setting, there is a fundamental need for places within the environment where children can be relaxed and restful. Although the practicalities of planning such areas will involve decisions about the physical environment, such provision is essential to children's well-being and an important element in the emotional environment that is created within the setting. Three- and four-year-olds are less likely to need a full sleep during the day than the younger children (although appropriate provision for those who do should be available), but will still have periods within the day when they want to be more 'passive', perhaps sitting or reclining in a quiet place watching others or cuddling a soft toy. At such times, stimulation and challenge is not appropriate.

Children, and adults, need time to 'unwind' and many of us will enjoy times, often at the end of a long working day, reading magazines or watching television programmes that do not engage us in deep thinking or learning but offer us an opportunity to take time out from our busy schedules and reduce the pace of our lives for a while. Children need 'safe' and cosy places, such as dens furnished with floor cushions and blankets, where they can just 'be', where they can escape from the fervour and excitement of the nursery and 'recharge'. Of course there will be quieter areas already on offer in the setting, such as the book area, but these will also serve other purposes and inevitably be accessed by children who are not ready to be restful, and are still operating with high energy levels. An area specifically designated for relaxation allows children to respond to their own need for rest as it arises and shows a respect on the part of the practitioner for children's individual rhythms.

> Provision should be made (space or partitioned area) for children who wish to relax, play quietly or sleep, equipped with appropriate furniture.
>
> (Department for Education 2012, Statutory Framework for the EYFS:
> Safety and suitability of premises, environment and equipment)

The role of the adult in supporting learning

Before discussing the adults' responsibilities in terms of challenge, it is important to remind ourselves of the vital role of understanding and supporting children's well-being. Unless children feel safe and secure, they will not be in a place emotionally that enables them to access all the learning that is on offer. The role of the key person is particularly significant in ensuring close attachments with the child, and in building trusting relationships with parents to ensure the best possible conditions for learning.

> 'When children's physical and emotional needs are met, they are more ready to take advantage of the play and learning opportunities on offer.'
>
> Principles into Practice card 3.2. Enabling Environments: Supporting Every Child
>
> (DfES Publications 2007)

In creating an enabling environment, the adult should also support children's developing social skills, helping them to make relationships with others and to manage their own behaviour. This support cannot be undertaken in isolation by each practitioner. There needs to be a sharing of information about children's individual needs and an agreed understanding of expectations of behaviour. It is important to develop a consistent approach towards supporting children's social learning and towards managing challenging behaviour. The whole team should be involved in drawing up policies around behaviour and aware of strategies to be employed in challenging situations. Again, unless practice supports children to develop appropriate and positive behaviours, the physical environment will be limited in terms of its effectiveness in promoting learning in other areas. It can be very interesting, as a team, to look at the factors impacting on children's behaviour in the setting. These may include tiredness, being hungry or thirsty on arrival, long hours spent at nursery, disordered lives at home, mixed messages/ inconsistent expectations between practitioners or between home and nursery, lack of routine, too much routine limiting scope for self-chosen activity, upset in the family or changed family circumstances. This type of discussion usually leads to a greater understanding of why children demonstrate particular forms of behaviour and more clarity around possible solutions, including changes in provision. For example, an audit of nursery routines may reveal that children are frequently being interrupted during times of deep involvement in their self-initiated play resulting in some children's frustration and resistance to adults' requests. Staff may decide to alter some routines to ensure longer periods of uninterrupted play. Of course, it would be impractical and inappropriate to change some routines, such as mealtimes, but such an audit does raise awareness of why routines are in place, and that they should meet the needs of the child rather than centre around convenience for the adult.

In terms of developing the physical environment, it is not enough merely to plan and set up good-quality areas of provision – the adult must actually value these areas as effective learning environments and spend time supporting children's learning in them. The role of the adult is crucial in identifying children's needs, assessing their stage of development and intervening in play to support individuals in moving forward. The timing and nature of such interventions will greatly influence the quality of the learning experiences that take place within the environment. Practitioners need to plan adult time in areas of provision to observe and engage in play, either supporting a planned focus or responding spontaneously to children's learning interests. 'The quality of interactions between children and staff were particularly important; where staff showed warmth and were responsive to the individual needs of children, children made more progress' (Sylva et al. 2004).

When working with young children, the following key points will be helpful in ensuring high-quality interactions:

- Be positive and respectful with children:
    a) Make sure that you are physically positioned at their level and maintain eye contact.
    b) Speak in a calm and interested manner making sure that your voice is clearly audible but not too loud.
    c) Praise children's attempts and achievements.
- Be aware of, and sensitive to, children's needs and interests:
    a) Find out about children's individual learning needs and interests by observing and listening to them in a range of contexts within the setting.
    b) Listen to, and share information with, parents and carers.

- Be prepared to support children's ideas and interests by adding resources to areas of provision or by planning an appropriate focus:

  a) Play alongside children and find out together.

  b) Make time to engage in 'sustained shared thinking', maintaining dialogue with children along a theme that interests them, listening genuinely and responding to their ideas.

  c) Support by role-modelling skills and ideas, and sharing your knowledge and experience with children, taking care not to lead or dominate their own ideas but helping them to make connections in their learning.

- Set high but realistic expectations. Be consistent in your expectations of children's behaviour. Make sure that your expectations are always appropriate to the child's stage of development and are rooted in observation-based assessments.

- Encourage children to be independent. Support them in making choices and decisions.

- Use questioning to challenge children's thinking and extend their learning.

  a) Ask open-ended questions, for example: 'What will happen if ...?', 'Why did you ...?', 'How can we ... ?' but resist 'bombarding' them with questions. Allow them time to process questions and to think about their response.

  b) Remember that children may need time to consolidate their learning in a particular area before being challenged to move on.

- Recognise when not to intervene in children's play, although you may still want to observe. Adult company is not always welcomed by children who are absorbed in their play. However, always intervene when play is offensive, e.g. racist or violent.

- Remember that sometimes children need time to observe before they are ready to join in.

  Sustained shared thinking helps children to explore ideas and make links. Follow children's lead in conversation and think about things together.

  (Department for Education 2012, Development Matters in the EYFS)

In order for the practitioner to fulfil all aspects of his or her role effectively, he or she must plan provision carefully, giving thought to all areas of learning and the full range of needs within the setting.

Planning the environment

In planning the environment, it may help practitioners to view provision as a structure which scaffolds children's learning but also allows them the freedom to experiment, investigate and pursue personal interests. Also helpful is the notion of the environment as the 'third teacher' as promoted by the educators of Reggio Emilia. Children should be encouraged to become active and independent learners, making choices and feeling confident to 'try out' ideas in a supportive and 'safe' setting.

Provision should be organised in a way that offers children opportunities for working individually, in pairs or groups, with an adult and for observation of other children at play. It should be constant enough for children to return to areas

---

'Making choices about things such as what they will do or what they will wear helps children feel some control over their day.

Remember that choices sometimes include choosing not to do something, such as choosing not to join in when everyone else is moving to music!'

Principles into practice card 1.1. A Unique Child: Child Development

(DfES Publications 2007)

---

over a period of days or weeks to develop ideas and modify their work. Children should have daily opportunities to become deeply involved in their learning, often through self-initiated activities or experiences over an extended period of time, and this means teams looking carefully at the structure of their day or session. Every time children are required to stop and conform to a routine, their play and learning is interrupted (see also 'The role of the adult'). Questions should be asked as to the justification for these disruptions and it may be that practitioners can find alternative ways of planning for activities such as whole-group snack time. A self-service snack system, supported as appropriate by an adult, will encourage independence and enable children to access a drink and snack during a natural break in their play. Similarly, if children only access the outdoor area as a whole group and for a limited period of time, opportunities for learning will be restricted. Over-long 'carpet time' sessions are inappropriate and also cut into children's time for being active. Of course, there will be occasions when group sessions are planned (although these should always meet the needs of all involved children) and expectations may change as children near the end of the reception year. However, throughout the Early Years Foundation Stage children must be supported as active learners, encouraged to make independent choices about their learning and allowed uninterrupted periods of involvement (see also the section in Chapter 6, 'Engagement and motivation').

Children need to know that some things will remain the same each day, for example that the woodworking bench and necessary materials and tools will always be there for them to use; that there will always be some paint; that those favourite books, or a story read today, will be there again to enjoy tomorrow. They need to know that if they begin something today they will be able to complete or add to it tomorrow, thus developing their own continuity of thought and action.

(Nutbrown 1999)

Displays have an important part to play in the creation of a stimulating environment and their role in promoting learning will be discussed in Chapter 5.

In developing long-term plans for areas of provision, practitioners will be able to ensure that sufficient, ongoing opportunities are provided across the areas of learning and that the curriculum is balanced. An overview of all the plans will show clearly how each area of learning is developed throughout the setting (see example on page 48). The process of long-term planning will help practitioners to focus their own thoughts and ideas and will, if undertaken collaboratively, establish a clear, whole-team approach and commitment to the curriculum. The plans should be regularly reviewed by the team and modified in response to assessments of children's use of, and observed learning in, each area of provision. (See Chapter 6, page 190 – 'Evaluating and improving the provision'.)

Long-term plans should be clearly written and follow a common format. They should be made readily available to any adult involved in supporting children in the learning process and also to adults visiting the setting in a monitoring or inspecting role. They offer a framework for teaching and learning and an explanation of curricular aims.

The depth of planning involved in creating a rich learning environment may not always be understood by visitors, and the 'free flow' system in operation in many settings is sometimes regarded rather dismissively as children 'just playing'.

However, as discussed in the Introduction, children learn to make sense of the world around them through play – it is their 'work' and as such should be afforded the high status and considered planning it deserves. It is as a result of thoughtful and informed resourcing and organisation of the environment in which children play that learning experiences of the highest quality consistently take place.

Planning an area of provision should start with the question: what opportunities for learning do we want to offer children? In all areas of provision, there should be planned opportunities for:

- Practising and refining skills
- Acquiring knowledge, developing concepts and consolidation
- Developing positive attitudes to learning.

Such opportunities for learning should be identified in plans. Also included in a long-term planning structure for areas of provision will need to be:

- Key areas of learning and pertinent early learning goals
- Resources: permanent, rotated, additional (e.g. to support a particular topic or focus activity) organisation of resources and area

- Anticipated learning experiences and activities; suggested extension or focus activities (see also Chapters 2 and 3)
- The role of the adult in supporting learning.

Teams of practitioners may decide to adopt a framework for long-term planning recommended by, for example, their LEA, or they may devise their own. If the latter decision is taken, practitioners should ensure that all the above points are addressed.

Practitioners may choose to display information, such as a brief explanation of learning intentions and a list of key early learning goals, in each area of provision. Such information can be a useful prompt to adults working with children in the area. It may also give parents and carers a deeper understanding of children's learning, enabling them to more effectively support their own child's learning. (Other ways of communicating information to parents and carers are explored in detail in Chapter 4.)

The inside area

Commercially-produced resources are numerous and vary enormously in quality and usefulness. Equipment should be selected according to its effectiveness in supporting planned learning and there will probably be a number of alternatives which will be equally successful in facilitating learning.

The following example illustrates the variety of resources that could be used to support children on their journey towards a specific goal in a particular area of provision.

Area of provision

- Sand

Key area of learning

- Mathematics

Working towards early learning goals:
- Use everyday language to talk about weight

- Bags of sand, empty bags (to be filled with sand and compared in weight)
- A range of stones and pebbles (to be compared with each other and against amounts of sand)
- A range of graded plastic cylinders (to be filled with sand and compared in weight)

- A selection of 'junk' containers, for example yoghurt pots, margarine pots and plastic bottles (to be filled with sand and compared in weight)

- Four identical containers to be filled with, for example sand, sawdust, cotton wool and water, and then compared in weight

- Simple balance

- Plank balanced on a narrow wooden block (children attempt to keep the plank horizontal by placing sand bags of equal weight on each end)

In order to encourage independent learning, resources in areas of provision should be readily available and accessible to children, and should be stored in clearly labelled drawers, boxes or baskets, or on templated open shelving or unit tops (see page 157).

It is a characteristic of many early years practitioners that they are 'hoarders' and reluctant to throw anything away in case it 'comes in useful'. It is true that such resources often prove to be very valuable in supporting learning and as practical storage equipment and, of course, reduce the strain on limited budgets.

The workshop area is usually a very popular area requiring a constant supply of 'junk' materials to feed children's enthusiasm for design and technology and it is a good idea to encourage parents to become hoarders of such materials too.

Other examples include the following:

- Large, transparent, plastic 'pop' bottles with the neck and top removed have a wealth of uses, for example as containers for growing beans, as containers for exploring capacity and volume, as containers for holding water (children mark-making using water and brushes outside). The cut-off tops of bottles can be used as funnels in the sand and water areas.

- Plastic film canisters make useful individual PVA glue containers – their tight-fitting lids ensure that glue remains in good condition.

- Old kitchen equipment can be used for making marks, exploring shape and creating texture in clay (e.g. forks, potato mashers, spoons, biscuit cutters, rolling pins), for investigations into the properties of water and sand (e.g. slotted spoons, sieves, tea strainers, colanders) and for imaginative play in the home corner (e.g. baking tins, plastic bowls, wooden spoons).

- Lengths of plastic guttering can be used to build exciting 'water ways' or 'marble runs'.

- Old car tyres can be used by children outside, as numbered 'targets' (for throwing beanbags into), or as part of an obstacle course.

- Large cardboard boxes (e.g. packaging for furniture or large electrical equipment) make exciting 'den' structures.

- Old, disconnected, telephones can be used very effectively in the office, home corner and other areas of provision to encourage children to engage in interactive conversation with adults and other children and to express thoughts and ideas verbally.
- Wire frames from old lampshades serve as frameworks for mobiles, for example to display children's model fish hanging above the water tray.

Practitioners may decide to make resources in order to ensure that they specifically fit their requirements, for example props to support story-telling or story-making, songs and rhymes such as laminated pictures of characters or parts of text and character puppets (very simple card cut-out characters attached to wooden lolly sticks are effective) or postboxes for the office displaying the name of the setting and session times.

Additional or rotated resources should be well organised and catalogued to ensure that all members of staff are aware of what is available and where it is stored. Practitioners may decide to catalogue under areas of learning, areas of provision or topic areas – there is no right or wrong way here, but the method of organisation should be a matter for discussion by the whole team. Systems should be easy to understand and use and storage arrangements should be practical within the setting.

Examples of additional or rotated resources include the following:

- Story boxes or bags, for example *Dear Zoo* by Rod Campbell (the book, letter to the zoo, plastic zoo animals in boxes or containers and 'puppy' soft toy) and *Billy's Beetle* by Mick Inkpen (the book, story tape, plastic beetle in a small box, 'Billy' puppet and 'sniffy dog' soft toy).
- Role-play resource boxes containing equipment for, for example a hospital, clinic, post office, travel agents and shop.
- Mathematical equipment[1] such as capacity jugs and cylinders, length measuring equipment, balancing or weighing equipment (standard and non-standard), dice, 'spinners' (number, colour, shape, etc.), sorting, matching or counting toys and pattern-making equipment – to be introduced to areas of provision as appropriate.
- Boxes of resources which will promote imaginative play in different areas, for example in the sand area – to create a desert or jungle environment – imitation plants (garden centres usually supply a wide range), rocks, pebbles, stones, plastic insects and reptiles. (NB Pineapple tops make very effective 'palm trees'.)
- Games – lotto, board games, card games, dice games.
- Resource boxes to support individual interests and schemas and predictable group interests, for example, 'Transport' – fiction and non-fiction books,

photographs or models of different modes of transport, road maps, underground maps, train/boat/bus/aeroplane tickets, road signs and equipment for setting up road systems in the outside area.

Some practitioners may be faced with the problem of sharing a hall or room with other groups and this has implications for organisation of the setting. In such cases, much of the equipment will probably have to be stored away at the end of a session and set out again at the beginning of the next session. It is vital, then, that all involved adults are aware of what provision should be offered to children in order to meet curriculum requirements and that a plan is available of how the basic provision should be organised. In drawing up such a plan, it is important to remember that the arrangement of furniture greatly influences the child's learning. Open areas allow children to observe other children working but more enclosed areas can enable them to concentrate for longer periods, leading to extended explorations and investigations.

Developing literacy and numeracy

In a well-planned environment, the development of literacy and numeracy will take place in all areas of provision and will form an integral part of activities and experiences. Although the areas of literacy and numeracy should not be viewed as any more important than other areas of learning, it is useful to look at how provision supports their development to ensure that children's experiences are appropriate, meaningful to them and enable them to explore purposefully.

Nigel Hall, in his book *The Emergence of Literacy*, states that:

> Children should never need to ask if they can engage in purposeful literacy acts. If a classroom provides an environment where the status of literacy is high, where there are powerful demonstrations of literacy and where children can freely engage in literacy, then children will take every opportunity to use their knowledge and abilities to act in a literate way.
>
> (Hall 1987)

The attitudes towards, and commitment to, literacy established during the early years are crucial in the development of children as readers and writers.

In the early stages of writing development, children will need time and opportunities to explore mark-making equipment. In time they will begin to look closely at the marks they have made, differentiate between their marks and then give meaning to marks. Through use of the mark-making equipment, and other activities that help to develop fine and large motor movements, children will gain control, developing and refining their marks over time. Plenty of opportunities for children to access physical activities should be available on a daily basis in order for children to make progress towards the early learning goals for handwriting, for example. using 'ribbon sticks' to encourage movement from the shoulder, using tools such as scissors and hole punches in the workshop.

Children's early mark-making experiences will not always be with conventional equipment such as crayons, pens and paper. They will explore marks using all sorts of media (planned or unplanned!), for example using their play cutlery to create marks in dry or wet sand (see Figure 1.1) or making circular marks with their fingers in spilt milk on the snack table. Although the latter of these examples may not be acceptable to the practitioner, it demonstrates the exploratory nature of children's early mark-making and practitioners should ensure that provision reflects all developmental needs within the setting.

Figure 1.1 Making circular marks with a finger in a mixture of salt and lentils

As children begin to understand that writing can be used to communicate meaning, mark-making equipment should be available in all areas of provision,[2] consisting of a range of mark-making tools (pencils, crayons, ballpoint pens and fibre tip pens, etc.), paper (the use of recording 'frames', shopping lists and memo pads will encourage children to write for a purpose, but plain paper should also be available), folded cards or sticky labels (for children to mark with their name and use to identify work such as models) and clipboards. Practitioners may want to provide two or three extra writing resource boxes in a central area which children can transport to, and use in, any activity.

Young children should be encouraged to use the equipment purposefully and to talk about the marks they make. Their achievements as emergent writers and readers should be celebrated and all developmental stages in literacy development recognised and valued by practitioners. The following examples of children's mark-making to communicate meaning show a range of purposes for writing within the early years setting.

Telephone message (Figure 1.2)

This message was written as the child (aged three years, six months) played in the office. Pretending to engage in a telephone conversation with her mum, she made marks in response to imagined contributions from her mum. During this activity, the practitioner scribed the child's talk (* indicates points at which the child made marks on the paper):

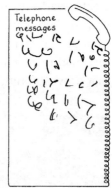

> 'Yes ... yes ... I'm at nursery. Yes ... Yes ... * No ... I'm going to the shop, what do you want? Fish and chips* ... Milk* ... Grandma is coming for me at nursery* ... I'm having my milk now ... Bye.'

Figure 1.2
Telephone message
(child's work)

Shopping list (Figure 1.3)

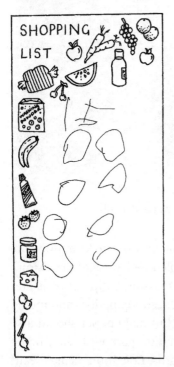

This shopping list was written by a child (aged three years, three months) during role-play in the home corner. He used a circular mark to represent each word on his list and 'read back' the list pointing to a different mark, moving down the page, each time he said a word: '... eggs – bread – chips – carrots – beans – pizza – sausages – apples'. The different marks at the top represent his name. He shows an understanding of features of lists and attempts writing to communicate meaning.

Lion's visit – building a den: recording frame (Figure 1.4)

This child (aged three years, eleven months) spent time building a den for 'Lion' in the construction area. She chose to make a record of her work and completed the 'frame' independently (having previously been shown how to use it). She then showed her work to the adult and gave the following verbal explanation:

> 'This picture [pointing to the drawing in the top box] is Lion – he is in his den. The leaves are on the top. That [marks to the left of the drawing] is Lion's name.'

Figure 1.3 Shopping list
(child's work)

When asked what she had used to build the den, she pointed to the marks in the bottom box and said 'boxes,

Name _____

I built a den for The Lion and his family. This is what the den looks like:

To build the den I used:

cardboard boxes
wooden bricks
paper
material
tape

Figure 1.4 Lion's visit – building a den: recording frame (child's work)

bricks, paper, material, tape'. The child has identified her work by making marks at the top of the page to represent her own name. This example shows that the child knows the difference between writing and drawing and makes that distinction in her own mark-making. She has written to inform, understanding that writing can be read.

Bear warning! (Figure 1.5)

This message was written by a child (aged four years) to an absent member of staff due to return the next day. The child had been enthusiastically involved in an imaginary 'bear hunt' in the outside play area during the morning. He asked another adult to give his message to the person concerned and offered this explanation:

'We've seen the bear. It's hiding. It's waiting to get us! [Pointing to his mark-making] Dear teacher ... there's a bear at nursery. Don't go outside ... the bear will get you. If you want to go out, wait for me and Michael ... we know where the bear's cave is.'

The child also drew a picture of the bear (with sharp teeth to show how fierce it was). A clear distinction is made between writing and drawing – marks (writing) are arranged in strings horizontally and display elements of letters (including a recognisable 's' and 'l').

Broken computer (Figure 1.6)

This observation of a child (aged three years, four months) shows the provision supporting a child's wish to communicate a message to other children in a genuine, and spontaneously arising, situation. He made his marks on a piece of paper on the practitioner's clipboard but knew that, to be effective, they should be displayed for others to see. Because the equipment and materials (scissors and masking tape) were readily available, and the child was confident in using them, he was able to attach his

Figure 1.5 Bear warning! (child's work)

sign to the computer by himself and was clearly satisfied at his achievement. Now everyone who approached the computer would know that it was broken and the child had been successful in his self-set objective.

Figure 1.6 Making a sign to tell others that the computer is broken

NAME:	DATE:
Reyez	16 June

OBSERVATION:

Watching me writing observations, Reyez asked if he could use my pen. He took the clipboard and, with great care, made a series of small marks in a line from left to right. As he finished the marks he turned to me and said 'It's computer name' and then added 'It says computer broken'. He wanted to attach his sign to the computer to tell other children that it was broken and he found some sprung scissors in the technology workshop to trim his piece of paper. He cut across the paper then took it to the computer and held it against the screen. Returning to the technology workshop, he found a roll of masking tape in a dispenser and brought it over to the computer. He tore off a few strips of tape using the serrated edge on the dispenser and used them to secure his notice on the screen working precisely and with energy. When another child asked him 'Why do we need writing on the computer?' he replied 'The computer is broken'. When happy that the task was complete, he stood back and said 'There!' with a big sigh of satisfaction and his hands on his hips.

Although it is essential to provide children with a good variety of high-quality fiction and non-fiction books (both in a designated book area and to support learning in other areas of provision), the environment must also offer children a much wider range of reasons and opportunities to read. The presence of bus timetables, recipe cards, magazines in racks and telephone directories in areas of provision will encourage children to incorporate reading into their play. Labels and signs which inform and instruct should be displayed in all areas of the setting, conveying meaning through the written word and through pictures and symbols.

Cards displayed in areas of provision which invite children to engage in a particular activity serve a dual purpose – to attract interest in the activity and to engage children in reading for a purpose (e.g. 'Would you like to write a party invitation? Who will you invite to the Teddy Bears' Tea Party?' – illustrated with a written invitation and a picture of a bear). It is a good idea to build up a bank of

Figure 1.7 Following a recipe to make pasta in the home corner

such 'activity cards' which can be used repeatedly. Displaying the cards in moulded, perspex photograph frames will ensure that they are protected from glue, water and paint.

Examples of children's mark-making should be displayed around the setting and their work used, where possible, as a resource by other children, for example, plans made by children of their 'construction kit' models, and lists (words or pictures) of components used, can be laminated and displayed[3] in the construc-tion area, or made into books, and used by others to reproduce an identical model. Practitioners may decide to scribe young children's verbal explanations or ideas and display them alongside drawings or photographs of models.

Children should have access to a card displaying their name which they can use in their play at any time, for example to support them when naming a painting or model, or when signing a card or letter. Some children will need to have a picture (probably a duplicate of the picture displayed on their coat peg) displayed along-side their name as they develop skills of visual discrimination. Children can also use their name card to register that they are waiting to work in a certain area. By attaching their card to a carpet tile on the wall in the area, or by writing their name on a list, they become 'first in the queue' to work there. When a space becomes available, the practitioner, or other children, will notify the child.

.Working towards early learning goals for literacy

- Read some common words.
- Write their own names and other things such as labels, captions.

Practitioners should be aware of the different goals for 'writing' and 'handwriting'. In the revised 2012 EYFS framework, 'handwriting' has been moved into the area of physical development (moving and handling) with the emphasis on physical skill for this aspect of learning. Understanding, and using, purposes for writing, however, remain in the domain of 'literacy'. Again, the planned environment can provide appropriate experiences for children in developing the skills required to eventually produce recognisable letters in their writing. The early developmental stages for handwriting include elements such as 'use one-handed tools and equipment'. Threading beads, cutting with scissors, making marks with fingers in dry sand or making circular shapes by waving a ribbon in the outdoor area are all appropriate ways of supporting children's handwriting development in the early stages.

> Phase 1 *(Letters and sounds teaching programme)* recognises the central importance of developing speaking and listening skills as a priority in their own right and for paving the way to making a good start on reading and writing. Put simply, the more words children know and understand before they start on a systematic programme of phonic work the better equipped they are to succeed.
>
> (DfES 2007)

It is essential that children practise in order to develop speaking and listening skills, and these skills are not always given a high profile in planning. However, in the 2012 EYFS framework, there is a clear recognition of the value of this area of learning with the inclusion of 'Communication and Language' as a prime area. The following example focuses on children's speaking and listening experiences, highlighting opportunities for supporting children's learning and including links to 'linking sounds and letters' and 'reading'.

Workshop area of provision

Activities and learning experiences

- Making imaginative and functional models using 'junk' materials. *Explaining how the model was made and what materials and equipment were used* (e.g. making beds for Goldilocks and the three bears – children could test the beds for strength and then *use them as a prop in their own story-telling*)

- Making musical instruments to produce a variety of sounds and *comparing children's musical instruments, discriminating between different sounds*

- Building large-scale models with other children, *discussing plans* and working collaboratively. *Children explain to others how to make a similar model*

- Following written and pictorial plans and instructions and *following instructions from an audio tape*

- Exploring properties of materials and *talking about characteristics using descriptive language*.

Working towards early learning goals for communication and language

- Children listen attentively in a range of situations.
- Children follow instructions involving several ideas or actions.
- Children express themselves effectively, showing awareness of listeners' needs.

Adults working in the setting should take every opportunity to model literacy skills (e.g. writing shopping lists, passing on telephone messages – written and verbal, writing letters, cards, invitations, writing 'reminder' notes, giving and responding to verbal instructions, following written plans, reading stories and information books) and to work alongside the children, supporting them in the development of writing, reading, speaking and listening skills.

It is important that numbers are displayed throughout the setting and accessible to children. Vertical and horizontal 'number lines' should be in evidence and can be presented in a variety of ways.

For example:

- Number train – each carriage numbered 1–10 (the corresponding number of 'lolly stick' puppets can be placed in each carriage, e.g. one rabbit, two frogs).

- Number washing line – children peg numbered clothes onto the washing line in the correct order.

- Number ladder attached to the wall – each rung is numbered and children help 'Monkey' (soft toy) to climb the ladder counting as he steps on the rungs.

- Autumn leaves – cardboard or real leaves (these will be preserved if laminated) numbered and hanging from trees outside or hanging from mobiles inside.

A 'bank' of numerals and number lines in each area of provision will encourage children to use numbers in their play.

Story boxes, as well as offering rich opportunities for development of language and literacy skills, can be planned with objectives for numeracy in mind. *Kipper's Toybox* by Mick Inkpen is an ideal story through which to develop counting skills. The provision of a cardboard box containing Kipper's toys and a copy of the book in the book area will inspire children to retell the story counting the animals in and out of the toybox.

The way in which equipment is stored and presented to children can, as well as encouraging independent learning, support the development of mathematical concepts as illustrated in the following 'water area' example:

Resources

- Three measuring cylinders (a range of sizes)

Organisation

- Children select cylinders from, and return them to, templates of the bases of the cylinders applied to the open shelf in size order. This will encourage discussion of size and use of language such as 'bigger', 'smaller' and 'circle', and of positional language such as 'next to'. 'Upright' templates applied to the back of a shelving unit will also encourage comparison of height and the use of related language. Numbering of the cylinders, 1, 2, 3, and corresponding numbering of templates, will encourage counting with one-to-one correspondence, and matching, naming and ordering of numerals.

Working towards early learning goals for mathematics

- Count reliably with numbers from 1 to 20, place them in order and say which is one more or one less than a given number.

- Children use everyday language to talk about size, weight, capacity, position, distance, time and money to compare quantities and objects and to solve problems.

In areas such as the workshop, painting area, malleable materials area and water area where children are required to wear aprons as they work, the provision of, for example, four numbered aprons in each area serves a few purposes. Numbered aprons hung on numbered hooks will encourage children to match and order numerals 1–4, to use the number names, for example, 'I'll use number 1 apron and you have number 2'. The number of children working in an area will be restricted by the number of aprons available (e.g. four aprons: four children) and children will soon begin to use vocabulary involved in addition and subtraction, for example, 'There are only three children in here – there's one more apron – you can come in, then there will be four'.

Working towards early learning goals for mathematics

- Count reliably with numbers from 1 to 20, place them in order and say which is one more or one less than a given number.

Sorting resources can be part of the 'tidying up' routine and to engage children in purposeful activities of this nature practitioners will, again, need to give careful consideration to the storage of resources in areas of provision. Storage containers should be 'sturdy' and clearly labelled with words, symbols and/or pictures.

Children will need to be taught how to sort the resources and given an explanation of the criteria used. Practitioners may decide to change the sorting criteria for a particular resource from time to time in order to encourage the development of certain concepts, for example interlocking bricks – these can be sorted according to colour, length, shape or purpose.

Long-term plans for areas of provision

This next section of Chapter 1 looks in detail at and gives specific guidance on long-term planning for children's learning in the following areas of provision:

- Construction
- Water
- Office/mark-making
- Role-play (home corner)
- Painting.

Figure 1.8 Selecting equipment in the water area

Long-term plans are organised under the headings:

- Learning opportunities
- Key areas of learning

- Early learning goals in key areas of learning
- Resources
- Organisation
- Learning experiences and activities
- Adult role
- Key questions
- Vocabulary.

These plans are offered as exemplars. It is hoped that practitioners will be able to adapt them for use in their own setting, and refer to the model when planning other areas of provision.

Where space is abundant and the setting well staffed, it will be possible to offer children a full range of equipment all the time, although staff will undoubtedly decide to plan additional resources to support topic work or focus activities. Other practitioners will need to carefully plan the rotation of resources to ensure that children have constant access to equipment that provides them with intended learning opportunities.

In every well-planned area of provision, valuable learning is likely to take place across the curriculum. Practitioners should always be aware of the numerous and diverse learning experiences possible and take every opportunity to extend children's learning in all areas. However, each area of provision has its own particular strengths in terms of promoting learning in key areas, and these are identified on the exemplar plans. Practitioners may wish to focus on different key areas of learning and this is perfectly acceptable as long as the resources reflect and support their focus, and the curriculum is broad and balanced across the setting as a whole. The goals included in each plan are those on which learning is most clearly focused in the key areas.

There will be a certain amount of repetition from plan to plan and practitioners will note that some goals are evident in a number of different plans. This is inevitable when producing separate and complete plans for each area of provision and only serves to emphasise, once again, how entwined the curriculum is with the environment.

'Organisation' and 'adult role' are other examples of sections in which certain points will be common to a few areas of provision. For the purpose of this book, these 'common points' are listed below, and only points exclusive to the area are included in each plan. However, in practice, it is advisable to produce long-term plans inclusive of all aspects of these sections. This will ensure that every plan is useful in its own right as a support for those adults working with children in that particular area – cross-referencing can be frustrating to the busy practitioner and confusing to the visitor.

In the interests of smooth organisation, it can be a good idea to designate coordination roles so that each practitioner is responsible for the maintenance of one or more (depending on the size of the staff team) areas of provision.

Aspects of organisation common to all areas of provision

- Resources easily accessed by children to encourage self-selection and independent learning.
- Clear cataloguing of and storage arrangements for rotated or additional resources and a rota or plans for their inclusion in the provision.
- Daily checking, and replenishing, of consumable resources (e.g. mark-making equipment).
- Regular focus activities and periods of observation planned.
- Key early learning goals displayed in the area.
- Children sign list, or engage in a similar activity, to register that they have worked in the area.

Aspects of 'adult role' common to all areas of provision

The adult will:

- Provide good-quality resources and organise the area
- Be aware of the goals in the key areas of learning and the steps taken on the journey towards the goals
- Interact with children asking questions and making suggestions to support their learning
- Be familiar with key vocabulary – model, and support children in their use of, key words
- Work alongside children, modelling skills and attitudes
- Read with children from fiction and non-fiction books, plans, instruction cards, etc.
- Scribe children's ideas and thoughts and display their work
- Observe children's learning and use of the provision
- Assess children's development and progress.

All long-term plans refer to examples of focus activities sited in that particular area of provision – detailed plans for these activities can be found in other chapters of this book and page references are given for each.

The wide range of children's learning needs within the EYFS is reflected in the planned provision and suggested learning experiences or activities and resources should enable progress to be made from individual starting points, towards the key early learning goals.

Construction area

Practitioners will need to provide as large a space as possible as work in the construction area often expands as it develops and frequently involves a number of children working on a 'project'. It may be that two or three children choose to work individually in the area in which case there will still need to be ample room to avoid frustrations and physical limitations on their work. The area will probably need to be carpeted or a rug provided as children tend to spend most of their time in this area sitting, kneeling or lying on their tummies.

'Small-world' equipment, although not construction equipment, is included in the 'resources' list. Its use by children in this area often results in the extension of an activity and in the development of language and creativity (for example, see 'Jungle Play' plans, Chapter 3).

Children should be taught to value other children's work and to celebrate achievements. An area for displaying children's models (e.g. a wall shelf, cupboard top, free-standing open shelving unit – see Chapter 5, Figure 5.7) should be made available and children encouraged to make a name card for display next to their work. Although the display area needs to be in a position where children can look at and talk about each other's work, they should be discouraged from touching or handling the work of others without their permission.

The following plan focuses on construction provision inside the setting – there will also be rich opportunities for construction on a larger scale in the outside play area and a list of appropriate resources can be found later in the chapter ('The outdoor environment').

Learning opportunities

Skills: Exploring, building, constructing, assembling, joining, planning, problem-solving, evaluating, modifying, adapting, recording, explaining, expressing ideas, observing, comparing, estimating, questioning, selecting and using equipment appropriately and writing or making marks to communicate meaning.

Attitudes: Valuing and showing respect for resources and other children's work, independence, cooperation, interest, enthusiasm, enjoyment, responsibility, concentration, perseverance and confidence.

Understanding and knowledge: Being familiar with the names, characteristics and uses of different construction kits and components, making comparisons (e.g. shape, size, length, colour), measuring length (non-standard), increasing spatial awareness, counting with one-to-one correspondence, developing understanding or use of mathematical language, finding out how to make a strong or balanced structure, using reference books or diagrams and plans to inform own planning and constructing, being aware of design purposes, making up or re-creating stories, and re-creating roles.

Key areas of learning

- Communication and language
- Mathematics
- Expressive arts and design

Working towards Early Learning Goals in key areas of learning (Department for Education 2012)

- Children give their attention to what others say and respond appropriately, whilst engaged in another activity.

- Children follow instructions involving several ideas or actions.

- Children express themselves effectively showing awareness of listeners' needs.

- Children count reliably with numbers from 1 to 20.

- Children use everyday language to talk about size, weight, capacity, position, distance, time and money to compare quantities and objects and to solve problems.

- They explore characteristics of everyday objects and shapes and use mathematical language to describe them.

- They safely use and explore a variety of materials, tools and techniques, experimenting with colour, design, texture, form and function.

Resources

- Open shelving, templated for, for example wooden blocks
- Open shelf unit on which to display children's models
- Plastic storage baskets and boxes clearly labelled with equipment names and pictures (e.g. cut out from catalogues)
- Carpet tiles on wall or free-standing board
- A range of appropriate fiction and non-fiction books
- Plans[4] (e.g. architects' plans, 'flat pack' furniture plans), diagrams, instructions, photographs of constructions (e.g. Eiffel Tower, fairground wheels and houses from different cultures) – displayed on wall or board
- Maps – roads and underground
- Examples of mechanical toys and clock workings
- Large set of wooden 'unit' blocks

- Construction kits (it is better to provide three to four well stocked sets which will enable children to develop a range of skills than lots of poorly stocked sets which will lead to frustration) – interlocking bricks, equipment with connectors, cogs and wheels, screws and bolts

- Train track and train

- Small-world people, farm animals, zoo animals, dinosaurs, cars

- Mark-making equipment – plastic carrying basket containing pens, pencils, rulers, small, blank, folded card labels (for children to name their own work), clipboards, plain paper, simple planning 'frames'

- Measuring 'sticks'

- An A4 file containing plastic pockets in which children can file their own work to create a central resource of children's plans for use by whole group

Organisation

Aspects exclusive to the construction area (see page 23 for 'common aspects'):

- Large, carpeted area to be available.

Learning experiences or activities

- Handling and exploring equipment.

- Making models with adult support.

- Making own models independently.

- Working collaboratively to produce a group model.

- Designing and making for a purpose, for example make a container for the straws on the milk table (such challenges can be repeated and children asked to use different construction sets).

- Talking about own and others' work, identifying successful areas and suggesting improvements.

- Explaining to an adult or other children how a model has been made.

- Following instructions (pictorial, written or from an audio tape).

- Giving verbal instructions to an adult or another child.

- Looking at non-fiction books and plans and using information to support own work.

- Recording own work (sequencing cards, drawings, lists).

- Naming work and signing the area 'register'.

- Dismantling models, sorting and counting components and matching resources to templates using mathematical language and correct names.

- Using stories or experiences as a stimulus for creative play and small-world equipment to build environments around their models.

■ **Examples of focus activities in this area:** see 'Jungle Play' and 'Lion's visit' plans, Chapter 3, pages 90–94.

Adult role

Aspects exclusive to construction area (see page 23 for 'common aspects'):

The adult will:

● Model skills involved in building and constructing

● Support children in making and reading plans

● Make diagrams and lists showing components used in a child's model.

Key questions

What did you use to make your model? How did you make it? What did you do first? What do you need to make a car? What does the plan tell us? Can you find the component parts shown on the plan? What is the purpose of your model? Which part do you think works the best? How could we make the tractor move? Will it go faster if we use bigger or smaller or more wheels? Is the garage big enough for the car? How could we make it bigger? What will happen if a car knocks into it – can we make it stronger? Can you build a bridge tall enough for the bus to go under?

Vocabulary

Big(ger), small(er), long(er), short(er), tall(er), circle, square, rectangle, triangle, sphere, cube, cuboid, cone, cylinder, names of component parts, number names (1–10), positional language (e.g. next to, in front of, on, under, behind), directional language (e.g. forwards, backwards).

Water area

The water area needs to be carefully positioned to allow staff easy access to taps and a sink. Some puddles on the floor are inevitable during enthusiastic investigations and surfacing should be 'non-slip'. There should be enough room for children to move freely around the water tray and also for them to construct water ways, siphoning systems, etc. Practitioners may want to restrict the number of children working in the area and, as mentioned earlier in the chapter, provision of a specified number of waterproof aprons is an effective way of limiting the group size. Aprons should be easy for children to put on and take off and should cover as much of their clothing as possible.

A tiled wall area around the tray is a good idea but not practical in all settings. Storage containers should be waterproof and, ideally, have holes in the base and sides as resources are often put away wet and soon become mouldy if not allowed to dry out properly – plastic baskets are suitable and readily available in many supermarkets and hardware shops.

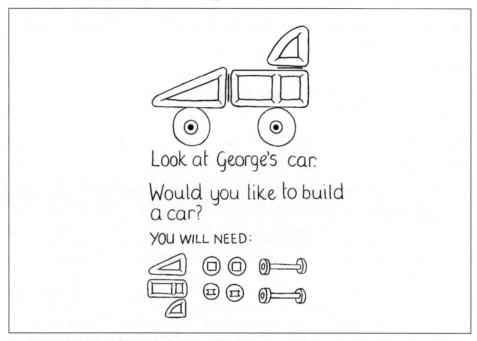

Look at George's car.

Would you like to build a car?

YOU WILL NEED:

Figure 1.9 George's car – practitioner's drawings of the components used by George in his model will support other children in their attempts to produce an identical car

It is difficult to display books in the water area without risking damage to them, although there are some book stands on the market which do offer protection (e.g. perspex cookery-book stands). Laminated blank sheets of paper for use with markers enable children to record without the worry of soaking their paper – these can be displayed on carpet tiles[5] on the wall or on a board, or can be attached to clipboards.

> **Learning opportunities**
>
> *Skills*: Investigating, experimenting, estimating, comparing, using descriptive or key vocabulary, problem-solving, selecting and using equipment appropriately.
>
> *Attitudes*: Sharing or turn taking, cooperation, collaboration, independence, enthusiasm, curiosity, motivation, concentration, confidence, respect for resources and the work or ideas of others.
>
> *Understanding and knowledge*: Developing an understanding of: volume, capacity, size, shape, number, displacement, forces (e.g. floating or sinking, siphoning), absorption, dissolving and heating or cooling. Being familiar with or using mathematical language related to these concepts.

Key areas of learning

- Communication and language
- Mathematics
- Understanding the world

Working towards Early Learning Goals in key areas of learning (Department for Education 2012)

- Children give their attention to what others say and respond appropriately, whilst engaged in another activity.

- Children follow instructions involving several ideas or actions.

- Children express themselves effectively showing awareness of listeners' needs.

- Children use everyday language to talk about size, weight, capacity, position, distance, time and money to compare quantities and objects and to solve problems.

- They ... explain why some things occur, and talk about changes.

Resources

- Water tray (with differing base levels)
- Water – sometimes coloured (using food colouring)
- Mop and bucket
- Wooden board to fit across the tray (perhaps with an arrangement of pipes fitted through holes drilled in the board)
- Open shelving templated for jugs, cylinders
- Plastic storage baskets, labelled
- Four waterproof aprons
- Graded sets of jugs, measuring cylinders, beakers, buckets
- Funnels, sieves, slotted spoons, ladles, water wheels, watering cans, siphons, tubes, pumps
- Natural materials such as sponges, corks, pebbles, pumice stones, shells, drift wood, fir cones, bark
- Transparent plastic bottles (different sizes or same size but marked at different levels with waterproof tape)
- Tea set – cups, teapot, jug, spoons
- A range of small-world creatures, people, boats
- Clipboard, laminated paper, markers

- Posters, photographs, poems (preferably laminated) and fiction and non-fiction books

Organisation

Aspects exclusive to the water area (see page 23 for 'common aspects'):

- Four children only allowed in the area (to be controlled by the provision of four aprons)

- Resources easily accessed by children, and equipment allowed to drain until dry

- Water tray to be emptied at the end of every session

- Colour to be added to the water as planned (in short-term planning).

Learning experiences or activities

- Observing other children working in the area

- Observing or exploring properties of water

- Pouring from and filling containers, counting how many of one fit into another

- Comparing and ordering containers

- Matching equipment to templates

- Investigating and experimenting using appropriate equipment and materials, for example: displacement – transparent plastic containers, pebbles, coloured water; heating and cooling water – ice blocks (perhaps coloured, or containing objects such as buttons) added to warm water in the tray, snow in the tray

- Discussing ideas with adults and other children

- Making predictions and drawing simple conclusions

- Simple recording – checklists, charts

- Imaginative 'sea world' play

- Using stories as a stimulus for imaginative play

- ■ **Examples of focus activities in this area:** see 'Making boats', Chapter 2, page 75 and 'Investigating snow', Chapter 3, page 121.

Adult role

Aspects exclusive to the water area (see page 23 for 'common aspects'):

The adult will:

- Ensure safety at all times (e.g. any excess water on the floor to be mopped up)

- Encourage children to experiment and 'find out'

- Work alongside children experimenting and modelling use of equipment.

Key questions

What do you think will happen if: We pour the water from this container into that one? We tip the jug this way? We lift up this end of the tube whilst the water is inside? We put a stone into this jug (full of water)? We put the sponge into the water? We squeeze the sponge in the water? Do you think the shell will float? Can you find something that you think will sink? Were you right? Why do think it sinks? How many jugfuls of water do you think will fit into the bucket? Do you think the jug holds more or less water than the cylinder? How can we make water travel upwards? How can we make the boat move in the water without touching it?

Vocabulary

Full(er), empty, emptier, big(ger), small(er), tall(er), short(er), wide(r), long(er), thin(ner), heavy, heavier, light(er), wet, dry, warm, hot, cold, freeze, melt, pour, flow, float, sink, equipment names.

Office and mark-making area

The office area is the obvious place in which to focus on developing learning in the area of communication, language and literacy. Resources should be provided which enable and encourage children to engage in reading, writing and speaking and listening activities for a 'real' purpose.

The area does not require the same amount of floor space as, for example, the construction area, but should be large enough to allow for movement of individuals without disturbance to other children. Many practitioners find that 'enclosing' the office area on two or three sides (using tall shelving units or screens) encourages children to concentrate for longer periods by excluding unnecessary distractions. This structure also reduces the volume of noise in the area, enabling the children to more easily engage in interactive conversation (e.g. using telephones).

Practitioners will need to be permanently looking out for resources to enhance the provision in this area, for example old catalogues, telephone directories, obsolete forms and used tickets. The rate at which children use consumable resources, such as paper, in the office is surprisingly fast – it can be quite a challenge to supply according to demand.

The provision of a variety of different papers and formats (e.g. lined, squared, headed writing paper and memo pads) will encourage children to engage in meaningful writing for a range of purposes. Practitioners can easily design these themselves and, if access to a photocopier is available, they should keep a file of master copies to enable them to quickly replenish stocks.

Learning opportunities

Skills: Recording; mark-making (to communicate meaning); using mark-making tools with control; reading (pictures, symbols, words); designing and making; decision-making; observing; forming relationships; listening; communicating through talk (explaining, expressing, discussing, negotiating, questioning and requesting).

Attitudes: Independence; enjoyment; motivation; confidence; concentration; cooperation; interest in and respect for the ideas and work of others.

> Understanding that meaning can be communicated through writing, and that reading is a way of accessing information from the written word; knowing the basic conventions of written English; developing a knowledge of the sounds and letters used in English; understanding that spoken language can be used to communicate, negotiate and discuss; understanding the importance of listening in an interactive conversation.
>
> (Department for Education 2012)

Key areas of learning

- Communication and language
- Physical development
- Literacy

Working towards early learning goals in key areas of learning (Department for Education 2012)

- Children follow instructions involving several ideas or actions.

- Children express themselves effectively showing awareness of listeners' needs.

- Children show good control and coordination in large and small movements.

- They handle equipment and tools effectively, including pencils for writing.

- Children read and understand simple sentences. They use phonic knowledge to decode regular words and read them aloud accurately. They also read some common irregular words. They demonstrate understanding when talking with others about what they have read.

- Children use their phonic knowledge to write words in ways which match their spoken sounds. They also write some irregular common words. They write simple sentences which can be read by themselves and others. Some words are spelt correctly and others are phonetically plausible.

Resources

- Round table and four chairs
- Wall space or large, permanent board (possibly covered in carpet tiles for use with 'hoop and loop fastening tape')[6] displaying, for example, greetings cards, invitations, signs, labels, alphabet, photographs of children writing for different purposes

- Large permanent board (or wall) displaying children's name cards (removable)
- Cork notice board
- Calendar
- Postbox
- Open shelving unit
- Two telephones
- Keyboard
- Bank of 'Can you ring this telephone number ...?' cards
- Telephone directories, catalogues, brochures
- Laminated message board (A4) with marker pens
- Address books, diaries, memo pads
- Bank of word or phrase cards (e.g. 'Happy Birthday', 'with love from', 'to')
- Paper, various sizes: blank, lined, squared, headed
- Forms, tickets
- Folded card (for making greetings cards), postcards
- Envelopes, used stamps
- Sticky labels, card labels, tape, glue sticks
- Hole punches, staplers, scissors, sharpeners, rubbers
- Pencils, biros, felt pens, crayons
- Clipboards

Organisation

Aspects exclusive to the office area (see page 23 for 'common aspects'):

- Different order forms, letter headings, blank invitations, etc. to be introduced regularly
- Area to be situated in a quiet position away from 'thoroughfares'.

Learning experiences or activities

- Mark-making using a variety of tools
- Writing for a range of purposes, for example invitations, letters, orders, greetings cards, postcards, telephone messages, envelopes, memos, lists, forms, diary entries
- Posting or receiving written communications
- Writing own name, for example signing letters

- Reading for a range of purposes, for example letters/cards/notes/invitations from friends, own writing, catalogues, brochures, telephone numbers

- Discussing work and ideas with adults and other children

- Dialling telephone numbers and holding two-way telephone conversations with adults and other children

- Example of focus activity in this area: see 'Jasper's Birthday', Chapter 2, page 70

Adult role

Aspects exclusive to the office area (see page 23 for 'common aspects'):

The adult will:

- Model reading and writing in a variety of situations and for a variety of reasons

- Hold telephone conversations with children in the area

- Ensure that all letters, etc. are collected from the postbox daily and distributed to the children concerned.

Key questions

Would you like to answer the telephone? Who is it? Why did they ring? Can you take a message? Can you read the message to me? Who would you like to ring up? What is their telephone number? What will you ask or tell them? Can you read your letter to a friend? How do you know who the letter is from? What will you write on the envelope? Which books would you like to order from the book club? Can you find your name card? Which is the first letter in your name? What sound is at the beginning of your name? Can you find the letter 'b'? Can you make a 'b' with your pencil? Would you like to send your friend a birthday card? Can you find her name card? What would you like to write? Can you find the label that says 'Happy Birthday'?

Vocabulary

Children will be expected to understand and use the following words: letters, words, numbers, write, read, send, receive, listen, talk, hear, and will be familiar with letter and number names (some or all) and vocabulary related to equipment and materials.

Role-play – the home corner

The home corner is an example of a role-play area. Through role-play, children learn about real life and relationships in a 'safe' situation, and can represent experiences and ideas creatively in their play. A well-planned role-play area should also provide rich opportunities for developing language and literacy, offering purposes for writing, reading, speaking and listening.

The possibilities for role-play in early years settings are almost infinite but the range and quality of provision is largely dependent on the fertility of the practitioner's imagination. Areas for role-play are often constructed to support a play theme and may be planned in response to a child's, or group of children's, interests. Practitioners should be mindful that what is meaningful and motivating to some children may be outside the experience of others. Where experience is limited or non-existent, children will be unable to make links and may be excluded from play. Often, some preparatory discussion and planned experiences can ensure that all children have enough knowledge and understanding to fully avail of all opportunities within a role-play area.

Listed below are some examples:

- Hospital, doctor's surgery or clinic
- Post office, bank
- Travel agents
- Supermarket
- Shoe shop
- Toy shop
- Hairdressers
- The 'Three Bears' House'
- Aeroplane, bus, train, boat
- Bear cave or lion's den
- Castle
- Hotel, café, restaurant
- Ice-cream van
- DIY store
- Library.

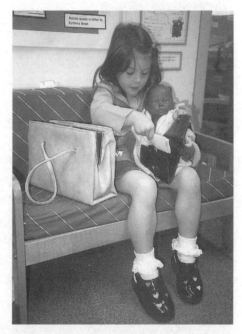

Figure 1.10 Preparing for a shopping trip

In many settings, if space allows, the home corner is part of the permanent provision and additional role-play areas are constructed temporarily in other sites, often in the outside area. Sometimes the home corner may consist of a kitchen with dining and sitting area, sometimes it will have a bedroom. Often a change, or rearrangement, of furniture will reawaken interest in the home corner, as will a focus activity such as a birthday party or the arrival of a new baby (doll). The home corner can also provide opportunities for discussing physical disability sensitively and positively through the use of persona dolls wearing, for example hearing aids or glasses or using wheelchairs.

The following long-term plan relates to a home-corner area comprising a kitchen and dining or sitting area:

Learning opportunities

Skills: Sharing, taking turns, observing, communicating, imagining, initiating and developing imaginative ideas, recreating roles and story-making.

Attitudes: Respect for self and others, independence, cooperation, caring, social awareness, sensitivity, self-assurance, resourcefulness and enjoyment.

Understanding and knowledge: Extending language; using skills for a real purpose; developing understanding of, and knowledge about, relationships or roles, cultures and needs of others or purposes of writing, reading and talking; 'real life' and home environment or social 'rules' and codes of behaviour and appropriate expression of feelings.

Key areas of learning

- Personal, social and emotional development
- Communication and language
- Expressive arts and design

Working towards Early Learning Goals in key areas of learning (Department of Education 2012)

- Children play cooperatively, taking turns with others.
- They are confident to speak in a familiar group, will talk about their ideas and will choose the resources they need for their chosen activities.
- Children talk about how they and others show feelings, talk about their own and others' behaviour, and its consequences, and know that some behaviour is unacceptable.
- Children listen attentively in a range of situations.
- Children follow instructions involving several ideas or actions.
- They use past, present and future forms accurately when talking about events that have happened or are to happen in the future.
- They develop their own narratives and explanations by connecting ideas or events.
- Children represent their own ideas, thoughts and feelings through ... role-play and stories.

Resources

- Home corner furniture at child height: cupboards, sink, washing machine, table, four chairs, sofa, cooker
- Draining rack, kitchen utensils, trays, chopping boards, saucepans, wok, colander and imitation food

- Cups, saucers, bowls, plates, cutlery (in coloured sets)
- Tea towels, oven gloves, table cloth
- Recipe cards, books
- Pegs, washing line, iron, ironing board
- Brush, dustpan, vacuum cleaner
- Open 'wardrobe' storage unit (on castors), coat hangers
- 'Dressing-up' clothes (from a range of cultures)
- Dolls (male, female with different skin colours)
- Baby clothes, blankets, shawls, bath, pushchair
- Mark-making equipment, note pads, shopping lists, paper, notelets, envelopes, invitations, birthday cards
- Telephone, address book, telephone directory

Organisation

Aspects exclusive to the home corner (see page 23 for 'common aspects'):

- Furniture arranged to create the feeling of a real room
- Enough space allowed for cupboard doors to open easily, and for children to be able to move freely around furniture.

Learning experiences or activities

- 'Playing out' real-life situations and personal experiences
- Fantasy play and story-making
- Dressing-up
- Discussing experiences and ideas, negotiating roles and delivering messages
- Making 'props' for play
- Writing for a purpose (e.g. shopping lists, telephone messages, invitations)
- Celebrating birthdays and festivals
- ■ **Example of role-play focus activity:** See 'Post office role-play', Chapter 3, page 118.

Adult role

Aspects exclusive to the home corner (see page 23 for 'common aspects'):

The adult will:

- Engage in role-play with the children
- Plan additional resources for celebrations.

Key questions

Who would you like to invite for tea? How will you invite him? (Telephone? Written invitation?) What will you make for tea? What does he like to eat? What do you need to make pizza? Can you find a recipe for pizza in the book? Why is your baby crying? How does she feel? What can you do to make her feel better? What are you going to buy at the shop? What do you need from the shop for your baby? What do you need to take with you to the shop?

Vocabulary

- 'Feelings' vocabulary, for example happy, sad, cross, angry, worried or frightened
- Vocabulary related to resources, for example, cup, saucer and plate

The painting area

The painting area should, ideally, be situated near to a sink so that children can fill up their own water pots and wash up utensils without leaving too long a paint trail on the floor.

Although ready-mixed paints are appropriate in some circumstances (e.g. printing), children should be offered frequent, and regular, opportunities to mix their own powder paint, exploring colour blending and a range of consistencies.

If children are mixing their own colours, it is not necessary to provide them with a large range, but the primary colours (red, yellow and blue) should be available, as these can not be mixed using other colours. By mixing two primary colours together, children will be able to produce the secondary colours (purple, orange and green). Blue and red mixed together will make purple, red and yellow produce orange, and blue and yellow make green. The addition of white will produce lighter tints, and black (which should be used sparingly), darker shades.

Children need to be taught routines and use of resources, and will probably need regular reinforcement until they feel confident in the area. Some younger children are much more interested in the process of mixing paint than in the application of paint to paper and should be allowed to pursue this interest.

Easels are very popular in early years settings and allow two children to work in a relatively small space. However, it can be frustrating for children, when using watery paint, if their marks are constantly distorted by 'trickles'. Some activities in this area are much more successful on a horizontal surface and, for obvious practical reasons, tables should be covered in a plastic-coated cloth or newspaper. It is not necessary to provide chairs in the painting area; children will be less restricted in their brush strokes if working from the standing position. Aprons should be provided in a place easily accessible to children.

Learning opportunities

Skills: Experimenting, recording, predicting, decision-making, describing, explaining, expressing ideas and opinions, mark-making, designing, imagining and creating.

Attitudes: Interest, motivation, independence, cooperation, perseverance, confidence.

Understanding and knowledge: Developing a knowledge about, and understanding of, the changes that occur when powder paint is mixed with water, and when colours are mixed together; understanding two- and three-dimensional representation and composition, organising colours and shapes to produce an image; increasing knowledge about line, tone, shape, space, pattern, texture and form (i.e. the elements of art); knowing purposes of tools and properties of materials and developing an appreciation of art and artefacts.

Figure 1.11 Mixing colours in the painting area

Key areas of learning

- Physical development
- Understanding the world
- Expressive arts and design

Working towards Early Learning Goals in key areas of learning (Department of Education 2012)

- They handle equipment and tools effectively, including pencils for writing.
- They ... talk about changes.
- Children represent their own ideas, thoughts and feelings through design and technology, art, music, dance, role-play and stories.

Resources

- Large, square table (at a comfortable height for standing to work) covered with a waterproof, self-coloured, cloth ('busy' patterns can be distracting when creating an image)
- Two easels with trays attached
- Trolley: surface templated for water pots, palettes, paint containers; tray storage for brushes (varying thicknesses, round and flat), spatulas, rollers, wooden printing

blocks, sponges, a range of 'found objects' for making marks with paint (e.g. cotton reels, washing up brushes, corks, plastic lids)

- Open shelved paper cupboard; rectangles of paper of varying size and proportions; textured paper (e.g. woodchip wallpaper cut into rectangles); white and coloured paper

- Drying rack (preferably holding work horizontally to avoid paint dripping)

- White, wooden cube (for displaying objects for observation)

- Reproductions of artists' work

- Powder paint (reds, blues, yellows, white, black) ready-mixed paint, water-based printing inks

- Instructions for paint mixing

- Pencils (for naming work)

- 'Gallery' displaying the work of children and famous artists

Organisation

Aspects exclusive to the painting area (see page 23 for 'common aspects'):

- Limit of four children working in the area

- A range of techniques to be explored, and skills taught, through focus activities.

Learning experiences and activities

- Mixing powder paint with water, mixing colours

- Applying paint to paper, drawing with paint using a range of tools

- Painting from observation and imagination

- Collaborative painting on large sheets of paper

- Printing, for example: with sponges, vegetables, leaves, hands, string, card; on fabric, paper, card, wood; taking mono prints (spread mixed paint on a perspex sheet, draw into the paint with finger, press paper onto the image); making bubble prints (mix washing up liquid with paint in a tray or bowl, blow with a straw until bubbles reach above the rim, place paper over the bubbles); press printing (draw an image onto a piece of specially produced polystyrene using a pencil or modelling tools, roll on ink or paint and press onto paper)

- Pattern-making (repeat and random)

- Painting own models made in the workshop

- Mixed media work

- Adding extra ingredients to paint to produce different textures

- Discussing children's work and the nursery gallery

- Looking at and discussing the work of artists

Adult role

Aspects exclusive to the painting area (see page 23 for 'common aspects'):

The adult will:

- Teach and reinforce routines and colour names

- Model skills and demonstrate techniques.

Key questions

What do you think will happen if you mix red with blue? Which colours did you mix together to make green? Which is your favourite colour? Is this blue lighter or darker than that blue? Which brush will make a thin or thick mark? What do you think will happen if you add more water to your paint? Have you used thick or thin paint? What is your painting about? What do you think this painting is about? What do you like best about this painting? What kind of line or shape have you made?

Vocabulary

Colour names: red, blue, yellow, orange, purple, green, white, black (other colours if children are ready), descriptive words related to the elements of art, for example, line: wiggly, straight, wavy, zig-zag; texture: rough, bobbly, lumpy, smooth.

The outdoor environment

'Being outdoors has a positive impact on children's sense of well-being and helps all aspects of children's development.

Being outdoors offers opportunities for doing things in different ways and on different scales than when indoors.

It gives children first-hand contact with weather, seasons and the natural world.

Outdoor environments offer children freedom to explore, use their senses, and be physically active and exuberant.'

Principles into Practice card 3.3. Enabling Environments: The Learning Environment

(DfES Publications 2007)

The outside play area is often described as an area of provision but should not be viewed merely as an additional area, more as a part of the whole setting in which all other areas of provision can be set up and all areas of the curriculum covered.

Planning for Children's Play and Learning

The size and features of outside areas vary tremendously from setting to setting and it may be necessary to plan areas of provision in the outside area on a rotational basis. Many teams organise their outdoor area into zones, for example wheeled toys, climbing and balancing, exploration and investigation (sand and water trays, digging plot, wild area), role-play and quiet area (books, seating). Equipment is then organised within each zone.

Staffing arrangements also have a bearing on the organisation of this area. All settings should aspire to the ideal of offering children free access to the outdoor area throughout the session, but where this is not possible, creative planning should ensure that children have as much access and choice as possible. Activities taking place in areas of provision inside can often be extended very successfully outside by introducing different resources, for example learning about how water travels and how it can be used to move objects:

- *Inside* – using tubes, marbles and 'pouring' containers in the water tray. Children pour coloured water into the tube and watch it travel along the tube as they lift up one end. They put a marble in one end of a tube and keeping the tube reasonably level, use water to 'push' the marble along inside the tube.

- *Outside* – using plastic drainage tubes, pipes and guttering (can be purchased from builders' merchants and are relatively inexpensive), two or three water trays, large buckets and bowls, marbles and balls of different sizes, 'pouring' containers. Children work together on a large-scale constructing complex waterways, investigating how water travels on inclines, moving water from a tray at one level to another tray at the same or a different level, and using water to 'push' balls along level guttering and transport them to another tray.

The outside area also offers opportunities for physical activity and development of gross motor skills which are largely impossible in the inside environment. It is important to ensure that children are allowed sufficient space in which to run, ride (e.g. bikes and scooters) and climb and that each of these activities is afforded its own designated area. Other activities should encourage the development of throwing and catching skills, balancing, jumping and hopping.

> **Working towards Early Learning Goals in physical development (Department for Education 2012)**
>
> - Children show good control and coordination in large and small movements. They move confidently in a range of ways, safely negotiating space.

Exciting investigations of the outside environment can lead to valuable learning taking place, particularly in the area of 'knowledge and understanding of the

Figure 1.12 Water investigations in the outside area

world'. Practitioners should anticipate such learning experiences and plan an outside area that will provide children with a wealth of opportunities to find out about the natural environment and a range of stimuli which will prompt them to ask questions about the world around them.

It is usually possible, even in the smallest of outside areas, to organise such activities as:

- A 'growth investigation' – a range of flowers and vegetables can be grown from seed in pots, troughs or tyres filled with compost.

- Developing a 'wild area' in which children will be able to observe seasonal changes – a small piece of land planted with grass and wild flower seeds, evergreen shrubs, spring bulbs, plants or shrubs that encourage butterflies, for example, buddleia.

Figure 1.13 Watering the plants

- A 'mini-beast investigation' – introduce a few logs and large stones to the wild area – children will be fascinated by the insect life they discover daily underneath the logs and stones.

Every effort should be made to promote literacy and numeracy in the outside area. Opportunities for children to practise and develop reading and writing skills are as numerous outside as they are inside but practitioners may decide to select some different resources for use outside; for example on a dry day, children will welcome the opportunity to make marks, and perhaps write their name, on walls and paving slabs using a paintbrush dipped into a pot of water (see Figure 1.16). Mark-making on a large scale allows children freedom of movement and expression – a roll of decorator's lining paper is inexpensive and, rolled out and secured to the

Figure 1.14 Searching for centipedes

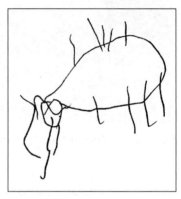

Figure 1.15 Beetle – drawn from observation in the outside area (child's drawing)

ground with masking tape, provides a 'canvas' large enough for a group of children to work individually or collaboratively with a range of tools. Laminated sheets of A4 card and marker pens can be more practical than paper in wet areas and can also be cleaned and 'recycled'. Portable baskets containing mark-making equipment (including clipboards) are also a useful resource in the outdoor play area.

Roadways (drawn in chalk on the ground) are always popular with bike riders and the addition of road signs and arrows encourages

Figure 1.16 Mark-making with brushes and water in the outside area

purposeful reading. Children will very quickly learn to recognise 'stop' and 'go' on a hand-held sign and to respond appropriately. Other examples of signs that can be displayed outside include 'bus stop', 'taxi rank', 'building site – wear hard hats', maps of the outside play area, shop and garden centre signs, 'follow the trail' arrows, 'are you wearing your outdoor shoes?' Children will often offer their own suggestions and should be encouraged to make and use their own signs.

A bank of illustrated question cards made available to children in the outdoor area will also encourage the development of reading skills, for example, 'Can you find a ladybird?' or 'Have you watered the carrots today?' If the pictures are clear and simple, even the youngest of children will be able to 'read' the card and, with support, respond to the questions.

Number plates on wheeled toys which children match to numbers on 'garages' as they park their vehicles encourage number recognition, matching and counting. As they become familiar with the system, children will begin to refer to bikes by their number: 'It's my turn to play on number three bike now!' – 'Look, 'two' bike is still in the garage, you can go on that.'

Other ways of developing mathematical learning outside include:

- Hopscotch and grid games painted on the ground
- 'Chant' games such as 'What time is it Mr Wolf?'
- 'Giant' dice games (roll a three – walk three steps across the playground – who will reach the other side first?)
- Playing positional language games, for example, hide the teddy behind the tree or in front of the den or in the sand tray
- Throwing beanbags into numbered boxes in the correct order (this activity could be presented as, for example, throwing fish to the sea lions)
- Making tally charts or tick lists – how many butterflies/cars/people/birds have we seen from the playground during the session?
- Observing insects in 'bug boxes' and counting legs and wings
- Following the 'bear trail' – children step on numbered paw prints to reach the bear's cave
- Posting activities – matching, for example, shapes on envelopes to shapes on postboxes around the area
- Drawing around children's shadows on a sunny day – comparing length and shape
- Measuring children's height against a wall and making a chalk mark for each child
- Growing sunflowers against a wall – comparing height and recording growth by marking the top of the sunflower in chalk on the wall every week

- Potting plants or planting seeds – comparing different pots – how much compost does this one hold? Does it hold more than that one?

- Fishing for numbered fish in a water tray: using laminated card fish (numbered, and with a metal paper clip attached) and string fishing rods with a small magnet attached – can you catch number one fish? Which number is left in the water?

- Comparing weights or balancing weights – using a rope thrown over a tree branch with a bag full of sand attached to one end, children fill the bag attached to the other end of the rope with sand until the two bags are balanced

- Selecting boxes of suitable size and shape to use as containers for stock in their role-play shoe shop.

All the Early Learning Goals for mathematics are worked towards through this range of activities.

Dens are guaranteed to capture the imagination of young children and the outdoor area is an ideal place in which to set up a bear cave, lion's den, camping holiday tent, teddy bears' hideout or desert-island retreat – the possibilities are endless. Wooden structures (e.g. a pyramid) provide a firm framework around which to build a den, but if these are not available large cardboard boxes, tables, etc. can be used effectively. Long lengths of fabric (old curtains or sheets are ideal) draped over the framework instantly create an exciting environment. Other resources can be introduced – the choice of these will depend on the nature of the children's play.

'Shadow play' on a sunny day also offers rich opportunities for creative development as illustrated in Figure 1.17. Following a story session during which the practitioner read *Where the Wild Things Are* by Maurice Sendak, children experimented with the shadows made by their own body shapes and created some very ferocious-looking 'wild things'.

Opportunities for personal, social and emotional development are many in the outdoor area. Well-planned and exciting activities taking place in this area often play a significant role in motivating children to learn and inspiring in them a desire to explore and investigate the world around them. Children learn to share, and take turns on, equipment and to follow clear codes of behaviour in order to work safely. They develop a responsibility for the care of living things and the environment and are offered opportunities to work independently, in pairs and as part of a group.

To list all the equipment used in the outdoor play area would be to duplicate much of the content of the long-term plans for areas of provision included in 'The inside area'. For this reason, only examples of resources that are exclusive to the outdoor area are listed next:

- Climbing equipment – frames, ladders, slides (positioned on soft surface)
- Fabric tunnels and plastic barrels

- Wheeled toys – bikes, scooters, go-carts
- Road signs
- Police/traffic warden/lollipop person uniforms
- Large wooden blocks, for example, hollow blocks, wooden planks
- Large plastic mats, carpet squares
- Old car/bus steering wheels
- Tyres
- Milk crates
- Cones
- Logs, tree stumps
- Bats, racquets, balls
- Beanbags
- Hoops and rubber quoits
- Skipping ropes
- 'Den' frameworks, lengths of fabric
- Lengths of guttering (can be stored on brackets attached to the wall)
- Large water trays, buckets
- Plastic sand tray or permanent, brick-built sand pit
- Shallow builders' tray, old wooden bricks (see Figure 1.18)
- Trowels, spades, rakes
- Hard builders' hats
- Wheelbarrow
- Watering cans, plant pots, troughs
- Portable mark-making resource baskets
- Plastic water pots, paint brushes and decorators' brushes.

Figure 1.17 Shadow play: creating 'wild things'

Figure 1.18 Builders at work

Examples of focus activity plan for the outside area: 'Going on a "Bear Hunt" – obstacle course' (page 82).

When all long-term plans have been completed, provision as a whole should reflect curricular breadth and balance. A simple overview such as the next example (Figure 1.19) will provide a record and also highlight any gaps.

Figure 1.19 Overview of areas of learning through long-term planning of provision

Areas of learning	Personal, social and emotional development			Physical development		Communication and language			Literacy		Mathematics		Understanding the world			Expressive arts and design	
Aspects	MR	SC&SA	MF&B	M&H	H&SC	L&A	U	S	R	W	N	SSM	P&C	W	T	M&M	BI
Sand Wet Dry				X			X					X		X			
Role-play	X	X	X			X	X	X	X	X			X				X
Mark-making				X					X	X							
Construction						X	X	X			X	X				X	X

Safety

The issue of safety is something that concerns many practitioners when planning for the outdoor area and of course it is crucial to protect children from serious harm. However, an environment with absolutely no risk is also an environment with no challenge. It is therefore important to create a balance, allowing children to learn how to assess risk themselves and to operate safely within the environment. In order to decide what is an 'acceptable' risk and to eliminate 'unacceptable' risks, it is useful to meet as a team to discuss the issue and to draw up a risk assessment. There are many formats available for this purpose and these include sections identifying the hazard and those at risk, judging the level of risk, outlining steps to be taken in minimising or eliminating the risk. Such assessments should be regularly reviewed and modifications made with the knowledge of all team members. Any incidents recorded in the accident book should be used to inform these reviews.

KEY POINTS FOR GOOD PRACTICE

- Offer areas of provision on a continuous basis to enable children to develop ideas and understanding over time. Where physical limitations dictate that areas are rotated, make sure that each area is available for a long enough period of time to allow for revisiting.
  - o Value continuous provision as a rich context for teaching and learning.
- Encourage children as independent learners and thinkers within the environment, organising provision to promote self-selection and decision-making.
- Make sure that routines do not unnecessarily interrupt children's learning experiences.
  - o Make sure that practitioners, routines and the physical environment support children's individual basic needs such as rest, sleep, food and water.
  - o Think about how you, as a team promote children's emotional well-being and support them in making relationships and managing their own behaviour, in order for them to effectively access the learning opportunities offered through areas of provision.
  - o Be aware of your role in identifying and supporting children's individual learning needs and interests within the learning environment.
  - o Ensure that all staff understand what constitutes high-quality interaction with young children.

- Draw up long-term plans as a whole staff team and link the planning to developments in provision.

- Identify key areas of learning in plans for each area of provision but reflect curricular breadth and balance through provision as a whole. Be aware that these identified key areas are merely a support for adults in planning but that outcomes will vary according to the choices children make over how they use the provision.

- Recognise the importance of outdoor learning and plan for all areas of learning through outdoor provision.

- Ensure that the learning environment is inclusive and that the needs of all individuals within the group are met through provision.

- Reflect a variety of cultures through provision.

- Regularly evaluate provision and review long-term plans.

The environment is the mechanism by which the teacher brings the child and different areas of knowledge together.

(Bruce 1987)

Notes

1 Much of this equipment will probably be included in the basic provision in certain areas, but duplicates and alternatives should be available for children to use in other areas in order to develop particular skills and concepts.
2 A wider range of writing equipment will be permanently available in the office area (see long-term plan for this area, page 32).
3 Carpet tiles attached to the wall in each area serve as a good display board – children's work, labels, signs, pictures, posters, poems, rhymes, numbers, plans and instructions will readily 'stick' to the tiles if 'hoop and loop fastening tape' is applied to the back of each. Resources can be changed quickly and frequently and children are able to move them around on the board. This may not be practical in all settings, in which case portable 'carpet tile' boards (sandwich board style) can quite easily be made for use in all areas of provision.
4 Include examples of children's work and photographs.
5 Markers can also be kept on the carpet tile if a strip of 'hoop and loop fastening tape' is attached to the shaft.
6 Children are more likely to use displayed labels and signs in their play if they can remove and transport them to where they are working.

CHAPTER 2

Planning for a focus

Each area of learning and development must be implemented through planned, purposeful play and through a mix of adult-led and child-initiated activity.

(Department for Education 2012)

The content of this chapter is organised as follows:

- What is a 'focus'? (page 51)
- Why plan a focus? (page 53)
- Deciding on a framework for planning focus activities – what should be included? (page 53)
- To what extent should focus activities be planned in advance? (page 54)
- Using an 'ideas bank' to support focus planning (page 55)
- Planning a focus (page 60)
- What should practitioners consider when evaluating the focus? (page 68)
- Examples of focus plans (page 69)
- Key points for good practice (page 84)

What is a 'focus'?

A focus is an activity or experience that is planned with particular objectives in mind. Basic provision is often enhanced in a way that will enable children to develop certain skills, knowledge, concepts and attitudes and the role of the adult in supporting their learning is clearly defined. Sometimes a focus on a particular area of the basic provision is planned to enable the practitioner to spend quality time in that area with a specific aim (see 'Why plan a focus?', page 53).

'Help children to build on prior learning by pitching activities, such as a play or a story, at a level that is demanding but still within children's reach.'

Principles into Practice card 2.3. Positive Relationships: Supporting Learning

(DfES Publications 2007)

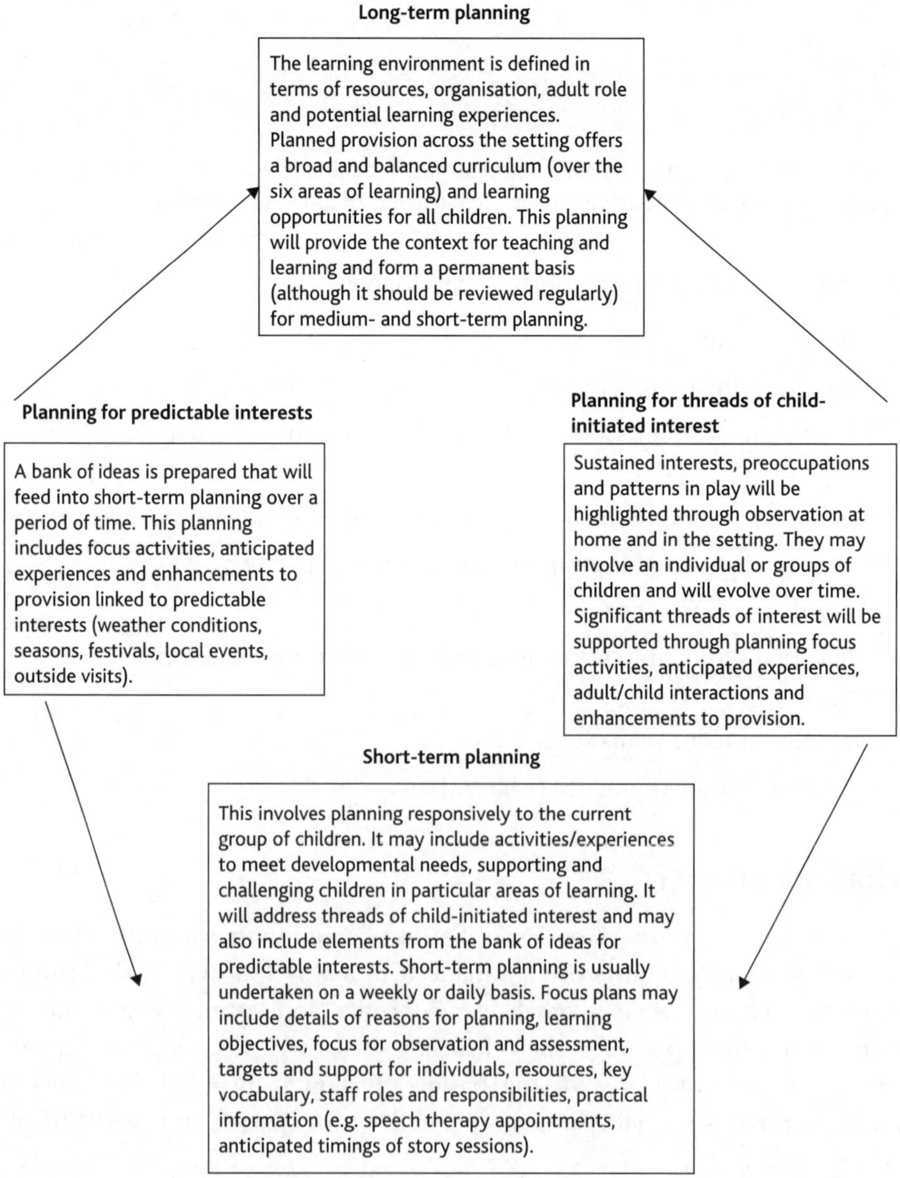

Long-term planning

The learning environment is defined in terms of resources, organisation, adult role and potential learning experiences. Planned provision across the setting offers a broad and balanced curriculum (over the six areas of learning) and learning opportunities for all children. This planning will provide the context for teaching and learning and form a permanent basis (although it should be reviewed regularly) for medium- and short-term planning.

Planning for predictable interests

A bank of ideas is prepared that will feed into short-term planning over a period of time. This planning includes focus activities, anticipated experiences and enhancements to provision linked to predictable interests (weather conditions, seasons, festivals, local events, outside visits).

Planning for threads of child-initiated interest

Sustained interests, preoccupations and patterns in play will be highlighted through observation at home and in the setting. They may involve an individual or groups of children and will evolve over time. Significant threads of interest will be supported through planning focus activities, anticipated experiences, adult/child interactions and enhancements to provision.

Short-term planning

This involves planning responsively to the current group of children. It may include activities/experiences to meet developmental needs, supporting and challenging children in particular areas of learning. It will address threads of child-initiated interest and may also include elements from the bank of ideas for predictable interests. Short-term planning is usually undertaken on a weekly or daily basis. Focus plans may include details of reasons for planning, learning objectives, focus for observation and assessment, targets and support for individuals, resources, key vocabulary, staff roles and responsibilities, practical information (e.g. speech therapy appointments, anticipated timings of story sessions).

Figure 2.1 The planning process

Why plan a focus?

Reasons for planning a focus activity include:

- To target, and address the specific needs of, individual children or a group of children

- To highlight a particular area of learning and offer rich experiences to support children towards the goals in that area

- To extend play initiated by the children and develop individual and group interests (this area will be covered more fully in Chapter 3, 'Starting points for developing learning')

- To provoke interest, stimulating and motivating children to learn

- To teach or model skills or use of new tools and equipment.

Practitioners may also decide to plan a focus in an area of provision in order:

- To monitor children's use of resources and the effectiveness of an area of provision in achieving aims stated in the long-term plans (see Chapter 1)

- To identify individual interests and support child-initiated learning.

- To monitor children's progress, assess needs, and record achievements (see Chapter 6).

Deciding on a framework for planning focus activities – what should be included?

It is important to bear in mind the purpose of the plan in terms of its use to the educator when deciding on a structure or format. The main questions to ask when determining what to include should be:

- Who will be using the plan?

- How will the plan support practitioners in structuring high-quality learning experiences?

- What information does the practitioner need in order to be well prepared and provide a rich learning environment?

- How will the plan support the adult in challenging children's thinking and extending their learning?

The plan must 'work' for those using it and standard formats may need to be modified to meet the needs of individual practitioners and teams of practitioners.

It may be that the plan will be used by parent helpers, students or temporary staff unfamiliar with the setting, as well as by the permanent members of the team. Content may vary according to the setting and the age of the children. The team need to discuss what to include in their planning structure, and then select or design a 'workable' format which helps practitioners to organise information in a way which is useful to them. Listed below are suggested elements for consideration:

- Focus areas of learning – the objectives may be cross-curricular or linked to a particular area of learning

- Learning objectives – these should be included in a prominent place on the plan

- DfE early learning goals – which particular goals will children be working towards during the activity?

- Target group – the activity may be planned to meet individual or group needs, or may be an activity open to all children but with opportunities for differentiation

- Children's prior learning – what knowledge and understanding can they build on?

- Date, time and expected duration

- Introduction, main activity, finishing off – content for each part of the activity presented in a clear sequence (if appropriate to the nature of the focus)

- The role of the adult

- Questions to ask in order to extend children's learning

- Extension activities

- Key vocabulary

- Resources – basic provision, equipment and materials needed to enhance areas of provision

- Opportunities for assessment – what will the adult observe? How will observations be recorded? How will the information be used?

- Evaluation of the activity

- Next steps – what does the practitioner need to do to support and challenge the child?

To what extent should focus activities be planned in advance?

Practitioners may want to think about the sort of activities and experiences that will motivate and support the learning of their particular group of children over a period of time. These ideas will probably be included in a medium-term plan. Opportunities for child-initiated learning may also be anticipated in advance and some may be included (on long-term plans for areas of provision, see Chapter 1). There will, however, be frequent occasions when the practitioner will want to respond to children's immediate interests, enthusiasms and needs and plan a focus accordingly. Decisions of this nature will obviously need to be taken 'in progress' and in response to staff evaluation. Weekly plans should be flexible enough to allow adults to plan a focus at short notice (see Chapter 3).

It is not a productive use of time to be re-writing large amounts of information and practitioners should guard against such practice. Medium-term banks of ideas (see next example) and long-term plans (see Chapter 1) should help to focus and support adults in their short-term planning, but are not concerned with activity details. Any planning in the medium term should never be so rigid or dominant as to exclude spontaneous planning in response to more recently observed needs and interests. Predictable interests such as seasons, community events, weather conditions or schematic interests (e.g. enveloping, containing, transporting, trajectories) can be prepared for in advance and plans kept on file (see 'Autumn' example on page 57). Current individual or group interests can also be supported by a medium-term plan, or 'ideas bank', outlining possible ideas for enabling children to further their interest and use it as a vehicle for extending learning across the six areas (see 'Spiders' example page 59). Ideas can then be drawn from these medium-term plans and fed into short-term planning to support interests as they arise. They can also be used to motivate children to explore new experiences. Plans should always be evaluated for future reference and adults should not worry that they have not covered *all* planned learning – this probably indicates that they have adopted a more responsive approach to planning and achieved a balanced of adult- and child-initiated activities.

Using an 'ideas bank' to support focus planning

It is possible to predict some interests but before drawing up a plan, or bank of ideas, to support these, it is a good idea to spend some time talking with children to find out what they already know and understand about the 'theme' around which you are planning. For example, staff decide to plan some activities in connection with the forthcoming annual community carnival. They anticipate that many of the children will be interested in, for example, preparing for a 'mini' carnival in nursery, making costumes and creating music and dances. On consultation with children, it becomes apparent that a few children have no concept of a 'carnival' and that even the word 'carnival' holds no meaning for them. They are reminded that one of these children has moved into the area since the last carnival and another has been away on holiday at the time of the carnival for the past two years. Two other children live in a different locality and have not attended the carnival. For these children, the staff needed to plan activities in advance such as showing the DVD footage and photographs of last year's carnival and dressing up in carnival costumes. Their parents were informed of the date and time of the carnival and encouraged to bring their children if possible. Situations such as this highlight the assumptions we make when planning for a group.

For some events, planning should focus on enabling children to revisit experiences rather than providing activities in advance. For example, Bonfire Night is often a very exciting experience for those children who attend a bonfire or firework display but follow-up activities are usually much more effective than those offered before the night. Children who have no prior experience of such events, or merely a hazy memory from the previous year, will make little sense of activities provided in advance but will approach the same activities with motivation when 'fired up' by their own exciting experience.

Likewise, it is nonsense to plan a topic on 'snow' just because it is winter season or the month of December. Many children may never have witnessed snow and there is certainly no guarantee of a snowfall within the period of a medium-term plan. Any focus on such weather conditions will be much more meaningful and engaging if offered as they occur and staff should be prepared to respond spontaneously (see Chapter 3, 'Investigating snow', page 121).

Another popular 'topic' for medium-term planning has historically been 'holidays' but, again, it is easy to overlook children's individual experiences and understanding unless practitioners take time to talk, and listen, to them. The word 'holiday' may mean very different things to different children. To some, it may mean Dad being 'off work', to another, something that Mum and Dad do whilst they stay with Granny. To others a holiday may be skiing in the Alps, playing on a beach in Majorca, going to a holiday camp or camping in a tent in the Lake District. Unless children have real experience to draw on, they will be unable, or limited in their ability, to access the activities we plan for them, however exciting we think they are. In any event, it is unlikely that a whole group 'topic plan' will be engaging or meaningful to all children.

A more effective way of planning is to identify children's experience and interests and to support these more specifically through a 'personal interest plan' (see 'Spiders' example, page 59) that outlines ideas for supporting the interest over a period of time. It may be that a group of children is interested in a similar 'theme' at the same time but it is likely that there will be a number of personal interest plans running concurrently. Observations and profiles should inform practitioners of any individual interests, patterns or repeated behaviours that may form the basis of a personal interest plan. Staff teams will need to decide on a system for feeding information from these plans into short-term planning sessions that is practical and realistic. Obviously, it is unreasonable to expect staff to draw up such a plan for each child every few weeks and it would be impossible to manage such a volume of information. It may be that each key person draws up a plan for one child in their key group each time and, over the course of, for example, a year, aims to address the interests of all the children in her or his key group. If possible, parents should be involved in drawing up the plans and should be encouraged to contribute information that would help to identify a strong interest. Of course, staff would still be responding on a day-to-day basis to children's immediate needs and interests. It is useful to keep a basic overview of which children have been particularly engaged by which personal interest plans and this may high-light children who have not been noticeably motivated by any of the additional activities and experiences planned. These children may then be prioritised for their own personal interest plan in the next round. Practitioners may also find it useful to take a retrospective look at the particular aspects of learning strongly promoted through each plan.

It is important, however, to emphasise that basic and continuous provision should be engaging and stimulating to children, enabling them to pursue inter-ests and determine the direction of their own learning. 'Predictable interest' idea banks and 'personal interest plans' provide an additional 'layer' to the planning and should not compromise, or take the place of, but should enhance, an ongoing good-quality learning environment.

Example 'ideas bank': predictable interests

AUTUMN

Date and duration

- October/November 2012. This plan will be implemented as seasonal changes are observed.

Possible key areas of learning

- Understanding the world (the world)
- Mathematics (numbers, shape, space and measures)

Suggested focus activities and anticipated experiences

- Walk around the nursery garden or school grounds observing changes
- Walk to park involving parents and carers
- Using collection trays to gather natural items of interest
- Gathering fallen leaves using wheelbarrows, long-handled brushes and rakes
- Putting small stickers on leaves on trees in the nursery garden and monitoring what happens to them, recording a mark on a sheet every time one of the leaves falls and is found on the ground
- Investigating what happens to leaves when they are wet and dry

- Handling and talking about autumn leaves, using language related to size, shape and colour

- Sorting (e.g. number of points) and ordering leaves

- Looking at skeleton leaves on black paper

- Constructing autumn collection display

- Making leaf prints, rubbings, collages

- Drawing from observation

- Colour-mixing explorations, for example, red plus yellow equals orange

- Discussing seasonal changes and features of the weather

- Photographing trees at various stages documenting the changes from summer through autumn to winter

Enhancements to provision

Outdoor area: Rakes, sweeping brushes, plastic shovels, wheelbarrows, buckets, leaf collection sacks, gardening gloves, trays, clipboards, pencils or crayons, digital camera, magnifying glasses, binoculars, wellington boots and rain coats, coloured stickers, number line.

Paint: Colour-mixing equipment (spatulas, yellow and red powder paint, palettes, water pots, brushes), photographs of autumn scenes.

Sand: Leaves, conkers, conker 'shells', acorns, etc.

Water: Autumn leaves.

Interactive display: Autumn posters, pictures, photographs, poems and story books. Natural items collected by children.

Book corner: Fiction and non-fiction books about autumn.

Vocabulary and questions

Vocabulary: Autumn, summer, winter. Weather vocabulary, for example rain, wet, dry, foggy, sunny, cloudy, frosty, windy. Tree, trunk, branch, leaf. Colour names: green, red, yellow, orange, brown. Shape and measure language, for example, triangle, long, short, small, big, smaller, bigger.

Questions: Have you noticed what is happening in the nursery garden? How many different colours can you find? What will happen to the leaves after they have changed colour on the tree? Can you find another leaf the same colour or shape as this one? Which leaf do you think will fall off the tree next? How many of our 'marked' leaves have fallen? How many are still on the tree? How is this wet leaf different from the dry one? What do you think will happen if we put the wet leaf on the radiator? Look at the pattern on this leaf – is it the same as that one?

Example 'ideas bank': Supporting an individual interest (personal interest plan)

Spiders

	OBSERVATIONAL EVIDENCE TOWARDS INTEREST:	OTHER POSSIBLE INTERESTED CHILDREN:
DATE: 25.06.12 CHILD'S NAME: Tom INTEREST: Spiders	*Every day, Tom has been observed looking behind the cupboard in the construction area since he found an enormous spider there! He is very excited when he discovers a spider and asks lots of questions about them. Mum says that he chose to spend some birthday money on a set of plastic spiders in the toy shop and has been hiding these behind cupboards and under beds at home for her to find.*	*Tim (often seen joining Tom on his searches for spiders in nursery!)* *Hayley (always interested in the outdoor mini-beast area)*
PSED (Possible enhancements to provision, activities and experiences) *Plan exciting activities to motivate children such as hiding model spiders around the nursery (e.g. in sand tray, under shrubs) for children to find.*	PD (Possible enhancements to provision, activities and experiences) *Provide tools and equipment that encourage handling and manipulation, e.g. magnifying glasses, small model spiders*	C&L (Possible enhancements to provision, activities and experiences) *Encourage children to express ideas, talk about observations and listening to others. Ask questions and encourage children to ask questions.*
L (Possible enhancements to provision, activities and experiences) *Share the story 'Billy's Beetle' (Mick Inkpen) substituting a spider for the beetle! Recreate the story through an organised search for Billy's spider.* *Learn 'Incy Wincy Spider'.* *Look at non-fiction books about spiders.* *Make information books about spiders using children's drawings, writing and photographs.*	M (Possible enhancements to provision, activities and experiences) *Count the legs on a spider. How many on each side?* *Record how many spiders you find each day.* *Compare the features of spiders using mathematical language such as big, small, long, short.*	UW (Possible enhancements to provision, activities and experiences) *Look closely at spiders to find out more about them using magnifiers and bug boxes.* *Take photographs of spiders documenting, for example, the different places they choose to go.* *Visit to 'Tropical Gardens' to look at the spiders.*

CD (Possible enhancements to provision, activities and experiences)		
Creating giant paper sculpture spiders and using these in the outdoor area to promote imaginative play and story making.		

EVALUATION:

18.07.12

Tom responded enthusiastically to many of the activities. He continued to look for spiders behind the cupboard every day but his interest was refined over time as he looked in detail at the features of the spiders he found. He became very interested in the ways in which, and the speed at which, the spiders moved and tried to imitate them through his own movements. 'Spider movement' was supported by an adult focus and children created 'spider music' using instruments from the music area.

Mum bought Tom two information books about spiders which he has looked at again and again. Dad set up a wild area in their garden (like the one in nursery) to enable them to look at other creatures such as woodlice and worms. Tom had been very excited by his discoveries in this area and he and Dad had made comparisons between the 'mini beasts'. Tom had attended his friend's fancy dress birthday party in a spider's costume made by Mum and him! The family trip to 'Tropical Gardens' to see the exotic spiders had proved very successful and Mum is planning return visit.

Nursery staff reported that Tom's deep motivation and involvement in the 'spider activities' had often led to high quality interactions and shared thinking between him and adults. These situations had been rich in opportunities for challenging thinking and extending learning across the six areas of the EYFS (see profile observations).

Although this plan had been drawn up primarily in response to Tom's interest in spiders, many of the activities engaged other children. Interest was widespread during the 'spider hunt' and most children showed an interest in looking at the spiders in 'bug boxes'.

The following children were particularly motivated by the theme of spiders and accessed many of the planned activities/experiences: Vivek, Hayley, Finlay, Emma, Jenny, Tim and Jordan.

Planning a focus

What will the children learn?

This is an important question to consider when planning any activity. What we want the children to learn will be identified on the plan, and the activity or experience will serve as motivating a vehicle for the children's learning.

Objectives may target a particular area of learning or be cross-curricular, but should always be clearly defined. Too many objectives become unmanageable – fewer (two or three will often be enough) carefully considered objectives will enable the adult to focus observations and interventions to support the child on their journey towards the intended outcomes. Focus areas of learning should be high-lighted on the plan, and pertinent early learning goals identified – this will help practitioners to assess children's achievements in terms of national expectations.

Identifying the reason for planning an activity is the first step towards defining objectives. The practitioner may want to target a particular group of children and relate objectives to their needs. In order to set objectives at an appropriate level for the targeted children, the practitioner should take into account prior learning and achievements, and consider where the children need to go next.

For example:

A group of children have spent time over a period of days investigating a range of containers in the water area. They have poured and filled and talked about their observations, for example: Adam, pouring water from a jug – 'Look! It's going – now it's gone! I'm going to put some more in – right up to the top!'; Sarah, using a large container full of water to fill a smaller one – 'It won't fit in it's going over the top'. The practitioner decides to build on this experience and extend the children's mathematical learning through a focus activity. The learning objectives are:

- To make comparisons between containers in terms of capacity
- To use mathematical language[1] when talking about their observations.

When the practitioner decides to focus on goals in a particular area of learning, and intends for many children to access the activities, learning objectives should reflect the range of needs, and opportunities for differentiation stated on the plan.

It is important to remember that, although objectives may target certain areas of the curriculum, other learning will take place during the course of the activity – this may or may not be anticipated but should be valued. The purpose of setting objectives is to focus, not restrict, learning. It should also be said that the intention may sometimes simply be to support a child in sustaining an identi-fied interest and, in such a case, objectives would probably relate to key goals for 'Dispositions and attitudes'. However, a retrospective evaluation of the focus would be likely to reveal a host of unanticipated learning opportunities.

Once learning objectives have been identified, the nature and content of the activity can be decided.

The activity – what will the children do?

The next step is to plan an activity that will help children to achieve objectives. The activity should capture their interest and should be embedded in a context that is meaningful to them.

Learning objectives

- To construct with a purpose in mind using a variety of resources.

- To describe main story settings, events and principal characters.

Activity: building houses for the 'Three Little Pigs'

To help the adult in structuring the activity, a sequence of elements will probably be identified in the plan. In the case of the 'Three Little Pigs' example used, these could include:

Introduction

The adult will read the story of *The Three Little Pigs* and encourage the children to discuss reasons why the wolf was able to blow down the first two houses but not the third.

Main activity

Children will construct three houses using straw, sticks and bricks (wooden, or plastic interlocking). They will talk about the story as they work, discussing characters and events.

Finishing off and follow-up

Children will test each construction for strength using bellows to emulate the wolf's 'blowing'. The made houses will be displayed, and resources made available all week so that children can revisit, and other children engage in, the activity. Laminated illustrations from *The Three Little Pigs* book will be displayed alongside the made houses and children encouraged to sequence these and retell the story to a friend.

Opportunities for differentiation and extension work

These should also be identified on the plan:

- Recording materials used in the construction of the house (tick lists, written lists, pictorial lists)

- Discussing which materials were the most successful and why (in terms of their properties)

- Looking at materials used to build real houses and architects' designs

- Making a plan of the made house or designing a different house

- Recording (audio tape) instructions for making a house

- Using 'Little Pig' puppets and puppet theatre to reconstruct the story

- Recording (audio tape) children retelling the story.

Where will the activity take place?

This is an important decision and there will often be a number of alternatives to consider. The nature and quality of the children's learning will be determined to a large extent by the environment in which it takes place. Practitioners may choose to site the activity in an existing area of provision (possibly enhanced with additional resources) or may decide to create a new 'area' which will serve as a particularly rich and appropriate setting for the intended learning. It may be that the activity could take place in a number of different areas of provision or across the whole nursery.

The following example illustrates the diversity of children's writing experience and the influence of the immediate environment on their learning.

Learning objective: to use writing to convey meaning

Table 2.1 The potential for writing in different areas

Example area	Potential writing experiences
Office	Letters, birthday cards, telephone messages, order forms, memos
Home corner	Party invitations, shopping lists, recipes, menus, telephone messages, catalogue orders, recounts, stories
Construction	Plans, lists, traffic signs, instructions
Water	Poems, lists, records of 'findings'
Book area	Stories, book reviews, information

The choice of area may be influenced by the interests of targeted children. Those children who prefer to spend their time building castles in the construction area may not be inspired to engage in a writing activity in the office – this would be good reason, then, to take the writing to the construction area and ensure that it had meaning for those children.

Activities could include: listing the resources they had used to build their castle, writing a story about their castle, writing invitations to the 'Castle Ball' and addressing envelopes to their favourite toys, making signs which direct the guests to the ballroom.

Alternatively, the adult may want to encourage children to work in an area that they rarely choose to frequent in order to develop certain skills and knowledge.

In this case, the nature of the activity needs to have appeal for those children. For example, a group of children who show little enthusiasm for working in the construction area, but who frequently choose to play in the home corner, could be encouraged to engage in a building and constructing activity in the construction area by being challenged to build a table for their teddy bears' picnic, or a bed for their dolls, which they could then transfer to, and use, in the home corner.

Figure 2.2 Taking a telephone message in the home corner

Resources – what should be added to basic provision?

The resources offered to the children will be very influential in shaping their learning and should always be of the highest quality. If an activity is sited in a permanent area of provision, it may be that the basic resources in this area are adequate in supporting the specific learning identified in the plan. It will almost certainly be the case that children use basic resources to some extent.

Practitioners may decide to 'enhance' provision in an area by adding extra resources in order to attract the children to the activity, stimulate imagination, help them to develop particular skills, knowledge and concepts, and as an extension of the basic provision.

Making musical instruments in the workshop

- *Basic workshop resources*: cardboard tubes, range of plastic tubs and pots, cardboard boxes, plastic bottles, treasury tags, paper clips, paper fasteners, rubber bands, glue (sticks and PVA), glue spreaders, sellotape, masking tape.

- *Additional resources*: a range of musical instruments, tape recorder and a range of taped music; for use in 'shakers': sand, dried peas, beads, buttons, pebbles, dried leaves; for use on 'drums': pieces of fabric, thin plastic sheeting; recording 'frames' (for use by children – see Figure 2.4).

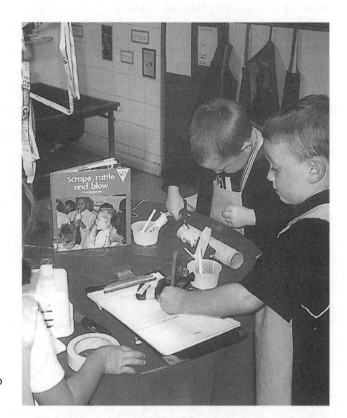

Figure 2.3 Making musical instruments in the workshop area

Figure 2.4 Making a musical instrument – recording frame

When a temporary area is set up, it will comprise mostly of resources additional to basic provision, although some will probably be duplicated in other areas of the setting.

> ### *Role-play: builder's office linked to a construction site*
>
> ● Duplicated resources: pens, pencils, crayons, paper, clipboards, scissors, glue sticks, telephones.
>
> ● New resources: builder's merchant's catalogues, invoice forms, order forms, architect's plans, walkie talkies/mobile phones.

It is important to remind practitioners at this stage of their role as a valuable resource in the context of children's learning.

Adult role – what will the adult do?

The precise role of the adult will vary according to the activity but in general terms it is to support, directly or indirectly, the children's learning. Direct support will involve:

● Stimulating children's interest in an activity

● Providing high-quality resources

● Listening and responding to children's talk

● Questioning children in order to extend learning (questions should be differentiated to address individual needs – see examples of activity plans)

● Working alongside children, modelling skills and use of key vocabulary

● Encouraging, reassuring and praising children

● Valuing and celebrating children's achievements.

A period of observation before intervening in children's play will help the adult to decide on the timing and nature of the support.

> To make certain that positive intervention does not become futile interfering in a child's learning process, it must be preceded by sensitive observation and interaction with the child.
>
> (Nutbrown 1999)

Indirect support includes assessment, which starts with observation of children at work. In some circumstances, observation will be the main role of the adult, but there will be times when balancing interaction with observation seems an almost impossible task. This aspect of the educator's role will be explored in greater depth in Chapter 6, but, with regard to the focus activity, practitioners may find that referral to the learning objectives on the plan helps them to focus their observations, as in the following example.

Learning objectives

- To identify and talk about features of living things.
- To use books as a source of information.

Activity: observing tadpoles

Observation

- Kylie, watching the tadpoles, remarked: 'Look! Their legs are growing – I can see them wriggling when they swim. They haven't got any arms but their tails are very long – their tails are swimming too.' Kylie spent a few minutes studying the tadpoles and then asked 'When will they go on the rock – when will they jump?' Supported by Mrs Taylor, she found a book about frogs and pointed to a picture of a tadpole saying 'That's like ours – it's got legs and it's got a tail'. She was interested in looking at the 'frog development' pictures with Mrs Taylor – they discussed what would be the next stage of development for their tadpoles and agreed to watch out for any changes.

Assessment

- Kylie shows a keen interest in living things. She is able to recognise and talk about features of living things using everyday language. Kylie understands that information can be found in books. She is able, with support, to read pictures in information books to extend her own learning.

How long should a focus activity last?

The answer to this question is dependent on a number of factors and, although practitioners will need to allocate a 'time slot' on the weekly plan for pre-planned activities, it may be necessary to review timing as the week progresses. For example, children discover a snail in the outside play area on Monday and staff recognise the potential for developing a valuable learning experience. They decide to respond to the children's excitement and fascination by planning time on Tuesday and Wednesday to observe and find out about snails. They postpone the focus activity originally planned for Tuesday, to Thursday. In making this decision they are ensuring that both the snail investigation and the planned focus activity receive the adult input, and enthusiasm from the children, that they need to be successful in extending learning.

Practitioners may decide to review the length of time allocated to an activity as they gauge the children's response. It is difficult to anticipate duration and children's interest in the activity is often the deciding factor. Evaluation of the activity as a learning experience may lead staff to develop ideas and plan follow-up activities and extension work. It is often a good idea to make the additional resources used during the activity available for children to access (with or without adult input) for some time afterwards – this allows for exploration of ideas in a less structured context and consolidation of knowledge and concepts. Alternatively, the response of the children may have been disappointing and staff may decide to plan a different activity, but with the same learning objectives. In the latter case, the decision to 'cut short' the activity may be taken – there can be little purpose in pursuing an activity that holds no interest for the children.

How 'rigid' should the plan be?

The activity plan should be seen as a supportive framework within which the practitioner can work to challenge children's thinking and help them to make progress towards achieving intended outcomes. Objectives need to be 'tight' but the plan should be flexible enough to allow for professional judgement – it is the skill of the early years practitioner in recognising when and how to intervene in children's play as it progresses, and the quality of questioning in response to their play, which ensures that children benefit fully from the provision.

What should practitioners consider when evaluating the focus?

In order for an activity evaluation to be useful, it must provide practitioners with information that will enable them to improve their practice and focus future planning.

This will require consideration of a number of elements and it can be helpful to work within a framework or to use standard 'prompt' questions:

- How did the children respond to the activity? Did it capture their interest?

- Was the context appropriate or would another activity (or focus in another area of provision) have been more successful in achieving objectives?

- Look at the planned learning objectives – have these been achieved?

- How far are individuals or groups of children on their 'journey' towards the key early learning goals?

- What incidental learning took place and in which areas of the curriculum?

- What were the most effective strategies used by adults to support children's learning? How did this vary with different children and at different stages during the activity? Did the adult take on any unexpected roles?

- How will your observations feed into future planning? How could you extend learning further and support children's developing ideas and interests following the focus?

- What would you do differently next time if you planned this focus again?

- Are there any resource implications, for example do you need to order new equipment or replace equipment?

Examples of focus plans

The following activities are planned in accordance with the guidelines given in this chapter. Learning objectives focus on particular areas of learning. Chapter 3 also includes examples of focus activity plans, some of which have cross-curricular learning objectives and others, objectives that focus on one area of learning. All activities have been 'tested' in an early years setting, have proved successful in achieving objectives and have been received with enthusiasm by children! However, each group of children is unique with its own range of interests and practitioners should bear in mind that plans may need to be modified to meet the needs of their children.

Examples of short-term planning for focus activities follow a common format and are organised under the following headings:

- Focus area of learning
- Learning objectives
- Background information and prior learning
- Introduction
- Main activity
- Finishing off and follow-up
- Adult role
- Key questions
- Resources.

'Jasper's Birthday'

This activity was planned at a time when a number of children were celebrating birthdays and attending parties. It inspired many reluctant mark-makers to attempt writing for a purpose. Jasper, a favourite puppet character, was used to motivate children and capture their imagination. The area of provision in which the invitation writing takes place is immaterial as long as adequate and appropriate resources are available to the child, although the most obvious choices are probably the office or the home corner. The initial activity will probably become the starting point for other imaginative and role-play activities which may offer additional opportunities for purposeful writing. It is a good idea to inform parents and carers of the focus of the activity so that they can support and extend their child's learning at home – children will probably want to invite their own soft toys to Jasper's birthday party!

FOCUS ACTIVITY:
JASPER'S BIRTHDAY

Focus areas of learning

Working towards early learning goals in:

- Physical development (moving and handling)
- Literacy (writing, reading)

Learning objectives

- To understand that print conveys meaning.
- To use own writing to communicate meaning.
- To practise and develop writing skills in a real context.

Background information and prior learning

All children will have experience of mark-making with a range of tools. They will be familiar with adults modelling purposeful writing and reading. They will be at different stages in their writing development and the adult will address individual needs in questions asked (adult role, key vocabulary and questions). All children will have met Jasper, the puppet, in other contexts on previous occasions. Most children will have first-hand experience of birthday parties.

Introduction

The adult will introduce Jasper and explain to the children that he is very excited because it is his birthday today. The children will be shown an envelope and parcel that have arrived in the post addressed to Jasper. They will be encouraged to guess what is inside and then a child will be invited to help Jasper to open his card and present. The group will sing 'Happy Birthday' to Jasper and be asked if they would like to join in his birthday celebrations.

Main activity

The children and the adult will discuss their own experiences of birthday parties. They will send birthday cards to Jasper, wrap up birthday gifts and plan a birthday party. Writing experiences will include signing names on cards and gift tags, writing envelopes, place names, menus and shopping lists for party food.

Finishing off and follow-up

The birthday party will be planned to take place in the home corner. Children will be encouraged to write party invitations to their own soft toys from home. Photographs will be taken of the party and displayed in an album in the home corner. Children may also help Jasper to write 'thank you' letters for his presents.

Adult role

The adult will:

- Provide resources

- Stimulate interest in the activity and engage in role-play

- Model writing skills

- Ask differentiated questions

- Be aware of each child's stage of writing development and support them at their own level

- Observe children (re: enthusiasm for mark-making, purposes for writing, pencil control and letter formation) and record observations.

Key questions

What do you think is inside the envelope? Who has sent it? Why? What do you think the writing says? Where do we start to read the writing? What information do we need to include in the invitation? Can you see where Susie has written her name? What is your doll's name? Can you write her name on the envelope? Where will you write your name? Can you find your name card and copy your name or write your name without your name card? Can you read back your writing?

Resources

- Birthday card (written) in envelope addressed to Jasper

- Wrapped present with Jasper's name written on it

- Mark-making tools (pencils, pens)

- Paper, card, folded card (birthday cards, shopping lists, labels, etc.)

- Commercially-produced, blank birthday cards

- Invitation writing frames

- Wrapping paper, tape

'Make a game'

This activity was planned as part of a focus on mathematical development and, although key goals have been highlighted, it offers numerous learning opportunities in all three aspects of this curricular area. The activity was particularly successful when children worked together to agree rules and then engaged in playing the game they had devised.

FOCUS ACTIVITY:
MAKING GAMES

Focus area of learning

Working towards early learning goals in:

- Mathematics (number, shape, space and measure)

Learning objectives

- To make up their own games.

- To count, and to recognise and use numbers, up to six and calculate using numbers beyond six.

- To explore pattern in their play using the language of position and orientation.

Background information and prior learning

Long-term plans for areas of provision include opportunities for children to develop awareness and understanding of number and attributes such as colour, size and shape in a variety of contexts. Children will have had a number of opportunities to play simple board games with an adult in the setting and some will have had similar experiences at home.

Introduction

The adult will introduce the new resources to the children, allowing them time to handle and explore equipment and to talk about their observations. The group will discuss the contexts in which children have used dice or spinners before and discuss their experiences of board games. The adult will then encourage children to use equipment in a more focused way, for example, by rolling a die and then moving a button the same number of spaces (as the dots shown on the die) on a grid.

Main activity

Children will make up their own games, selecting from the equipment available and experimenting with rule structures. They will play games with each other and the adult. (See Figure 2.5 for examples of games made up by children.)

Finishing off and follow-up

This activity will be available over a period of time to enable children to develop their ideas and modify games. Children will be encouraged to explain the rules of their games and their instructions will be scribed. Rules will be recorded on 'game cards' (see Figure 2.5). Parents will be invited to play children's made-up games in the setting and 'game sets' will be put together in boxes for children to borrow overnight. Adults will take opportunities to develop children's understanding of number and calculation within the context of their play primarily through modelling and questioning.

Adult role

The adult will:

- Gather resources and present them in an organised and attractive way, for example sorting equipment stored in segmented trays or labelled baskets

- Stimulate interest in the activity, modelling ideas and involving children in playing games

- Model use of key vocabulary

- Support children in making links and agreeing rules

- Challenge thinking through differentiated questioning

- Observe children and record evidence of their achievements towards the key goals.

Key vocabulary and questions

Vocabulary: Number names (one–six), colour names, 'more', 'less', 'add', 'count', 'count on', 'next', 'first', 'last', 'same', 'different'.

Questions: The dice shows red, can you find a red reel to put on the grid? Whose turn is it now? How many more spaces does the blue button need to move before it reaches the end? How many spaces has your reel moved already? Your two dice show two and three – how many is that altogether? What colour do you need next to carry on your pattern?

Resources

- Laminated grids (some blank, some with a colour in each space and some with a number at the end of each column)

- Paper copies of blank grid

- Dice and spinners (spots, numerals and colours)

- Coloured* pencils or felt pens

- Coloured* sorting equipment (e.g. buttons, plastic reels, transport sorting set)

* Colours should correspond to colours on the dice

'Making boats'

This activity was planned following an investigation of materials in the water tray. The practitioner wanted children to use their prior knowledge in responding to a challenge and solving a practical problem. The story *Where the Wild Things Are* by Maurice Sendak was a familiar tale and Max, a favourite character. The story was used to motivate the children, give purpose to their designing, and criteria for success when testing their boat 'structures'. The activity is a good example of using two areas of provision (water and workshop) in one activity, and could take place inside or outside.

Figure 2.5 Children's games

Children's Games

Spotty patterns

Rules:

- Roll the colour die.
- Choose a pen the same colour as the colour shown on the die.
- Make a coloured spot in a space on the grid.
- Carry on until all the spaces are filled and look at the pattern you have made!

Numbers and spots

Rules:

- Roll the number die.
- Draw the same number of spots in a space on the grid as the numeral shown on the die.
- Carry on until you have filled the spaces.
- Count how many spots are in each column – which is the 'winner'?

Bear race

Rules:

- Roll the colour die and, whatever colour shows, find a bear of the same colour and match it to a coloured spot on the board.
- When all the spots of one colour have been covered, the game is over and that colour has won!

Figure 2.6 Making up games

FOCUS ACTIVITY:
MAKING BOATS

Focus area of learning

Working towards early learning goals in:

- Expressive arts and design (exploring and using media and materials)

Learning objectives

- To design and construct for a specific purpose.
- To use prior knowledge in problem-solving.
- To select tools and materials appropriately.
- To evaluate the success of a design and make necessary modifications.

Background information and prior learning

Children will have been given opportunities for exploration of materials. They will have talked about properties and investigated how different materials react when placed in water. Children will understand the concepts of 'floating' and 'sinking' and will be familiar with the key vocabulary. They will have experience of using a range of tools and materials in the workshop area. Children will be familiar with the story *Where the Wild Things Are*.

Introduction

The children will be reminded of the recently read story *Where the Wild Things Are*. The adult will explain to the children that Max's boat has a leak and cannot be used, but that he is desperate to visit the 'Wild Things' again. The adult will show the children models of Max and the Wild Things (Max placed at one end of the water tray and the Wild Things at the other) and ask for suggestions as to how Max could cross the 'ocean'. They will discuss suggestions (see 'Key questions') and children will be challenged to build a boat that will carry Max to the 'Wild Things'.

Main activity

The children will build a boat for Max using tools and materials in the workshop (see 'Resources'). They will look at information books about boats. They will talk about prior investigations and use their knowledge from these to inform their decisions. They will test their boat in the water tray to determine whether or not it floats and will make any necessary modifications.

Finishing off and follow-up

Children will put the 'Max' model in their boat and transport him to the other side of the 'ocean' and the 'Wild Things'. Some children will record their work (see 'Resources').

Adult role

The adult will:

- Provide resources

- Stimulate children's imagination and interest in the activity

- Be aware of children's prior learning and build on their knowledge

- Ask questions in order to extend learning

- Support children in recording their work

- Observe the children re: appropriate use of tools and materials, ability to design for a purpose and evaluate success of their design or modify their design, ability to record work.

Key vocabulary and questions

Vocabulary: Float, sink

Questions: How can we help Max to cross the 'ocean'? Examples of suggestions: Make a bridge – how could it stretch all the way across? What could we use to support it? Would it be too far for Max to walk? He could swim – is Max strong enough to swim all that way? How could he carry his suitcase? What would happen if there were sharks in the water? Make a boat – what would we use for the bottom of the boat, the cabin, the sail or the mast? What happens to this material if it gets wet? Do you think this plastic pot will float? Let's test it in the water tray – were you right? How could you stop your boat from sinking? Where will Max sit in your boat? Does your boat still float when it is carrying Max? What did you use to make your boat? Which materials were successful or unsuccessful?

Resources

- *Where the Wild Things Are* by Maurice Sendak

- Max and 'Wild Things' models

- Information books about boats

- Basic provision in workshop area and water area (see long-term plans for these areas of provision)

- Recording frames

Story-making and imaginative play

It seems that anything that is introduced to children out of a sealed box, bag or envelope can be exciting to them. Such an introduction, especially when children are encouraged to anticipate what might be inside, is usually very effective in stimulating imagination and inspiring enthusiasm for an activity. In the following

Figure 2.7 Testing Max's boat in the water tray

case, a key inside a decorated box is the stimulus but other resources could be just as successful in prompting creative ideas, for example:

- A tiara in a jewellery box
- A purse in a handbag
- An ornate silver spoon in a velvet pouch
- A photograph (e.g. a character or building) in an envelope
- A gem stone or piece of crystal in a small satin-lined box
- A large, exotic shell wrapped in tissue paper.

Whatever the stimulus, during an activity of this nature the practitioner should provide children with the necessary resources for them to develop their imaginative ideas. The introduction of this particular activity took place in the book corner. This area was chosen because it was enclosed on three sides (and relatively free from distractions) and because there was ample provision for all children to sit comfortably. The story-making and imaginative play took place throughout the setting but, as play progressed and it was agreed that the key probably opened a box of treasure lost at sea, children and staff decided to build a ship in the outside area so that they could search for the treasure.

FOCUS ACTIVITY:
STORY-MAKING AND IMAGINATIVE PLAY

Focus area of learning

Working towards early learning goals in:

Expressive arts and design (being imaginative)

Learning objectives

- To respond imaginatively to a stimulus.
- To express thoughts and ideas through imaginative play.

Background information and prior learning

Children will have experience of listening to stories and of engaging in and observing imaginative play.

Introduction

The adult will show the children a 'very special box' and ask them to guess what is inside. The box will be opened to reveal a key (see 'Resources'). Children will be encouraged to handle the key in turn and describe how it looks and feels.

Main activity

The adult will lead and support the children, through questioning (see 'Key questions'), in creating a story around the key. They will express ideas which the adult will scribe. The children will then be encouraged to work as a group to develop their 'key story' ideas through imaginative play. Children will use the key, and other props (see 'Resources'), in their play.

Finishing off and follow-up

Children will be encouraged to share their stories and ideas with other children at a group gathering. Some children will record their story ideas pictorially and/or in a written form. A book will be compiled using photographs taken of resources and children's play, and children's story ideas (recorded by them or scribed by the adult). Copies of the book will be available for children to take home and share with their families. Children will be allowed continued access to resources, and time, to develop ideas.

Adult role

The adult will:

- Provide resources
- Stimulate interest in the activity and build up anticipation (re: opening the box)
- Ask questions, and make suggestions (without dominating), in order to develop imaginative ideas

- Encourage children to express ideas, and value their contributions

- Scribe children's ideas

- Support children in recording their ideas at their own level

- Observe children's play re: response to activity, use of imagination, ability to express ideas

- Record observations in individual profiles

- Photograph children at play

- Compile a book of their work.

Key vocabulary and questions

Questions: Where do you think the box was found? Who left it there? What do you think is inside the box? Who does the key belong to? What has happened – has the person lost the key? – Has it been stolen? What will the key open – a secret door? – A box? – A cupboard? – A treasure chest? – A case? What will you do with the key? Where will you go – how will you use it? How will you find the owner of the key? Who will go with you? What happens on your journey to find the owner of the key?

Resources

- A 'special box' (e.g. painted gold and decorated with 'jewels') containing an elaborate key

- Additional resources such as large cardboard boxes, pieces of fabric, a variety of hats

- Mark-making tools, paper

- Camera

Introductory circle session

This 'circle session' was the first in a series of sessions planned to establish a forum for addressing issues around PSED. The intention was that, once children were familiar with the weekly model, practitioners could introduce a focus that was pertinent to that particular group of children at that time. For example, at a time when construction equipment in the setting was not being put away after use resulting in children not wanting to access the chaotic area, a similar scenario could be recreated using the regular puppet (Tig) and another puppet with boxes of construction equipment. Children would then able to view the issues objectively and become part of the solution, rather than the problem, as they make suggestions to the puppets. Hopefully, the ideas discussed, and agreements reached, during the circle session would be transferred to the children's free play in the construction area and impact positively on the behaviour of the group as a whole. The circle session can offer children opportunities to explore feelings, talk about experiences, agree rules and learn about sharing, taking turns and negotiating. They can also be a very genuine forum for adults to consult with children over issues concerning them, e.g. lunch-time routines, changes in the learning environment.

These sessions should be a 'safe' and non-threatening forum for children and some may want to observe for a few sessions before actively taking part. Sessions are often organised in key groups and led by the key person with whom children will already have a comfortable and trusting relationship. Ideally, they should take place in a quiet area free from distractions. Sessions should be short and engaging.

There are a number of established circle session models, most of which work around a routine and clear rules. The following plan is offered as a suggestion but may need to be altered to suit the needs of different children and settings.

FOCUS ACTIVITY: CIRCLE SESSION: INTRODUCTORY SESSION

Focus area of learning

Working towards early learning goals in:

- Personal, social and emotional development (making relationships, self-confidence and self awareness, managing feelings and behaviour)

Learning objectives

- To introduce children to the circle session puppet.
- To familiarise children with the routine and rules of a circle session.

Background information and prior learning

Attitudes of respect for the feelings of others and interest in the experiences and work of others are promoted through all areas of provision and learning. Children will be familiar with the following expectation during group sessions (such as story time): sit quietly and listen when it is someone else's turn to speak.

Introduction

The key person will gather children together and ask them to find a chair to sit on. She will explain that they are going to meet a special visitor.

Main activity

The key person will introduce Tig, the circle session puppet, and invite each child to say 'Hello' to him as he is passed around the circle. She will encourage children to tell the puppet their names. Tig will give each child a 'Welcome to Tig Time' card. The key person will explain to the children that there are important rules to remember during Tig Time. Tig will help the children to learn the rules:

- Sit quietly on your chair and keep your feet still.

- Listen when someone else is speaking.

- When you are holding Tig's special shell, it is your turn to speak (and you can expect others to listen).

Tig's shell will be passed around the circle and children will be asked to tell him what they like to do at nursery. The key person will introduce the 'ring game' arranging the ribbon so that it stretches around the circle with each child holding it in both hands. She will ask children to pass the ring around the ribbon circle taking only one hand off the ribbon at a time. Once the children are confident with the aims of the game, she will suggest that they play it with their eyes closed.

Tig will pass around his 'bag of smiles' and invite each child to take an imaginary smile.

Finishing off and follow-up

Children will sing the end of circle session song:

Tig Time has finished now, finished now, finished now.

Tig Time has finished now, see you next week! (to the tune of 'Here we go round the mulberry bush')

They will be reminded that they will meet Tig again next week. Children will take their welcome card home. Parents will be informed of the purposes of circle sessions through a display and leaflets. Further sessions will be planned. All sessions will include reinforcement of the rules, interaction with Tig, a game, an invitation to take a smile from the smile bag and the closing song.

Adult role

The adult will:

- Help the children to feel relaxed in a calm, comfortable and welcoming environment

- Encourage the children to speak but respect their right to stay silent or 'pass'.

- Remind children of the 'rules' when necessary.

- Always be positive – thank children for their contributions and praise them for their adherence to the rules.

- Discuss with children the features of a good listener (i.e. looking at the speaker, being quiet and still)

- Take photographs of children and scribe their comments, compile book

- Observe children re: general response to the session, confidence in speaking in a group, ability to use language to express themselves.

Key vocabulary and questions

- Puppet's name (Tig)
- Shell
- Next, pass, turn
- Speak/talk, listen

Resources

- Seven child-sized chairs (one adult, six children) arranged in a circle.
- Puppet (Tig)
- Exotic shell
- Welcome cards (with Tig's photograph on the front)
- Empty, attractive decorated bag ('bag of smiles')
- Length of ribbon threaded through a wooden curtain ring and tied to create a circle.

'Bear Hunt' – obstacle course

This is another example of a favourite story being used as the starting point for an activity (Chapter 3 offers further examples of stories as starting points). The 'Bear Hunt' took place in the outside area and this is the ideal site for the activity. A large hall could be used as a 'wet weather' alternative but, if the hall is not accessible on a permanent basis, use of the resources over the following few days (as recommended in the plan) may be difficult to organise. The activity allowed staff to observe a range of skills, enabling them to make clear assessments of children's physical development. Most children chose to participate in the activity and some continued to set up their own bear hunts long after the 'focus' had passed.

FOCUS ACTIVITY:
GOING ON A 'BEAR HUNT' – OBSTACLE COURSE

Focus area of learning

Working towards early learning goals in:

- Physical development (moving and handling)

Learning objectives

- To develop jumping, balancing, climbing, hopping, running skills.

- To move with imagination and confidence.
- To develop spatial awareness.

Background information and prior learning

Children will have had daily opportunities to develop gross motor skills. There will be children at different stages of physical development – the activity will be open to all children and the adult should be aware of the range and nature of needs in order to give effective support.

Introduction

The adult will read the story *We're Going on a Bear Hunt* by Michael Rosen, the children will join in with the words and actions. The adult will ask the children if they would like to go on a bear hunt. They will pack imaginary bags and begin their hunt.

Main activity

The children, with the adult, will follow the obstacle course to the bear cave. For example:

- Climbing over a mountain – climbing up a ladder and over the climbing frame
- Going through a dark tunnel – crawling through the barrel
- Walking over a bridge – balancing on a plank
- Wading through a muddy swamp – walking over tyres
- Crossing a river on stepping-stones – stepping on different-sized wooden hollow blocks
- Following a narrow path – walking on a wavy chalk line
- Walking through a thick forest – weaving in and out of cones
- Jumping over a stream – jumping over two parallel chalk lines.

Children may want to chant the words from the 'Bear Hunt' story or make up their own chants. When they reach the bear cave, they will go inside, discover the imaginary bear and run to the other side of the play area.

Finishing off and follow-up

The 'Bear Hunt' obstacle course will be set up in the outside play area for a few days to allow children to revisit the activity and practise skills. The resources may be organised in a different way each day, or new resources introduced, in order to add interest or extend learning.

Adult role

The adult will:

- Set up obstacle course and bear cave in outside play area

- Read the story and stimulate interest in the activity
- Lead the 'Bear Hunt'
- Encourage children to join in
- Talk to them using suggested vocabulary
- Support children at their own stage of physical development
- Observe children re. physical skills, confidence, spatial awareness, and record their achievements.

Key vocabulary and questions

Vocabulary: The adult will use, and encourage the children to use, words such as 'through', 'over', 'under', 'in', 'out', 'up', 'down'.

Questions: Can you go over or under the bridge? How will you get to the other side of the river? Is there enough room for you and Tom to be on the bridge at the same time? Can you step across the stream or do you need to jump? Can you walk in between the cones without touching them? Can you step from the middle of one tyre to the next without touching the rubber? Can you balance on the top of the tyre?

Resources

- *We're Going on a Bear Hunt* by Michael Rosen
- Tyres, wooden planks and blocks, barrel, ladders, climbing frame, cones, chalk

KEY POINTS FOR GOOD PRACTICE

- Remember that inspiration for focus planning can come from a variety of sources. Long- and medium-term plans will offer banks of ideas but children's observed needs and interests should always be the paramount consideration.
- Remember that activities and experiences should be offered to children but not imposed on them. Any topics or themes should relate to children's experience and current interests and are unlikely to be relevant or interesting to all children.
- Be aware that a focus should take place in a meaningful context within the learning environment.
- Link plans to key early learning goals and differentiate them to address the needs of all children accessing the focus.
- Be prepared to abandon a pre-planned focus in favour of pursuing a spontaneous and more exciting interest. The original focus can always be introduced, if appropriate, at a later date.

- Value children's individual responses to a focus and support them in following up their own ideas.
- Recognise the importance of evaluating a focus and the positive impact that this can have on future practice. Make sure that there are systems in place so that practitioners can share such information.

The valuing and sharing of children's play by adults can only serve to increase the status of the activity and the self-esteem of the child.

(Abbot and Rodger 1994)

Note

1   Key vocabulary should be identified on the plan, in this case 'full', 'empty', 'more', 'less'.

CHAPTER 3

Starting points for developing learning

Children learn by leading their own play, and by taking part in play which is guided by adults.

(DfE 2012, Statutory Framework for the EYFS)

The content of this chapter is organised as follows:

Chapter 2 looked at why and how to plan a focus. This chapter aims to explore different stimuli for developing learning in the early years environment. It consists of ideas and plans which are offered as examples of starting points. These are intended to be of practical use to the reader but many will not transfer directly. Those based on the interests and experiences of particular children are presented more as examples of an approach rather than for direct use, although elements may be relevant to other children. As emphasised throughout this book, each child, and each group of children, is unique. With them they bring a set of experiences, knowledge and interests that provide a rich foundation for teaching and learning but that will never be exactly replicated in another group of children. This makes planning in the early years both exciting and challenging. One thing is for certain, it should never become dull or monotonous!

A responsive approach to planning

It is useful at this stage to redefine our understanding of what is included in 'planning'. So far we have looked in detail at planning formats for areas of provision and for a focus. Clear frameworks for planning are important and ensure that systems are rigorous and thorough, covering all elements agreed to contribute to the support of children's learning. However, there is a danger that, in a culture of evidence-based accountability, what is written down in a formal plan becomes much more important than those actions taken more spontaneously, but with thought, throughout the day or week. It is often these informal actions that are effective in enabling and motivating children, and in sustaining momentum. Where teams recognise the importance of these day-to-day interventions and understand that they cannot always be anticipated at a weekly meeting, they have developed planning systems to include, and raise the status of, incidental practices. This has resulted in a more responsive and 'organic' approach to planning. This type of planning is 'live' and ongoing, embracing both freedom and rigour. Its success is dependent on a well-planned learning environment and it will include detailed focus planning for some activities or experiences where practitioners consider there to be a need. It will show clearly how observation has informed planning, how children have responded to ideas and the learning that has taken place. It will involve all adults, including parents, and will reflect children's ownership of their own learning. As a shared document, such planning is often recorded somewhere visually accessible to all audiences, for example on a wall display or in a floor book. The advantages of using a large floor book over a display are that it can easily be moved to a place where children can look at it, reflect on it and contribute to it and it is easily stored as evidence or for future reflection. Because of the ongoing nature of the planning, adults and children will be able to add to it at any point although a regular weekly team meeting will provide a valuable forum for review and discussion around threads of play and learning (see 'King Lanzarote' example, page 100). This approach supports not only the children's learning but also the adult's learning and professional development.

This type of planning is:

- Growing, evolving, inspired by children's development and interests
- Visible and shared by practitioners, children and parents
- Embracing all aspects of 'planning', everything that impacts positively on children's learning
- Telling a story about children's learning and development
- A celebration of a journey involving children and adults.

It is also helpful to discuss in a little more depth the term 'child initiated'. This is a term which is widely used but not always clearly understood within the complex context of how young children learn. Within a rich learning environment, children will be able to discover and pursue individual or group interests and develop a creative approach to learning. An open-ended activity planned by an adult can also stimulate interest and ignite individual ideas. Children will bring ideas and experiences from home to the setting and vice versa. All of these will be a powerful and motivating force for future learning and it is the practitioner's responsibility to recognise and support them. This supportive role will involve guidance, teaching and the offer of further motivating activities and experiences that 'fuel' the journey and sustain the commitment to learning. It is a skilled role that should be undertaken with deep consideration and sensitivity and with open-minded attitudes to outcomes. The practitioner, whilst enabling the child to navigate the direction of their own learning will, in the knowledge of the child's stage of development and capabilities, use the interest as a vehicle for challenge. So, it is right that 'child-initiated' learning is high on the agenda of all practitioners, but an effective approach to supporting this is dependent on enabling an environment that includes the interventions of a knowledgeable and understanding adult. A young child, however motivated and competent, is likely to come to a point in their pursuit of an idea where they need the support of an adult whether this be, for example, help with a technical skill, the provision of additional equipment or the shared talking through of options. This working partnership between adult and child is very different from a more formal 'adult-led' activity where the content, direction and outcomes are defined in advance by the adult. However, the support for learning should no less rigorous and the common perception that, unless children are unsupported, their learning cannot be defined as 'child initiated' can lead to unnecessary limits being placed on their explorations and resulting understanding.

This responsive approach to planning can be used as a vehicle for promoting learning, and for challenging children in particular areas of learning, perhaps where a need or gap has been identified. A balance should be struck between 'following' children's interests and being one step ahead of them in terms of understand their learning needs and what is motivating them. This does not mean that the adult will be leading the direction of play and learning, but will adopt a very conscious approach to support and challenge based on ongoing observation.

In identifying a meaningful interest, the 'characteristics of effective learning' (Department for Education 2012) are a useful tool (see also Chapter 6). Where a child is involved, concentrating, persisting and showing satisfaction in their achievements, the practitioner can feel confident of the child's commitment, and in their own use of the interest as a starting point for planning. Where an interest is more fleeting, there will be less depth of involvement. These characteristics can also be used to evaluate children's responses to planned activities or experiences and to help the practitioner to know if they are on the 'right track' or making inaccurate assumptions about what is motivating children.

An effective early years curriculum recognises the need for children to be 'active learners'. Through interacting with, and responding to, the world around them, children acquire skills and knowledge and develop concepts. Well-planned provision in the early years environment will offer them a wealth of exciting opportunities for exploration and investigation (see Chapters 1 and 5).

> In planning and guiding children's activities, practitioners must reflect on the different ways that children learn and reflect these in their practice.
>
> (Department for Education 2012)

In addition to the planning for identified group interests, there will be a need for the key person to be aware of, and support, any personal interests or explorations that are not captured through planning for the group. These may be documented through a regular summary in the child's learning journey.

Early years practitioners are on a constant quest for new and exciting ways of inspiring young children's learning and the sharing and pooling of ideas is to be encouraged. It is a privilege to work with young children, for whom learning is an exciting voyage of discovery, and also a great responsibility, since experiences in the early years play a vital part in shaping future attitudes to learning and in inspiring a continuing thirst for knowledge. It is the role of the early years practitioner to nurture and respond to children's natural curiosity and motivation and to engage them in the learning process.

Planning from children's interests and enthusiasms

(See also Chapters 4 and 6 for further examples of planning from children's interests.)

A great deal of children's learning takes place outside the setting and this should be recognised by the practitioner. Interests and experiences that children bring from home should be valued, celebrated and, if appropriate, used as a starting point for developing learning in the early years setting. Children also develop interests within the setting and may even be inspired by another child's interests, becoming involved in related activities – this situation offers rich opportunities for the sharing of knowledge and ideas and can lead to valuable learning experiences across the curriculum.

'On Safari'

Joe visited a safari park at the weekend and returned to nursery on Monday full of enthusiasm for the experience. He was given an opportunity to talk about his visit to a small group of children and to show the brochure and plastic elephant he had brought back. Other children were encouraged to ask him questions and a child was asked to bring the box of 'jungle animals' from the construction area. They looked at each animal in turn, naming them and discussing their features – Joe, and the other children, were encouraged to share knowledge and to use information books to further their knowledge.

A group of children (including Joe), inspired by the discussion, went to the construction area and spent the rest of the session building 'jungle environments' and story-making. The adult observed parts of their play and decided to plan a focus in the construction area the next day (see activity plan: 'Jungle Play').

FOCUS ACTIVITY:
'JUNGLE PLAY'

(See Figure 6.9)

Working towards early learning goals in:

- Personal, social and emotional development (making relationships)
- Communication and language (listening and attention, understanding, speaking)
- Expressive arts and design (exploring and using media and materials, being imaginative)

Learning objectives

- To use resources imaginatively.
- To take part as a speaker and a listener in a small group.
- To express thoughts and story ideas.
- To negotiate and work cooperatively.
- To use language to imagine and re-create roles and experiences.

Background information and prior learning

Joe visited a safari park at the weekend. He enthusiastically shared his experiences with a small group of children and has inspired some imaginative 'jungle play' and story-making in the construction area. After observation of children's play, staff agreed that adding extra resources (see 'Resources') to the area and planning some adult focus time would be likely to extend their learning in the focus areas. Targeted group: Joe, Lucy, Sameena, Jake and Andrew (this group will not be exclusive if other children choose to participate in the activity).

Introduction

The adult will show the children the extra resources and explain the purpose of these (i.e. for use by children in their 'jungle play').

Main activity (construction area)

Children will continue their 'jungle play' and story-making using basic provision in the construction area and additional resources (see Figure 6.9, Chapter 6).

Finishing off and follow-up

Additional resources and the children's constructions will remain in the area to allow for re-visiting of the activity and continuation of imaginative play and story-making. The precise nature of any follow-up work will be determined by the direction taken by the children in their play. There may be possibilities for making information or story books using photographs of the children's play, their ideas scribed by the adult and examples of their drawings and writing.

Adult role

The adult will:

- Value children's experiences outside the setting
- Provide resources
- Recognise when to intervene in children's play and when to 'stand back'
- Scribe children's imaginative and story ideas
- Question children about their play
- Observe children re: response to activity, ability to work cooperatively and express ideas, use of imagination in play
- Make a book or display (e.g. children's ideas, photographs of their play).

Key vocabulary and questions

Vocabulary: Animal names, for example elephant, lion, giraffe, gorilla, crocodile.

Questions: How many different animals live in your jungle? Can you name the animals? Why has this lion climbed to the top of the mountain? Would you like to explain to Lisa why the snake is hiding under the leaves? Are there any people in the jungle? Why are they there? How did they get there? Would you like to go to this jungle? What can you feel, see and hear in the jungle?

Resources

- Basic resources in the construction area including box of 'jungle animals'
- Additional resources: fiction and non-fiction books about jungles and animals, pieces of fabric (different textures, natural colours), crepe and tissue paper, cellophane, cardboard tubes and boxes

The children's interest in the 'jungle theme' deepened. They revisited the construction area over the course of a few days, modifying their 'jungles' and creating more elaborate and imaginative stories. By this time other children were showing an interest in their work, some attempting to join in and others choosing to observe.

At this point the practitioner decided to plan another focus activity in order to develop particular skills using the jungle interest as a starting point. This time the whole group was involved as a letter from 'Lion' was read out:

FOCUS ACTIVITY:
'LION'S VISIT' (BUILDING A DEN)

Working towards early learning goals in:

- Expressive arts and design (exploring and using media and materials, being imaginative)

Learning objectives

- To explore properties of materials.
- To select and use tools and materials appropriately.
- To design and construct for a specific purpose.
- To make plans and lists of the materials they have used.

Figure 3.1 Lion arrives in his box

Background information and prior learning

A group of children have been pursuing a 'jungle interest' in the construction area. The focus activity planned in response to this interest has been successful in achieving its objectives and children are still very enthusiastic about the jungle theme. Staff have therefore decided to use the theme again, this time as a starting point for developing technology skills. This activity will be open to all children.

Introduction

The children will be shown a large, 'camouflaged' cardboard box and invited to guess who is inside. 'Lion' will then appear from inside his box and 'tell' the children that he has come to spend some time with them. He will present them with a letter (see 'Resources') asking them to build a den for him and his family. Lion will explain to the children that he has brought a box of additional resources with him to help them in this task.

Main activity (workshop, construction area and outside play area)

Children will handle and talk about the resources in Lion's box. They will then use basic resources and Lion's additional resources to build a den to Lion's specifications. This activity can take place in any suitable area (see previous suggestions). They will be encouraged to make plans and lists as they work.

Finishing off and follow-up

Children will talk about the dens they have built, explaining what they did and used. They will test the dens according to the criteria in Lion's letter, for example size, safety and warmth.

Adult role

The adult will:

- Make Lion's box and provide all other resources
- Stimulate interest in the activity, building up excitement and anticipation during the introduction
- Work alongside children asking questions, modelling (building, drawing plans, writing lists), scribing children's ideas (lists, plans)
- Observe children re: appropriate selection and use of tools and materials, ideas, enthusiasm for and ability to record ideas.

Key vocabulary and questions

Questions: Who do you think is inside the box? Where has he come from? How did he get here? What will you use to build the walls of the den? How can we make the walls stronger? How can we make and support the roof? Is the den wide and tall enough for Lion and his family? How can we make it wider or taller? How can we make the den warmer? What shall we use to cover the floor? What did we use to build our den?

Resources

- Lion (soft toy) inside a box camouflaged with, for example, brown and green paper, paint or material
- Lion's letter (see Figure 3.2)

- Lion's box of additional resources, for example, cardboard boxes, lengths of fabric, paper (crepe, tissue, etc.), balsa wood, scissors, string, masking tape
- Photographs of lions and jungle environments, maps of Africa, safari travel brochures
- Paper, pens, pencils
- Recording frame (see Figure 1.4, page 15)
- Outside resources: milk crates, large cardboard boxes, tyres, wooden hollow blocks, planks, lengths of fabric, 'den' frame
- Outside equipment tick list (see Figure 3.3)

Where practitioners have identified an ongoing interest, this will provide a rich context for planning further learning experiences (see also Chapters 4 and 6). The interest may be motivating one child or a group of children over a period of time but any plans that are rooted in one child's interest are likely to excite other children too. This is true of planning to support children's schemas as it will often be the case that a number of children are exploring a similar schema at the same time. Any focus planned to support an ongoing interest will probably be part of a wider plan that includes enhancements to provision and specific adult support which will enable the child to develop the interest and use it as platform for further learning.

Dear Children,

Thank you for welcoming me to your nursery. Your teachers have told me about the exciting jungles you have created in your construction area and I was wondering if you would build a den for my family and me to stay in during our visit.

The den would need to be big enough for 3 cubs, their mother and me. It would also need to be warm and safe.

Can you help?

Yours hopefully,
The Lion.

Figure 3.2 Lion's letter

Figure 3.3 Outside equipment tick list

Figure 3.4 Lion's den in the construction area   **Figure 3.5** Lion's den in the outside area

'The budding engineer'

Figures 3.6 and 3.7 show how a child's interest in cars was supported in nursery. Liam's mum and dad had noticed that Liam was spending long periods of time playing with his toy cars at home, pretending to drive them and take them on journeys. He had also been very interested in the controls on the family car asking Dad about their functions and wanting him to demonstrate how to operate, for example, the lights and horn. Practitioners in nursery had recognised that Liam was often choosing to play with vehicles in the small world area and had also been interested in being a 'mechanic' in the outdoor garage role-play area. Liam was asked about his interest in cars and said that he would like to find out more about how they worked. After discussion with Liam's key person, and his mum and dad, it was decided that a focus, a visit to the centre car park, would be planned to enable Liam to look more closely at cars. A risk assessment was drawn up in advance of the visit to identify any potential hazards and minimise risks in order to ensure safety for Liam at all times. A practitioner took Liam into the car park (at a time when cars were not coming in or out) and they looked at a number of cars, noticing differences and similarities between shape, wheels, lights, etc. Liam was provided with a camera and took photographs of cars, and parts of cars, that interested him. He was particularly fascinated when the practitioner showed him a car engine, explaining in simple terms the functions of some of the components. On return to the centre, Liam's photographs were printed and the image of the engine (Figure 3.6) was produced in A4 size. Liam immediately took this large photograph to the technology workshop and began work on building his own engine. As he worked, he enjoyed the company of the adult with whom he had

Figure 3.6 Liam's photograph of the car engine

Figure 3.7 Liam building a car engine in the technology workshop

shared the experience, talking through his ideas with her and reflecting on what they had seen and learnt. Throughout the experience, Liam was focused clearly on pursuing the car theme and the opportunities for engaging in sustained shared thinking with him were plentiful.

Although, in this case, no curricular outcomes were highlighted by the adult in advance, and the activity was planned purely to support a sustained interest of Liam's, the learning opportunities that arose were diverse and numerous. The learning that took place was on a deep level because of Liam's high level of involvement and the sensitive support of the adult. Learning opportunities identified retrospectively:

- Characteristics of effective learning: Showing high levels of involvement and excitement about learning.
- Communication and language: Discussing the experience and using talk to connect ideas.
- Physical development: Using tools and materials effectively, and with control, to build his engine.
- Mathematics: Using developing mathematical ideas to solve problems when creating his engine.
- Understanding the world: Looking at similarities and differences and asking questions about how things worked. Using the camera to record parts of the car that interested him.
- Expressive arts and design: Building his own engine based on experience of looking at a real engine and using his photographs as a point of reference. Using one object to represent another, and a range of tools and techniques, to construct his model engine.

With such a keen interest, it is unlikely that this would be the end of Liam's eagerness to pursue it. The 'engine' theme could be used again as a starting point for planning, this time with increased knowledge about the nature of it based on observations. It could be a powerful tool for further promoting an area of learning, for example writing – recording the materials needed to make a model engine and the steps in the process.

'The DIY enthusiasts'

Figure 3.8 shows Ethan and Kelvin (twins) enjoying painting the walls in the outdoor area. This activity was planned following observations of them engaged in self-initiated role-play around 'home improvements'. For example, practitioners noticed, on a number of occasions, Ethan gathering up all the planks from a wooden construction set and arranging them in lines against the skirting board. Puzzled as to his intentions, his key person shared the observation with Mum who was immediately able to enlighten her – they were having laminate flooring laid at home and Ethan had been very interested in this process and the techniques involved. Mum said that they had recently undertaken a lot of home improvements, particularly decorating work, and she had noticed Ethan pretending to lay carpets and hang wallpaper at home. Equipped with this knowledge, practitioners were able to talk to Ethan about his play and his experiences at home. They also decided to support the boys' current interest by planning a number of activities and enhancements to nursery provision. 'Decorating' the outdoor brick walls was such a focus. Staff collected old emulsion paint tins (empty) and filled them with thickly

Figure 3.8 Decorating like Daddy in the outdoor area

mixed powder paint – washable and easily hosed off the walls later! They provided a range of decorators' brushes and a large expanse of wall! Sheets of lining paper and 'paste tables' with rollers were also offered. Both Ethan and Kelvin accessed this provision repeatedly and Ethan delightedly told staff, 'I'm decorating the walls like Daddy!' As the work finished at home, so the boys' interest in the nursery DIY plans diminished. In evaluation of this work, the team agreed that the plans were so successful because staff had acted immediately to support a current interest and Kelvin and Ethan were able to mirror experiences in nursery as they happened at home. A similar 'topic' could have been planned with a block of activities offered to the whole group at a time decided by the adult but this would not necessarily have engaged Kelvin or Ethan in such an inspiring way. Unless children had had real experience of activities such as wallpapering or painting walls, their ability to access such role-play in the nursery was limited. It is therefore crucial that planning is responsive to the interests, experiences and developmental needs of the current group of children.

At this point it is worth including an example of a planning format that supports practitioners in documenting how observations are used to inform planning (see also Chapter 6). Using a simple sheet such as the one shown (see Table 3.1) enables the whole team to be aware of children's interests and all practitioners to be involved in 'responsive' planning. A new blank sheet would be available each week and made accessible to all staff. It may be that the

Table 3.1 Planning in response to observed needs and interests

Day of the week	MONDAY 17 May	TUESDAY 18 May	WEDNESDAY 19 May	THURSDAY 20 May	FRIDAY 21 May
Observation	Dry sand very shallow at one end of tray – Ryan discovered that he could make circular marks with his finger but was frustrated by other children disturbing his sand.	Water tray: Group of children deeply involved in filling/emptying containers and interested in water levels.	On arrival, lots of children reported on new road works next to the school building.	Torrential downpour! Children excited by the sound of the rain on the corrugated roof and watching rain bouncing in puddles through windows.	Still raining!
Response (e.g. enhancements to provision, adult support, planned focus)	Provide smaller, shallow trays containing dry sand so that Ryan and other children can explore mark-making. Also provide chopsticks/twigs/clay modelling tools as mark-making tools.	Add food colouring to water to make levels more visible through transparent containers. Mark half-full levels on containers with waterproof tape. Model use of key vocabulary: 'full', 'empty', 'more', 'less'.	Outdoor area: Provide cones, hard hats, etc. Take digital photographs of road works to display and discuss with children.	Abandoned planned focus today. Took children out in small groups wearing splash suits and wellies. Covered umbrellas with foil and listened to sounds. Splashed in puddles.	Rain collection focus – key area of learning: knowledge and understanding of the world (exploration and investigation). See focus plan.
Evaluation comments	21/5 Trays popular with a large number of children. Next week a focus will be planned to support development towards handwriting goals using large shallow tray and salt. Look at stepping-stones in this area.	21/5 Offered lots of opportunities for assessing learning in area of shape, space and measures (mathematical development). Display key vocabulary in area. Include ideas in long-term plan for water area.		20/5 Children fascinated by rain pouring down drainpipes into drains. Plan for a focus on rain collection if weather conditions continue tomorrow. Gather resources: lengths of guttering, water trays, buckets, funnels.	21/5 Need to order two more splash suits. Include rain collection plan in the rain resource box.

response is merely to add an appropriate item of equipment to an area of provision or the practitioner may decide to plan in more detail for a focus. The information collected on this sheet should then feed into evaluations and may impact on future planning. Introducing this type of documentation can help to raise the profile and status of supporting child-initiated learning where there has tended to be an overemphasis on adult-led activities. It can be a preliminary step to adopting an approach to planning as illustrated through the 'King Lanzarote' example (below) or can be used as an integral part of such an approach.

'King Lanzarote'

Figure 3.9 Prince Tenerife

King Lanzarote, and his son Prince Tenerife, became significant characters in a setting following an imaginative story-making session. Although the initial session group comprised only six children, they became so ignited with ideas that they motivated many other children to become involved with their story play and the world of King Lanzarote, in one form or another, continued for months. The aim of the group story-making session (see also Chapter 2, page 78 for an example plan 'Story making and imaginative play') was to provoke imaginative thought and ideas through the use of open-ended items presented in a bag. In this case, a piece of fabric, a bunch of keys, a piece of 'fool's gold' and a torch were included. The session was carefully planned with a clear aim in mind but ideas and outcomes were directed by the children. It was these ideas that provided the starting blocks for further planning that evolved over time. Photographs, observations and focus plans related to this play theme were displayed on the entrance wall. Also included on the planning display were brief 'incidental planning statements' (e.g. where enhancements had been made to provision), links to learning, evaluations at key points, staff reflections and references to literature and research.

Initial ideas generated by the group session:

- The fabric became a 'flying rug' and took the children to Jamaica and Lanzarote (two involved children had been to these destinations on holiday recently). The children 'flew' on their rug to see 'King Lanzarote'.
- The 'fool's gold' was treasure and they searched for more on the beach.
- The key was a special key for opening treasure boxes.

How learning was supported following the initial group session:

- A practitioner called into the charity shop on the way home to buy some 'treasure'.
- Travel brochures were provided so that children could decide on destinations for their 'flying rug'.
- The team wrote a letter from King Lanzarote to the children asking them to look for his stolen treasure and to keep his precious crown safe.
- The King's 'treasure' was hidden around the outdoor area and maps provided.
- A practitioner made a treasure box with the children to keep the treasure in.
- Staff made treasure maps with children.
- 'Royal writing paper' was provided for the children to write back to King Lanzarote.
- A practitioner built a pirate ship with the children and made telescopes.
- At the children's request, a party was organised with the children for King Lanzarote's birthday. Two practitioners took some children to the shop to buy ingredients for making a cake. They supported children in making 'party outfits'.

What was recorded on the planning display?

- Observations of individuals/groups
- Photographs/samples of children's work
- Adult responses and reflections
- Parents observations/comments
- Summaries of interests/play themes at key points
- Notes of actions taken by adults to support learning (see example 'Making party clothes')
- Focus plans (see alternative format in Table 3.1)
- Links to areas/aspects of learning
- Links to EYFS principles and characteristics of effective learning
- Relevant quotes from literature.

Incidental action to support learning: making party clothes

Figure 3.10 Making party clothes

Statement on planning display:

Paula discovered a group of children excitedly painting marks on pieces of fabric found in the technology workshop. 'We're making party dresses for King Lanzarote's party!' R said. When their painted fabric dried, they were disappointed to find that the paint cracked and fell off. Paula talked with the children about why this had happened and discussed other options. She suggested they try a dying technique using paint in a bucket. The children squeezed their fabric in buckets of different coloured water and then went with Paula to hang the fabric in the laundry to dry. They were delighted with the result and draped the material around themselves ready for the party.

Involved children: T, R, S, S and Z.

Links to learning: PSED: SC&SA, MR UW: W EA&D: M&M

Date: Week beginning 12 November 2012	Lead person: P

Reason for planning:

Children asked if King Lanzarote could visit the nursery. After discussion, we decided to let the King remain in the children's imagination but decided to send another letter from him, asking if his son, Prince Tenerife, could visit.

Planned experience/activity:

A letter and parcel will arrive through the post from King Lanzarote. The letter will thank the children for looking after his treasure and ask if the children will take care of his son, Prince Tenerife, when he visits them. The parcel will contain a silver spoon and bowl for them to use with the prince at meal times. Children will be asked to write to the King to let him know how the Prince is getting on. They will also be invited to take the Prince home for a night and look after him. All staff will be receptive to, and support, children's ideas as their play with the Prince develops.

Preparation – Resources/organisation:

Small empathy doll, cloak. Silver spoon and bowl wrapped up in a parcel with the King's letter. Prince Tenerife's diary (for home use) and 'overnight' bag including face cloth, hair brush, toothbrush, bowl and spoon.
Writing set to be provided including 'Dear King Lanzarote' formats, crown stamps and envelopes.
Interested children to be gathered together at an appropriate time for the introduction of the parcel. Prince Tenerife to be placed in the outdoor area for the children to 'find'.
Rota to be organised for taking home the Prince.

Possible links to learning: PSED: SC&SA, C&L: L&A, U, S L: R, W PD: M&H, CD: M&M

Figure 3.11 Planning in response to observed interests

Planning for Children's Play and Learning

What made the difference to the successful support of this play theme?
Adults who:

- Shared the children's excitement about their ideas

- Responded quickly with support and resources

- Knew when to offer a 'bridge' to enable children to sustain their play theme

- Helped children to realise their ideas

- offered an environment that enabled children to pursue their ideas independently.

What did children learn?

Planning for this play theme continued for eight weeks but even after this period, some children continued to pursue ideas related to the thread and planning was kept 'open' for these children. Children's individual responses and learning were documented in their personal profiles. Planning was reviewed at key points to identify what was motivating which children and to evaluate the effectiveness of learning opportunities. A quick analysis of 'links to learning' referenced on plans and observations identified that much learning had taken place in the areas of 'Communication and language', 'Literacy' and 'Expressive arts and design' but that there had been missed opportunities in 'Mathematics'. This helped to raise awareness of opportunities and impacted on future planning, for example the treasure box was used in a more focused way to promote and support children's learning about number and calculating. Photographs and observations showed clear evidence of children's engagement, motivation and creativity.

What are the benefits of a responsive or 'organic' approach to planning?

- Children are 'in charge' of the direction of their play and exploration.

- Parents are showing interest and sharing information from home.

- Parents with EAL can access information from the sequence of photographs.

- Practitioners talk to each other about developing ideas throughout the week. 'Planning' is something that happens all the time rather than once a week.

- Practitioners who can't attend the planning meeting can still contribute.

- There is a clear link between observations and planning.

- We are now 'uncovering the curriculum in the child' rather than 'covering the curriculum'.

- Children and staff are motivated and 'energised'.

Goldfish poem

The following example illustrates again how an experience that excites and engages a child can be used as a motivational 'springboard' for follow-up learning. In this particular nursery, children had been busy preparing for the arrival of two goldfish. When the fish were actually introduced, a number of children chose to spend a large part of the morning watching and talking about them. The practitioner took advantage of this opportunity for extending children's ideas and language and also scribed their comments. These words and phrases were crafted by the practitioner and children into a simple poem. The poem was then shared with other children, adults in the setting, parents and carers.

Our Goldfish
Fishes flying and dancing in the water,
Their tails wobbling from side to side.
Fishes laughing and talking – pop, pop,
Their mouths sucking and blowing in and out.
Fishes looking for food, playing hide and seek,
Their eyes moving like a wheel – black and gold and shiny.
Fishes sleeping quietly in their home,
Bubbles going up and up – bump, bump, bump.

Festivals and special occasions

The experiences that children bring from home will influence the nature of self-initiated learning and will also impact on how they access planned activities in the setting. In many settings there will be a range of cultural and racial backgrounds but in others the spectrum will be narrower. Where the community reflects diversity, there will be a wealth of natural opportunities to celebrate festivals and special occasions within the context of children's real lives. Of course it is important to share these significant times with children and cultural experiences can provide exciting starting points for planning a focus. Families and friends of children will usually welcome an invitation to become involved with celebrations. They can also help practitioners to build up a knowledge and understanding of cultures that vary from their own.

However, where this 'real' context for celebrating certain festivals does not exist, difficulties related to authenticity and meaning for the children may arise.

It is important that such celebrations do not become a 'token gesture', simplistic activities planned merely to satisfy perceived requirements of the curriculum. When festival celebrations are planned, they should be genuine and meaningful. They should not be seen as the definitive 'multi-cultural curriculum' but as enriching experiences planned within the context of a setting that embraces and celebrates diversity.

Ongoing opportunities for exploring and beginning to understand their own and other cultures must be woven into the fabric of the whole curriculum. Imaginative and creative play can offer a meaningful context in which to explore cultures and lifestyles that are outside their real-life experience. It can also highlight for children the variety of ways in which a particular occasion can be celebrated, for example, birthdays will be associated with certain traditions for one family but these will differ between families. Exploration of, and discussion about, such differences at this stage will help children to learn acceptance and respect. It is therefore crucial that opportunities for creative experiences of this nature are planned and starting points for furthering children's understanding recognised.

Training and sharing of knowledge between settings can help to deepen the understanding of practitioners and to increase their confidence in approaching other cultures. Reflection about their own culture can also lead practitioners to a deeper understanding of others.

'Practitioners ensure that their own knowledge about different cultural groups is up-to-date and consider their own attitudes to people who are different from themselves.'

Principles into Practice card 1.2. A Unique Child: Inclusive Practice

(DfES Publications 2007)

Stories and nursery rhymes as starting points

Stories are a frequently used starting point for developing learning across all areas of the curriculum. Sometimes practitioners will choose a familiar and favourite story, or a well-known story character, as the stimulus but in other circumstances may decide that a new story would be more successful in exciting the children. Of course, even though key learning objectives may be focused on an area of learning other than communication, language and literacy, using a story book in this context will help to foster a love of books and to develop skills involved in learning to read. There is a wealth of beautifully illustrated children's literature on the market that provides practitioners with an almost infinite source of inspiration. Here are a few ideas.

The following 'bridge-building' activity was planned after staff had noticed that, although the large construction equipment was available to children outside on a daily basis, they were not using it with much intention. The aim was to give children a purpose for design and construction, and *The Billy Goats Gruff* story, as well as being a group favourite, offered a real purpose.

The activity should take place in the outside area if possible. Children will need plenty of space to manipulate equipment and time to test and modify structures. If a large group of children is keen to engage in the activity, it is a good idea to provide a long 'river' so that a number of bridges can be constructed.

FOCUS ACTIVITY:
BUILDING A BRIDGE FOR THE BILLY GOATS GRUFF

Focus areas of learning

- Mathematics
- Expressive arts and design

Learning objectives

- To solve problems and to build for a specific purpose.
- To use key mathematical language (see key vocabulary and questions).

Working towards early learning goals in:

- Mathematics: shape, space and measure
- Expressive arts and design: exploring and using media and materials, being imaginative

Background information and prior learning

Most children will understand the concept of big and small. Some children will have been introduced to the concept of heavy and light. All children will have experience of working with the resources used in this activity. All children will be familiar with the story *The Billy Goats Gruff*.

Introduction

The adult will read the story of *The Billy Goats Gruff* to the children, encouraging them to join in, for example 'Who's that trip-trapping over my bridge?'

Table 3.2 Starting from a story: activities and goals

Story	Possible activities	Most applicable early learning goals
Handa's Surprise by Eileen Browne	• Circle time: being kind to friends • Making a 'carrier' for fruit • Tasting exotic fruits • Writing letters to Handa • Looking at features of our environment and comparing it with Handa's environment	• Have a developing awareness of their own needs, views and feelings and be sensitive to the needs, views and feelings of others • Build and construct with a wide range of objects, selecting appropriate resources and adapting their work where necessary • Investigate objects and materials using all of their senses as appropriate • Attempt writing for various purposes, using features of different forms such as lists, stories and instructions • Observe, find out about and identify features in the place they live and the natural world
Titch by Pat Hutchins	• Talk about own growth and development from babyhood, remember significant experiences • Measuring height	• Find out about past and present events in their own lives, and in those of their families and other people they know • Use language such as 'more' or 'less', 'greater' or 'smaller', 'heavier' or 'lighter', to compare two numbers or quantities
Brown Bear, Brown Bear, What Do You See? by Bill Martin Jnr	• Playing with rhyme: anticipating the next animal	• Listen with enjoyment and respond to stories, songs and other music, rhymes and poems and make up their own stories, songs, rhymes and poems
Owl Babies by Martin Waddell	• Talking about nocturnal animals and features of night and day • Exploring a dark den with torches • Circle time: 'settling-in' – helping new children to feel secure and happy in the setting	• Find out about, and identify some features of, living things, objects and events they observe • Ask questions about why things happen and how things work • Have a developing awareness of their own needs, views and feelings and be sensitive to the needs, views and feelings of others
Rosie's Walk by Pat Hutchins	• Setting up a Rosie's Walk obstacle course around the outside area • Looking at how flour is made, and using flour in baking • Making maps and plans: route to the park, plans of the outside area	• Move with control and coordination • Look closely at similarities, differences, patterns and change • Find out about their environment, and talk about those features they like and dislike

Book	Activities	Learning objectives
Where the Wild Things Are by Maurice Sendak	• Role-play – sailing to see the 'Wild Things' • Drawing/painting making collages of Wild Things • Making up monster poems/chants • Floating/sinking investigations • Making boats (see page 75 for activity plan)	• Use their imagination in art and design, music, dance, imaginative and role-play and stories • Explore and experiment with sounds, words and texts • Investigate objects and materials using all of their senses as appropriate • Build and construct with a wide range of objects, selecting appropriate resources, and adapting their work where necessary
The Billy Goats Gruff (traditional)	• Sorting and ordering toy goats according to size • Building bridges (see page 107 for activity plan) • Making goat and troll puppets • Puppet show/role-play	• Use language such as 'circle' or 'bigger' to describe the shape and size of solids and flat shapes • Build and construct with a wide range of objects, selecting appropriate resources, and adapting their work where necessary • Use their imagination in art and design, music, dance, imaginative and role-play and stories
Kipper's Toybox by Mick Inkpen	• Counting toys in and out of the toy box • Making 'Sock Thing' puppets • Looking at toys from other times	• Count reliably up to ten everyday objects • Select tools and techniques they need to shape, assemble and join the materials they are using • Find out about past and present events in their own lives, and in those of their families and other people they know
The Very Hungry Caterpillar by Eric Carle	• Looking at the life cycle of a butterfly • Looking at colours and patterns on a butterfly's wings and make 'butterfly' prints or collages • Counting the pieces of fruit eaten by the caterpillar	• Find out about, and identify some features of, living things, objects and events they observe • Explore colour, texture, shape, form and space in two and three dimensions • Count reliably up to ten everyday objects

Main activity

The adult, with the help of the children, will create a 'river' and 'fields' using lengths of fabric. Using wooden blocks, planks, etc. (see 'Resources'), the children will then work together to construct a bridge(s) over the river.

Finishing off and follow-up

The children will, with adult support, talk about their bridges, for example successful features, resources used, modifications made (see also 'Key questions'). They will use the river, fields and bridges in their play, recreating *The Billy Goats Gruff* story and making up stories of their own.

Adult role

The adult will:

- Provide resources

- Read the story and stimulate interest in the main activity

- Model use of key vocabulary

- Be aware of children's prior learning

- Intervene in children's play as appropriate, asking questions in order to extend learning

- Observe children re: response to activity, use of key vocabulary, understanding of concepts, ability to problem solve, use of resources.

Key questions and vocabulary

Vocabulary[1]: Big/bigger, small/smaller, middle-sized, heavy/heavier, light/lighter, under, on, over.

Questions: Who do you think is under the bridge? Where does the troll live? Who will go over the bridge next? Why does the goat want to go over the bridge? Who is on the bridge now? Which goat is bigger or smaller than the middle-sized Billy Goat Gruff? Which do you think is heavier than the small Billy Goat Gruff? Is your bridge strong enough to support the goats? How could you make it stronger? Is your bridge tall enough for the troll to live underneath? What have you used to build your bridge? Have you used the same resources as William?

Resources

- Story book – *The Billy Goats Gruff*

- Long lengths of fabric (e.g. blue/silver/grey/white for the river, green/yellow for the fields)

- Construction resources: wooden hollow blocks, wooden planks, milk crates, tyres

Table 3.3 Starting from a nursery rhyme: activities and goals

Nursery rhyme	Possible activities	Most applicable early learning goals
Humpty Dumpty	• Building a strong wall for Humpty Dumpty • Looking at brick patterns	• Build and construct using a wide range of objects, selecting appropriate resources, and adapting their work where necessary • Talk about, recognise and recreate simple patterns
Jack and Jill	• Finding ways of pulling/ pushing objects up a 'hill', rolling objects down a 'hill'	• Ask questions about why things happen and how things work
London Bridge is Falling Down	• Looking at different bridge structures • Building bridges for different purposes	• Ask questions about why things happen and how things work • Build and construct with a wide range of objects, selecting appropriate resources, and adapting their work where necessary
Baa Baa Black Sheep	• Counting 1-2-3 • Looking at properties of wool, use wool for collage, weaving, sewing, threading, etc. • Weighing/balancing bags	• Count reliably up to ten everyday objects • Investigate objects and materials using all of their senses as appropriate • Use language such as 'more' or 'less', 'greater' or 'smaller', 'heavier' or 'lighter', to compare two numbers or quantities
Incy Wincy Spider	• Looking at, and drawing, spiders and their webs using magnifying glasses • Counting spiders legs	• Find out about, and identify some features of, living things, objects and events they observe • Count reliably up to ten everyday objects

FOCUS ACTIVITY: PLAYING WITH RHYME

Focus area of learning

• Literacy

Learning objectives

• To listen attentively.

• To enjoy and respond to nursery and other rhymes, and rhyming songs.

• To show an awareness of rhyme and offer contributions of rhyming words.

Working towards early learning goals in:

● Literacy: reading

Introduction

The children and adult will say some of their favourite nursery rhymes, and sing rhyming songs, together. The adult will invite children to play percussion instruments in accompaniment. They will listen for, and identify, the rhyming words.

Main activity

The adult will introduce some new, humorous versions of traditional nursery rhymes.

For example:

> Twinkle, twinkle, chocolate bar
> Your Dad drives a rusty car
> Press the starter
> Pull the choke
> Off he goes in a cloud of smoke
> (Taken from Foster 1991)
>
> Humpty Dumpty sat on a chair
> While the barber cut his hair
> Cut it long
> Cut it short
> Cut it with a knife and fork
> (Taken from Rosen and Steele 1993)

The children and adult will try to think of some versions of their own – the adult will encourage children by making suggestions and asking children for contributions of words to complete the rhyme. For example:

> Humpty Dumpty sat on a log
> Humpty Dumpty saw a _____

Children and adult will make up other rhymes (for example using the children's names).

> Josh is sitting on a chair
> Kate is eating a juicy _____
> Tom is standing on his head
> Liam is sleeping in his _____

The adult will scribe the children's ideas.

Finishing off and follow-up

The children's rhymes will be displayed on the wall and a book of children's rhymes will be compiled. Involved children will be encouraged to share their rhymes with other children. A note of explanation will be sent home with examples of the children's rhymes and parents and carers encouraged to make up rhymes with their children at home. Other poems, rhymes and stories with rhyming words in the text will be read to the children during the course of the week (see 'Resources'). In other aspects of children's play, adults will capitalise on opportunities for developing awareness of alliteration, rhythm and rhyme, for example, in the sand area 'squishy and soft in the sand, cold and wet in my hand', in the outdoor area, 'we're splishing, splashing in the puddles', naming soft toys in the home corner 'Happy Harry' and 'Bobby Bear', singing or chanting whilst tidying up in the book area 'pick up the books and put them away, tidy and safe for another day'.

Adult role

The adult will:

- Provide resources including a range of rhymes
- Read new rhymes to the children
- Encourage children to make rhyming connections by giving examples and through repetition and emphasis of rhyming words
- Reassure and praise the children
- Display children's rhymes and make rhyme book
- Observe children re: enjoyment of and interest in activity, awareness of rhyme, contributions to new versions of nursery rhymes.

Key vocabulary and questions

Vocabulary: The word 'rhyme' will be used by the adult.

Questions: Can you hear the word that rhymes with wall? Can you think of another word that rhymes with wall and fall? Listen to these words, can you add any more? – dog, bog, jog, fog, _____. Can you read our new rhyme?

Resources

- Books (rhymes, stories, poems) for example, *Round and Round the Garden* by Sarah Williams, *Each Peach Pear Plum* by Janet and Allan Ahlberg, *Hairy Maclary* by Lynley Dodd, *There's a Wocket in my Pocket* by Dr. Seuss, *All Join In* by Quentin Blake, *Dragon Poems* by John Foster and Korky Paul, *Machine Poems* collected by Jill Bennett
- Large sheets of paper, pens

Starting from works of art and music

Reproductions of artists' work, original works of art and artefacts from the present and other times, and from different cultures, can provide a stimulating starting point for learning across all areas. In using such stimuli, practitioners are giving children opportunities to become familiar with a selected work of art, or the work of a particular artist, and encouraging them as 'consumers' of art. Visits to art galleries can be very enriching and exciting experiences for young children but if these are not practical, galleries and museums often offer a 'loan service'.

'Belvedere' by M.C. Escher is a particularly good starting point for 'story-making' by children of all ages.

FOCUS ACTIVITY: STORY-MAKING AND IMAGINATIVE PLAY

Focus areas of learning

- Communication and language
- Literacy
- Expressive arts and design

Learning objectives

- To respond to an artist's work.
- To talk about observations.
- To use language and imaginative role-play to express ideas.
- To show an understanding of the elements of stories.

Working towards early learning goals

- Communication and language: listening and attention, understanding, speaking
- Literacy: reading
- Expressive arts and design: being imaginative

Background information and prior learning

Children will have experience of expressing ideas through role-play and circle time activities. They will be familiar with looking at, and talking about, works of art (see long-term plans for areas of provision: painting, Chapter 1).

Introduction

The adult will explain to the children that he or she has brought a very special and exciting picture to show them (the reproduction will be displayed on a board but initially covered by a curtain). The adult will invite suggestions from the children as to what the picture might be about. The picture will then be revealed – 'Belvedere' by M.C. Escher.

Main activity (small group of children)

The adult will ask questions about the picture (see 'Key questions') and encourage the children to share their observations. On a large piece of paper, the adult will scribe the children's ideas and together they will make up a story[2] about the characters and the building depicted.

Finishing off and follow-up

Children will be encouraged to use 'Belvedere' ideas in their play (additional resources will be provided as required to support play). The children involved in the story-making activity will share their ideas with the rest of the group. The picture and stories will be displayed for all children to look at and talk about. A 'Belvedere' story book using children's ideas will be compiled by the adult.

Adult role

The adult will:

● Provide all resources

● Question children and encourage them to express their ideas

● Scribe children's ideas

● Join in children's imaginative play as appropriate

● Observe children re: use of imagination, ability to express ideas, understanding of elements of stories

● Display picture and children's work and make 'Belvedere' book.

Figure 3.12 Revealing the work of art

Key vocabulary and questions

Questions: Where do you think the building is? What are these people doing in the building? Who are they? Where do you think the door at the bottom of the building leads to? Where is the key to the door? Find the man behind the barred window – why is he there? What is he saying? What is the woman at the top of the building looking at? What can she see? Who is the man on the bench? What is he making? What will he use it for? Look at the man and the woman climbing the stairs – what are they talking about? Would you like to go to the building? Who would you go with? How would you get there?

Resources

- A reproduction of 'Belvedere' by M.C. Escher (included in 'Taschen' poster pack: M.C. Escher)

- Large board and 'curtain'

- Large piece of paper, pens

- Additional resources (role-play props) as required

Similarly, listening to music can be a powerful stimulus particularly in terms of creative and language work. There are many commercially-produced tapes and CDs which are suitable for use with children (e.g. instrumental 'mood' music, classical collections) but it is often a good idea to produce a compilation tape with which practitioners feel comfortable, and which will be tailored to fit intentions. For example, after talking about *The Snowman* story (by Raymond Briggs) with children, the adult may decide to plan an activity with a creative focus. She or he would then select appropriate pieces of music for each part of the story and encourage children to respond to the music through dance and movement. The music chosen to relate to James and the Snowman flying through the air would be a calm and serene piece, whereas the party music would be lively, loud and with a 'dance beat'.

Working towards early learning goal for creative development

By the end of the foundation stage, children will be able to:

- Use their imagination in art and design, music, dance, imaginative and role-play and stories

Looking at musical instruments, and making their own music, can also inspire children's learning across a range of curricular areas, as illustrated in Table 3.4.

Table 3.4 Music as a stimulus: activities and goals

Stimulus	Possible activities	Aspects of learning
Listening and responding to music	• Movement and dance using, e.g ribbons, scarves • Expressing feelings: how does this music make you feel? Is it happy/sad/ angry music? Listen to the sad music, look in the mirror – can you make a sad face? • 'Painting to music': making marks to match the mood of the music (e.g. large swirling patterns, stamping footprints, splatter painting, angular zig-zag patterns)	Personal, social and emotional development: managing feelings and behaviour Physical development: moving and handling Expressive arts and design: exploring and using media and materials, being imaginative
Handling/listening to musical instruments	• Discriminating between instruments/ matching sounds to instruments • Looking at/handling/playing/drawing instruments from own and other cultures • Looking at how musical instruments are made/making own instruments • 'Sound' word poems (listening to different instruments), e.g. tinkling, ringing triangles, booming, banging drums	Literacy: reading Understanding the world: people and communities, the world Expressive arts and design: exploring and using media and materials
Making music	• Using musical instruments (own and commercially produced) to accompany own singing/dancing • Exploring rhythm: counting beats, clapping names, playing simple rhythms on an instrument, marching to music/songs • Composing own tunes/sound strings and using a simple system of notation (e.g. based on colour or shape) to record own music • Perform own music to an audience • Record own music on audio tape	Literacy: reading Mathematics: numbers Expressive arts and design: exploring and using media and materials

Visitors and outside visits

Outside visits, and visitors to the setting, offer a host of opportunities for planning exciting learning experiences. Practitioners may choose to link visits to a project, or plan them with a particular area of learning in mind – whatever the original intentions, adults should be prepared for unplanned 'spin off' activities.

Outside visits do not have to be sophisticated, or involve weeks of organisation. A simple walk around the local area can provide the starting point for a range of learning experiences and activities. The following role-play activity was inspired by the visit of a post office worker known to many of the children as their local postman.

FOCUS ACTIVITY: POST OFFICE ROLE-PLAY

Focus area of learning

- Literacy

- Understanding of the world

- Expressive arts and design

Table 3.5 A walk around the local area: activities and goals

Possible activities	Most applicable early learning goals
• Looking at different buildings/shops, using knowledge in role-play in the setting	• Use language to imagine and recreate roles and experiences
• Looking at numbers/words in the environment (door numbers, street signs), making signs for the setting	• Recognise numerals 1–9 • Read a range of familiar and common words and simple sentences independently
• Discussing and drawing 'landmarks' and features of the area, making plans of an area/route maps	• Observe, find out about, and identify features in the place they live and the natural world
• Counting how many buses go past the park, making tally charts	• Count reliably up to ten everyday objects
• Observing seasonal changes, bringing back, for example, autumn leaves for observational drawing/further investigation	• Find out about, and identify some features of, living things, objects and events they observe

Learning objectives

- To develop an understanding of the role of the post office.

- To use knowledge of the post office in role-play.

- To use writing as a means of communication.

Working towards early learning goals

- Literacy: reading, writing

- Understanding of the world: the world

- Expressive arts and design: being imaginative

Background information and prior learning

Children will have experience of writing for a variety of purposes. Children will be at different stages in their writing development – the adult will be aware of each child's prior achievements.

Introduction

The post office worker will visit the setting and explain to the children how the post office works – the service it offers the community, the different roles of the people who work there, the journey of a letter, etc. They will show the children the uniform worn and equipment used when delivering post. Children will be encouraged to ask questions.

Main activity

Children will:

- Work in the post office role-play area, for example filling in forms, selling stamps and stationery, stamping passbooks and handling money

- Write letters to friends, family, etc., address envelopes and post letters

- Collect letters from postboxes

- Read labels and signs (see 'Resources').

Finishing off and follow-up

Before the children go home, a child will be invited to deliver the post (with adult support). Children will take home letters written to them and to their family members.

The post office role-play area will be available for children for as long as they show an enthusiasm for working in the area.

Adult role

The adult will:

- Arrange the post office worker's visit and prepare the children for the visit

- Support children in asking questions during the introduction

- Provide role-play resources and ensure that the area is well stocked at all times

- Intervene in children's play as and when appropriate

- Ask questions in order to be aware of the extent of children's knowledge and to extend their learning

- Observe children re: purposes for writing, progress in writing development, use of language in role-play.

Key vocabulary and questions

Vocabulary: Children will be familiar with 'post office' vocabulary, for example stamp, letter, envelope, address, postbox.

Questions to visitor: What is the role of people who work behind the counter? Where do you deliver post? How many houses do you deliver to? Which streets do you deliver to? What happens to a letter after we put it in the postbox? Where does it go before it reaches its destination? Why do people go to the post office? How do you help them?

Questions to children: Who are you writing to? Why are you writing to them – what would you like to tell or ask them? Would you like to send a birthday card to Simon? Where do they live? Can you write their name on the envelope? Do you need to go and buy a stamp? Look at the post office signs – where can you buy a stamp? How much does it cost? Do you need some money from your post office account? Can you fill in a form? Where do you write your name?

Resources

- Post office worker
- Post office role-play area: an area of the setting with furniture arranged to provide a counter, a writing surface and a sitting area (where children can look at leaflets, read letters, etc.)
- Tills, money, stamps, forms (for different purposes), leaflets
- Writing paper, notelets, postcards, greetings cards, envelopes, pens, pencils
- Signs (words/pictures/words and pictures), for example 'Buy your stamps here', 'Money bank', 'Postbox – times of collection: 11.00 am and 3.00 pm', 'Open' or 'Closed', children's name cards
- Fiction and non-fiction books about the post office or letters (e.g. *The Jolly Postman* by Janet and Allan Ahlberg)

(See also 'Eeyore's visit to nursery', Figure 4.1.)

Responding to the weather

The weather in Britain is characteristically unreliable and most practitioners will know the frustration of planning a paddling pool activity during a heat wave, only to wake up on the morning of the planned activity to torrential rain! This makes the task of 'timetabling' focus activities related to weather, or seasonal changes, almost impossible. Practitioners should be prepared to respond to weather conditions as they occur, although possible learning experiences and activities can be anticipated in advance. The arrival of snow is invariably greeted with great glee by children but is not always predicted and rarely lasts for more than a day or two. In the event of a snowfall, the practitioner will probably want to put other plans on hold and take full advantage of the opportunities offered by the 'snow experience'. It is a good idea then, to be prepared with ideas for developing learning and the following plan suggests ways in which children can learn about 'freezing' and 'melting' using snow as a starting point.

FOCUS ACTIVITY: INVESTIGATING SNOW

Focus areas of learning

- Communication and language
- Understanding of the world

Learning objectives

- To investigate the characteristics and properties of snow.
- To understand that water freezes and ice melts in response to changes in temperature.
- To talk about their observations using key vocabulary.

Working towards early learning goals

- Communication and language: understanding, speaking
- Understanding of the world: the world

Background information and prior learning

Children have made ice lollies and been introduced to the words 'freeze' and 'melt'.

Introduction

Children will enjoy the snow outside, handling it and building and modelling with it, etc. They will look closely at snowflakes as they fall, 'catching' them on black paper.

Main activity

Children will collect snow in buckets and transfer it to the water tray. They will dig, build, mould and imprint and, as they play, will observe the snow melting. More snow will be introduced to the tray and the adult will offer children a jug of warm water to 'mix' with the snow. The adult will also introduce some large blocks of ice[3] (e.g. water frozen in margarine tubs) and encourage children to watch what happens to the snow when it is placed on an ice block.

Finishing off and follow-up

Snow will be introduced into the indoor water tray. During the few days following the activity, small ice cubes containing objects such as pebbles, shells, buttons, beads, wedges of citrus fruit, will be placed in the water tray. Children will collect the 'hidden' objects in a special container as the ice cubes melt. A balloon full of water (with a length of string inserted) will be frozen. The balloon 'skin' will then be removed and the 'ice balloon', on a string, made available to children.

Adult role

The adult will:

- Be prepared to respond immediately to the arrival of snow
- Prepare ice blocks and cubes in advance and store in readiness in the freezer
- Work alongside children, asking questions and introducing warm water or ice blocks at an appropriate time
- Model, and encourage use of, key vocabulary
- Observe children re: their observations, understanding of freezing and melting, use of key vocabulary.

Key questions and vocabulary

Vocabulary: Warm, cold, freeze, frozen, melt.

Questions: What does the snow feel like? How do your hands feel after holding the snow? What could you use to make a 'snow castle'? How long do you think a snowflake will stay on your hand? What do you think will happen to the snowball if we pour warm water onto it? What will happen to the warm water when it is mixed with the snow?

Resources

- Snow!
- Water tray, spades, buckets, plastic pots, shells, brushes, tubes, black paper
- Jugs of warm water (not too hot as safety is the paramount consideration – tepid water will serve the purpose)
- Ice blocks
- Ice cubes (containing 'hidden' objects)

KEY POINTS FOR GOOD PRACTICE

- Be aware of the holistic nature of children's learning.
- Be flexible in your use of plans – if children's 'agenda' is different from what you have planned for them, abandon or postpone your plans in order to support their interest.
- Remember that identifying and understanding children's needs and interests starts with a period of observation. Sometimes observations in a number of contexts reveal a schematic interest.

- Use the characteristics of effective learning to identify what is meaningful to children and to evaluate their responses to provision and activities in order to identify directions for planning.
- Maintain a balance between children leading play and adults guiding their learning.
- Share information with parents and carers and find out more about children's current enthusiasms at home. Also share observations of children with other members of the team.
- Recognise and respect children's varied cultural experiences. Reflect and share these in the setting.
- Recognise the importance of the adult in supporting interests and extending learning.
- Remember that a child's interest can be used as a starting point for learning across a number of curricular areas.
- Value the learning process, fostering children's creativity and guarding against an overemphasis on concrete results.
- Never underestimate the power of a child's imagination as motivation for learning.

We need to feed the child's natural curiosity, the urge to explore, to try things out, to look more closely, to see what happens. We need to build on the child's disposition to explore and investigate, to satisfy the 'rage to know'.

(Fisher 1990)

Notes

1   Some children will be ready to use comparative vocabulary. Other children will need more experience of using, for example, big and small but will benefit from adults and peers modelling the use of comparative vocabulary.
2   Children could make up their own stories and use pictures or writing to record their stories.
3   Take care that children do not 'burn' themselves on the ice.

CHAPTER 4

Establishing and developing positive links with home

Foundation Stage
Nothing can be achieved without working with parents.

(Field 2010)

The content of this chapter is organised as follows:

First contact

Prior to entering the setting, and during their early years, parents and the home environment will be central to a child's world and, in particular, to their emotional well-being. Many children will also have secured close bonds with professional carers, or carers within their family or circle of friends. Whatever the circumstances, for many children, starting nursery, pre-school, playgroup, or beginning a new relationship with a childminder can be a big milestone in their life. For both parents[1] and children, the prospect of entering this next stage, although exciting in many ways, is often tinged with apprehension. The role of the practitioner is crucial in allaying anxieties and in building up trust between home and the setting. Experiences in the early days form the foundation for future attitudes and relationships.

A happy and open relationship with parents, based on confidence and trust, is crucial to the building of a successful relationship with their children.

(Whitebread 1996)

It is important, then, that practitioners consider carefully how to ensure that the child's and parents' initial contact with staff and the setting is an enjoyable experience. Many settings organise induction or open days, or arrange visits to the setting, prior to the child's starting date. Parents and children will often be sent individual invitations and will be offered the opportunity to 'sample' activities whilst becoming familiar with staff and the physical surroundings. There may also be an explanation of the aims of the setting in the form of a talk by staff, perhaps illustrated by a slide show or displays.

Other practitioners visit children and parents in their own home at a time and date mutually agreed beforehand. This system has the advantage of allowing both parties freedom from distractions and is also a more intimate atmosphere in which parents may feel able to talk about concerns or personal circumstances which could affect the child. Young children will usually feel more relaxed and confident in familiar surroundings and visiting practitioners will find, in many cases, that the child sets the agenda, enthusiastically showing off their toys and pets! It is important to remember that the aim is to make the first contact between home and setting a positive experience, and the parent should always feel comfortable about the venue and nature of that first meeting – for this reason, any approach that is adopted by the practitioner, or team of practitioners, should be flexible.

However, practitioners should be aware that, even when they are approachable and friendly, some parents may still feel uneasy at the prospect of a home visit or indeed about becoming involved in the setting beyond dropping their child off and picking her up. There could be a number of reasons why parents are reluctant to engage. They could have had negative experiences of education in their own childhood resulting in a lack of self-confidence or a mistrust of professionals, or perhaps they have literacy issues. The perception of some parents is that it is the responsibility of the nursery or school to educate their child and they do not realise the potential impact they can have on their child's learning. All parents should feel included in the community of the setting and teams should consider how they welcome different groups, for example fathers who may feel that they have no place in an environment dominated by female workers or parents with English as an additional language (EAL) who may feel anxious about handing over their child without being able to communicate effectively with practitioners. Whatever the barrier, practitioners should adopt a creative approach to engagement and endeavour to reach all parents.

There is consistent evidence that fathers' interest and involvement in their children's learning (which was measured in terms of interest in education, outings and reading to the child) is statistically associated with better educational outcomes.

(DCSF 2008b)

The first meeting marks the beginning of a shared journey. The child's developing self-confidence and self-esteem is much more likely to flourish in a climate of respect and understanding between his or her parent and teacher. The child will already be part of a culture within the family and within the wider community and it is important that the practitioner understands this culture. At home and in the setting they must be supported in building up confidence in their own cultural identity. Families should feel confident that their experiences and traditions are valued and that they will be treated with dignity and sensitivity at all times.

If 'home visiting' is chosen as the preferred first contact, follow-up opportunities should also be planned for the child and parent to visit the setting before the official starting time; young children will feel more assured if they are able to visualise the provision and are familiar with some of the routines.

Planning, and carrying out, home visits

As any adult who works in an early years setting will appreciate, time is at a premium – there never seem to be enough hours in the day to fit all the jobs in! However, in the case of home visits, although there will be a limited amount of time available, it is important to allocate time-slots long enough to enable relaxed conversations between adults, and interaction with the child, to take place. Many settings plan time during working hours for visits – some school nurseries close for two or three days at the beginning of each intake term to enable staff to make home visits, although this is not always possible. Whatever the arrangements, practitioners need to be well organised and prepared in order to ensure maximum benefit to all involved. It is advisable for practitioners to visit in pairs (one being the child's designated key person) both from the safety aspect and also because this allows more flexibility during the visit, for example, a parent may want to talk about a serious issue concerning the child's health or safety – in the event of two adults being present, one could talk with the parent, recording any necessary information, whilst the other engages with the child. It is important to discuss and define roles prior to visiting and each adult needs to be clear about their responsibilities. Before embarking on visits, practitioners should always remember to inform an adult in the setting of their schedule, i.e. times of visits and addresses.

The following plan outlines some of the reasons for home visiting and offers suggestions for organisation, resources and the sharing of information. It is an example specific to one setting (arranging to carry out a number of visits over a period of a few days) – practitioners will need to tailor it to their own needs, may decide to adopt the framework for planning their visits, or may just choose to try out some of the ideas.

ORGANISING AND CARRYING OUT HOME VISITS

Dates: 5–8 September

Duration of each visit: 30 minutes

Aims of each visit

- To establish positive links between home and the setting.
- To begin to develop a relationship between the child and key person.
  - Establishing and developing positive links with home.
- To find out information about the child, e.g. personal interests, recent experiences, identified needs.
  - To share information (e.g. practical suggestions, policy information) about the setting with the parent.

Resources needed

- List of names, telephone numbers and addresses; timetable of visits
- Street map of local area
- Home visit record forms and questionnaires[2]
- Photograph album – a collection of annotated photographs showing children at play in the setting
- Soft toy character – Oscar the clown (see Figure 4.18, page 150)
- Small present for the child, for example drawing book and crayons
- Booklet containing information about the setting
- 'About Me' leaflet[3]

Organisation and adult role

Arranging visits:

- Contact families to confirm that a visit is required and to arrange a suitable time.
- Ensure that all information in booklets is correct and up-to-date.
- Check that there are sufficient forms, booklets, etc. for every visit.
- Gather all resources together, compiling individual packs of leaflets, forms, booklets, etc. in labelled bags.

Carrying out the visits:

- Introduce staff by name to the parent and child.
- Talk with, and listen to, the child putting her or him at ease (use props such as the photograph album, the drawing equipment and Oscar the clown to encourage conversation). Encourage the child to show and talk about his own toys or experiences.

○ Talk with the parent about what their child likes to do and the special people in his life.

● Informally observe, in particular, the child's social, physical and language skills if opportunities present.

● Explain to the parent, for example, how the setting and staffing is organised, strategies for settling children in to the setting, routines, systems of assessment, how information is communicated between staff and parents, rotas for parent help in the setting. Show the parent the photograph album and talk about activities.

● Ask parent if there are any questions they would like to ask, further information they need to share (if this has not already been recorded on a form or questionnaire) or any issues or concerns they would like to discuss. Allow plenty of time for this part of the visit.

● Inform parent of any equipment the child will need, for example, a spare set of clothes, inside shoes.

● Ask standard questions (if these have not already been answered during the course of conversation) and complete records.

● Remind parent that they are welcome to visit the setting, with their child, prior to the official starting date.

Following up visits:

● Plan starting dates for children, staggered if necessary

● Inform parent of the official starting date for their child

● Prepare individual equipment such as name cards, milk tags, coat peg labels

● Begin child's profile (see Chapter 6, page 184) by making a 'home visit' entry.

The settling-in process

When practitioners are very familiar with the environment it can be easy to overlook or dismiss the feelings of children and their parents, who are reluctant to go beyond their usual space. We only have to think back to an experience when we entered unfamiliar territory, such as starting a new job or entering secondary school for the first time, to remember and understand the fears and insecurities of young children and their families.

(Nutbrown and Page 2008)

Children's responses to starting their new setting will vary enormously. Some will enter on the first day full of enthusiasm and confidence and eager to explore. Others will be much more reticent, preferring to observe from a 'safe' distance. Many may cope with a full session or day whilst some will benefit from shorter sessions in the beginning. Every child is different and practitioners must take their lead from the individual when devising programmes for 'settling-in'. Settings also vary as to what is an appropriate or practical approach. In a school situation where all EYFS children are together in a unit, transition from nursery into 'reception' should not cause any problems. But if children are arriving from other settings, reception class staff will find that children usually settle more easily if links are made with settings attended prior to starting school. The transition period should be carefully planned to allow children opportunities to experience activities in the class (e.g. an invitation to a story session, or to lunch) and, where possible, should include visits by reception staff to children in their own setting or home (see home visits, page 126). Similar transition arrangements should also be planned for children who are transferring from one setting to another at an earlier point during the foundation stage.

As a general rule, for three-year-olds starting in a new setting, parents should be encouraged to stay with their child for at least the first session, and for parts of, or complete, subsequent sessions until the child is settled. It may be that the child is happy to venture away from the parent immediately in which case the parent may decide to keep their distance, within the setting, on the first day. After observing the child's behaviour the parent may feel confident in leaving the child for a short period the next day. Invariably the child will soon be entering the setting confidently and be happy to wave 'goodbye' to the parent as soon as the routines have been completed. However, it does sometimes happen that a seemingly very confident child becomes 'clingy' after a few days in the setting, as if the novelty of the experience has worn rather thin. In such a case the practitioner and parent will need to review the situation and may decide that the child needs more support than originally anticipated.

Occasionally, a child will be happy to play with other children and explore the setting with a parent present but, even after a period of time, will be extremely reluctant for the parent to leave. It may be that the child is anxious about the possibility of the parent not returning. The child should not feel under pressure to 'make the break' before feeling ready and, in order to build up the child's confidence, the separation process will need to progress in small steps. The 'break' can also prove to be emotionally difficult for the parent, who may need support and understanding from the practitioner. The length of time could be built up gradually over a period of a few days until both parent and child feel comfortable about the parent leaving the building for part of the session. As the child realises that the parent always comes back, he or she will become less anxious about the separation until eventually he or she is happy to attend the whole session without the presence of the parent.

The key person role

Early Years Foundation Stage states the statutory requirement for all children to be assigned a key person. Particularly in settings caring for very young children, and for those offering full day care, the importance of developing close emotional attachments should never be underestimated. It is imperative that the key person role is established in a genuine and effective way in order to foster a sense of well-being in the child and to offer a consistent point of contact for parents. Even for children at the older end of the EYFS, it is important that they have a 'special' person within the setting on whom they can depend although, due to practical staffing constraints, the key groups may be larger in a reception class. In order for a key-person system to become effectively embedded, it is important that all members of management and all staff understand, and are committed to, the principles behind this requirement. If a whole-team commitment to the principle of secure attachment is established, even where organisational challenges present themselves, staff will endeavour to reduce barriers to ensure that they are able to offer children the essential elements of the key-person role.

From a position of safety and security, children will feel confident to explore. By being able to depend on a trusted adult, they learn to become more independent themselves. The role of the key person is to understand the child's physical and emotional needs and to be an advocate and an 'anchor' for them. The key person will not spend all their time with the child but he or she should be sensitive to the child's feelings and be there for them during times of uncertainty, in new situations and when the child is unwell or upset.

> 'A key person develops a genuine bond with children and offers a settled, close relationship.
>
> A key person talks to parents to make sure that the child is being cared for appropriately for each family.'
>
> Principles into Practice card 2.4. Positive Relationships: Key Person
>
> (DfES Publications 2007)

Of course, there will be times when the key person is not available for the child, for example they may be on holiday, attending a course, on sick leave or on a late shift. Because it is impossible to ensure that one person is always on site, it is good practice to, where practical, to operate a 'significant second' system. In larger staff teams, practitioners often work in pairs to support each other's key children when the primary key person is unavailable. This approach has organisational implications for management, for example, pairs should be on opposite shifts to ensure that one or other of the pair is present at the beginning and end of the day or session. If possible, they should also take their holidays at different times. Where a child needs intimate care, it is particularly important that he or she feels comfortable with the adult involved. Such care should be given by the key person or the significant second.

Children are able to make a number of close attachments and the relationship developed between a child and their key person will not undermine the child's bond with their parents. However, it is important that the designated key person is sensitive to the parents' anxieties about their child's new attachment and reassures them that the parent/child relationship will not be compromised by the child's closeness to an adult at nursery.

Adults must always be consistent, reliable and truthful – a child should always be told when a parent is about to leave the setting and when he or she will return. Slipping out of the door whilst the child is temporarily preoccupied, or distorting the truth about where they are going, are not actions conducive to building up a relationship of trust with a child.

It is not the responsibility of the key person to write all the observations about their key child for his or her profile. Indeed this approach would give a limited picture of the child offering only one person's perspective on their learning. Contributions should be made by all members of staff for all children and the role of the key person in most settings is to collate the observations, compile the profile and analyse the evidence with a view to assessing the child's stage of development. He or she will then feed this information into team planning meetings in order to effectively support the child's learning.

At times of transition, the child's key person will support the child in becoming familiar with new environments and a new key person. Where a child is moving setting to a distant location, making links may be challenging but time spent talking about feelings and looking at photographs of the new setting and staff will help to prepare the child (see also Chapter 6, 'Tracking progress and summative reporting', page 211).

Welcoming parents into the setting

'Children feel a sense of belonging in the setting when their parents are also involved in it.'

Principles into Practice card 1.4. A Unique Child: Health and Well-being

(DfES Publications 2007)

It is the policy of most settings to encourage parents to spend time in the setting throughout their child's time there, and some parents are able and happy to come in on a regular basis. There is often an abundance of strengths and enthusiasms to be 'tapped' amongst the parents and carers – some may be able to play a musical instrument, others will have a particular interest in woodwork, sewing or gardening – whatever skills they have to offer, the practitioner should encourage them to share with the children in the setting. There are numerous other activities, many of them ongoing, with which parents can become involved on a day-to-day basis, for example reading stories with the children, making models, building dens, baking, teaching routines in the painting area, joining in imaginative and role-play in the home corner.

Beginning of session routines, such as the self-registration systems and the 'question table' (see Chapter 5), provide a focus for children and parents on entry to the setting as well as offering sound learning opportunities for the child. Self-registration usually involves the child, supported by the parent, taking a label or tag (displaying their own personal motif or photograph of self and/or name) and placing it in a designated place in order to register their presence in the setting. The labels may be hanging on coat pegs when the children arrive, or may be arranged on a table requiring children to select their own cards. The label may then, for example, be hung over a milk bottle or a named photograph attached with 'hoop and loop fastening tape' to a train or house displayed on the wall. A glance at the labels will inform the practitioner which children are present. Details of the 'question table' are included in Chapter 5, page 167.

Practitioners may also decide to organise social events and these are often run alongside planned activities involving the children, for example a Christmas concert or 'sing-along' may be accompanied by coffee and mince pies. Such occasions offer parents opportunities to meet other parents and to chat informally with staff. It is advisable to give plenty of notice when planning events of this nature to allow parents with other commitments to make the necessary arrangements in order to attend. In many settings parents organise fund raising or social events themselves and this kind of involvement can be beneficial in helping to bind the partnership between practitioner and parent, as well as in providing very worthwhile experiences for all.

Parents are often invited to share experiences with their children and Figure 4.1 illustrates an example of such an occasion. Parents were invited to the nursery to meet 'Eeyore', a visiting donkey. Eeyore was accompanied by staff from the local donkey centre who talked to children and parents about caring for donkeys and the work of the Elisabeth Svendsen Trust for Children and Donkeys. The children were enthralled and eager to talk about their experiences. Because of the parents' involvement, they were able to discuss the visit with their children in detail, and with enthusiasm. The nursery decided to 'adopt' a donkey (on a sponsorship basis) from the centre and parents were very supportive. Parents, children and staff now had a shared commitment to the charity which not only benefited the Trust, but also served to strengthen links between home and setting.

The setting itself should feel welcoming to the parent. Provision (a safe distance from the children's play area) of tea- and coffee-making facilities and an area where parents can sit comfortably and talk will be an attraction. Not all parents will be keen to spend time working with children in the setting and some find it difficult because of caring for younger siblings, but they may be happy to offer their support by making or cataloguing resources – a 'working party' could be set up to, for

Figure 4.1 Eeyore's visit to nursery

example, make up story boxes or catalogue posters. Although the practitioner would be involved in the content of the work, parents could organise the rota and decide responsibilities for tasks. This can be a very successful way of involving parents in their child's learning and can also have positive social repercussions for many. The provision of a box of toys suitable for younger children and babies is also a good idea – parents will often be happy to contribute to this collection. Parents can be involved in the organisation of a book and toy lending library within the setting, sharing responsibility for the smooth running of the system, and for the maintenance of the resources, with the practitioner.

A 'parents' notice board' is an effective way of communicating information to parents such as forthcoming events in the setting, new staff appointed to work in the setting and holiday dates. Useful leaflets about local clinics, support groups, toy libraries, etc. can also be displayed and the board can be used by parents to inform each other about happenings in the community, for example, school fairs, jumble sales, aerobics classes. The provision of such a board will help to give parents a feeling of inclusion in the setting, will encourage social interaction between parents and will also convey the message that the setting does not work in isolation – that it is an integral part of the community.

Practitioners may also decide to take information (such as a summary of aims, session times, dates of open days and social events) about the setting into the wider community, displaying posters or leaflets in libraries, doctors' surgeries and clinics. This will serve to raise awareness of the setting in the community and encourage prospective parents to visit.

Working with parents to support and extend children's learning

For all children, the quality of the home learning environment is more important for intellectual and social development than parental occupation, education or income. What parents do is more important than who parents are.

(Sylva et al. 2004)

Planning for Children's Play and Learning

In acknowledging parents as educators, practitioners must recognise that their own role is inextricably linked to that of the parents. The learning process does not take place exclusively in the setting, nor does it only happen at home – experiences in all aspects of children's lives combine to broaden and deepen their learning. It is the role of the practitioner and parent to support the child in that process. Parent and practitioners have much to learn from each other and an efficient system of communication should be in operation to facilitate the sharing of information. This will involve both parties in making time to talk and listen.

Experience and training will equip the practitioner with the professional expertise needed to plan an appropriate and broad curriculum within the setting. But their expertise can have a wider impact when their approach includes involvement of parents in planning support for their child's learning both at home and in the setting. For children with special educational needs, it is crucial (and a legal requirement) that parents are involved in the planning process. In these circumstances, an Individual Education Plan (IEP) will be drawn up to identify and address those needs that are additional to the setting's usual curriculum. Parents know their child better than anyone and have a vital contribution to make, as equal partners in the team, to discussions about the plan.

This section of Chapter 4 focuses on building an effective partnership between parents and practitioners as educators, and on developing a high-quality home learning environment.

> 'Effective communication means there is a two-way flow of information, knowledge and expertise between parents and practitioners.'
>
> Principles into Practice card 2.2. Positive Relationships: Parents as Partners
>
> (DfES Publications 2007)

Working with parents to support children's learning is not about one party holding the balance of power as can sometimes seem to be the case for parents, for example when attending a school parents' evening where the five-minute time slot is consumed by the teacher imparting information about the child's attainment and behaviour at school. It is about genuine partnership, the exchange of information about a child with a shared aim of ensuring the child's involvement in the learning process and improving outcomes for that child.

Positive relationships form the basis of effective partnerships and it is crucial to establish trust and respect between parent and practitioner before expecting to be able to engage on a deeper level to support the child's learning together. However, practitioners should bear in mind that a 'relationship' with the setting is not enough to ensure an impact on the home learning environment, it is how that relationship is used as a vehicle for working with parents to engage them more deeply in their child's learning that will make the difference.

It is important to engage with parents regularly in a relaxed and mutually respectful context. The practicalities of organising such get-togethers will be easier with some families than others, and in some settings than others, depending on circumstances. Where working parents have a tight schedule it can be difficult for them to make time at the end or beginning of the day and, for example, in reception classes where ratio requirements result in less staff, organisation of individual meetings may be problematic. Some settings are able to offer more flexibility within their staff team and may even have a room designated for meetings with parents. Whatever the challenges, a practitioner committed to the principle of meaningful partnership work with parents with look for creative ways of overcoming barriers. Children's individual profiles can be a very useful focus for discussions about their learning and interests and many settings offer opportunities to take the profile home so that the child can share experiences with their family in the comfort of their own home. For parents unable to access the setting very often, DVD film of their child showing the sort of experiences that are currently engaging him could be sent home. Where cameras and camcorders are available to lend, parents could film significant experiences at home. Where flexibility is an issue, a regular time slot for group meetings with parents may be more practical. Of course, all involved parents would need to be comfortable in sharing information about their child's play and learning but, where this is the case, some very worthwhile discussion can be generated through group meetings.

> The key person must seek to engage and support parents and/or carers in guiding their child's development at home.

> (Department for Education 2012)

Before looking at examples of partnership working with parents to support children's learning, it is important to mention the power of aspiration. It is not only what parents *do* with their child, but also what they expect of them, and hope for them, that will make a difference to outcomes. Parents expectations and aspirations will be influenced by their own experiences and sometimes work with parents to build confidence, and a realisation that they can help their child to achieve more, can have as much long-term impact as work with the child.

Figures 4.2–4.9 illustrate how a practitioner and parents worked together to find out more about a child's interests and to plan support for her learning both at home and in the nursery. (See also Figure 3.8, 'The DIY enthusiasts'.) At nursery, staff had noticed that Megan was preoccupied with making lines. They had observed this interest in a number of contexts for example, lining up equipment in the outdoor area and then, very carefully, walking along her line and arranging parallel lines using polished stones (see Figures 4.2 and 4.3). When Megan's key person shared this observation with Megan's mum, she too reported that she had noticed similar behaviour at home (see Figures 4.4–4.7). Megan often lined up her

Figure 4.2 Megan walking along her line of bats, cones and stilts in the outdoor area

Figure 4.3 Making lines with polished stones

Figure 4.4 Megan's line of Barbies

Figure 4.5 Lining up cars in her bedroom

Figure 4.6 Sitting in a line of teddies!

Figure 4.7 Making a line of cushions in the sitting room

Barbie dolls and her teddies and also made long lines of toy cars in her bedroom. She even made lines by arranging the cushions in the sitting room! Nursery staff and Mum recognised that the repetition of these 'lining up' actions may be significant. As yet they were not exactly sure what it was that was interesting Megan about the lines she was making but decided to plan further opportunities for her explore trajectories.

Staff at the nursery offered Megan a range of interesting objects to make patterns or lines with, for example buttons, shells, leaves. Mum and Dad also provided collections of objects at home. They offered equipment that would enable Megan to make lines in space, for example sponge balls, bean bags. Megan enjoyed rolling bicycle wheels in lines across the outdoor area at nursery (Figure 4.9) and sending marbles and balls down tubes on a 'ball run' that she built with her Mum and brother at home (Figure 4.8). Her deep involvement in the experiences offered indicated to nursery staff and Mum that they were 'on the right track' but there was still more to learn about her preoccupation with lines.

Both Mum and Megan's key person documented her interest through photographs and these proved to be a very useful tool for reflection with Megan. For example, during discussion about the photographs at a later date, Megan's comment about the equipment line she made in the outdoor area was 'That's my

Figure 4.8 Building a ball and marble run

"long way" pattern' as she walked along her 'pattern' until she came to the end. It may have been that she was interested in direction, travel or journeys, and perhaps the play with cars may be linked to such an interest. Sometimes adults never really get to the bottom of what is motivating a child but the discussion about observations of repeated actions are bound to give a deeper insight into the child's world.

It is worth mentioning at this point the many commercially-produced resources on the market which claim to be aids to 'home learning', some of which can be useful if carefully selected. Some others, however, are at best a 'gimmick', and at worst inappropriate for the child's stage of development and likely to lead to bad practice or confusion. Parents eager to

Figure 4.9 Rolling a bicycle wheel across the grass at nursery

give their child the best educational start in life are vulnerable to marketing ploys and are frequently persuaded to spend large amounts of money on so-called educational toys, videos and 'work books' of dubious quality. The reality is that very often, equally, or more, valuable learning experiences can take place at little or no expense in the home or local environment. Practitioners have an important role to play here in sharing their expertise and knowledge of how young children learn, in helping parents to interpret their children's play in terms of learning, and in offering suggestions of how learning can be supported at home. It may be appropriate to point out that children's learning should be contextual and purposeful, and to emphasise the value of conversation between adult and child.

Providers should make sure that information about the EYFS, and how it is delivered in their setting, is available to parents. This information may be presented through displays or leaflets about early learning, or through a range of forums. Alongside such information, they should explore ways of sharing ideas for learning at home. It is important at this stage to highlight the value of discussing the 'characteristics of effective learning' with parents as well as suggesting practical activities. It is an understanding of *how* children learn that will equip parents with the confidence to try out ideas and plan experiences to support their child's learning in ways that are appropriate to their stage of development.

Many parents will be keen to learn more about the early years curriculum, the activities planned for their children at nursery and the ways in which they can support learning at home. An effective way of sharing ideas and curricular aims in a relaxed atmosphere is to hold an open day or evening and to invite parents to have 'hands-on experience' of activities at a workshop event (some settings may organise a similar event prior to children starting the setting). Practitioners would be available to talk about children's play and learning, and to answer questions. A brief explanation of learning objectives, and photographs of children engaging in a range of activities, displayed in each area of provision can also provide some helpful information.

'Stay and Play' sessions are an effective way of enabling parents to see how their child responds to the nursery provision. This type of involvement will enable parents to observe the strategies that practitioners use to support children's learning and offer practitioners an opportunity to model particular skills that may be useful to the parent when interacting with their child at home.

> Parents are particularly predisposed to understand play and its learning potential if invited to curriculum or topic sessions in school and allowed to experience for themselves some of the materials and resources children use.
>
> (Moyles 1989)

Some practitioners produce guidance leaflets on learning opportunities offered through provision and these can be a very welcome support to parents and students helping in the setting[4]. However, practitioners should guard against overwhelming the parent with too much 'paperwork' – information should be useful, concise, easy to read and attractively presented. The content may be of a general nature (e.g. explanation of routines, areas limited to four children at a time, encouraging independence) but can also be specific to an area of provision, including information such as suggested activities, and ways in which the adult can support children's learning across the curriculum in, for example, the sand area. Reference to long-term plans may help practitioners in writing 'area of provision' leaflets.

Leaflets may also be produced which focus on the seven areas of learning. These will offer information on how learning in a particular curricular area can be developed in different areas of provision (see for example Figure 4.10). Figure 4.11 aims to help parents to support their children's learning within the area of literacy.

If aware of the practitioner's plans for activities and experiences within the nursery, many parents will have exciting ideas of their own for developing their children's learning at home and should be encouraged to share these. Information can be displayed on a board in the setting or can be communicated through a letter from the staff as illustrated in Figure 4.12.

Practitioners may decide to include other information in the letter such as notification of a planned coffee morning, or they may choose to produce separate

MATHEMATICAL DEVELOPMENT IN THE NURSERY

You can support children's mathematical development in all areas of the setting. Listed below are some suggested activities:

- *Construction area*: looking at and comparing shapes of bricks; matching shapes to templates; sorting components (by colour, shape or size); counting the amount of component parts used to make a model, counting how many wheels altogether in two sets.

- *Painting area*: printing flat shapes; creating or recreating patterns and sequences looking at colour, size and shape.

- *Malleable materials*: making solid shapes; comparing length (who has made the longest snake?); sharing the dough (three children: three amounts of dough).

- *Home corner*: matching 1:1, for example, laying the table – spoon, cup, saucer for each child; shopping – dealing with money; counting and matching numbered clothes on a washing line; knock four times on the door before entering; counting candles on a birthday cake, calculating how many candles there will be if we add two more.

- *Office*: reading and dialling telephone numbers; writing numbers (e.g. house numbers on envelopes); matching numbered stamps to numbered postboxes.

- *Water area*: comparing containers (shape and size); filling and emptying containers; counting the number of jugs of water needed to fill a bowl.

- *Music area*: using instruments to explore rhythm – counting beats; clapping names (e.g. Sam – an – tha, 1 – 2 – 3); singing number songs, for example, 'Five Little Speckled Frogs'.

- *Sand area*: looking at solid shapes – using cuboids as moulds (wet sand); filling and emptying containers with sand; feeling sandpaper numbers on the wall; ordering size graded containers; weighing bags of sand.

- *Workshop area*: comparing and measuring lengths of wood; solving problems (e.g. how long does the piece of string need to be to go around the box? How many more boxes do we need?)

- *Book area*: looking at fiction and non-fiction books which involve, for example, counting, size, shape, height and length comparison; listening to number rhyme audio tapes.

Talking with the children as they play helps to develop their mathematical understanding as well as their language. They should be encouraged to use the following vocabulary and will learn the meaning of words through hearing you use them:

Numbers and counting: 1, 2, 3, 4, 5, 6, 7, 8, 9, 10 (higher number names if children are ready).

Calculation: add, one more/less, count on, altogether.

Shape: circle, square, triangle, rectangle, cylinder, sphere, cuboid, cone.

Size: big, bigger, small, smaller.

Length and height: long, longer, short, shorter, tall, taller.

Weight: heavy, heavier, light, lighter.

Capacity: full, fuller, empty, emptier.

Pattern: same, different, next to.

There are also a number of computer programs available which support children's mathematical learning. A member of staff will be happy to talk about these with you.

Figure 4.10 Mathematical development in the nursery guidance leaflet

---

Preparing for 'phonics'

Early phonics develop through a wide range of experiences. Before they are able to identify sounds in words, children need plenty of opportunities to really listen to, and discriminate between, sounds. You can support your child's learning in this area by:

- Playing games such as making a sound (e.g. rustling paper, shaking a cereal box) behind a screen and asking your child to guess what has made the sound.

- Encouraging your child to listen to, and recognise, sounds in the environment (e.g. car engines, taps dripping, birds singing).

- Encouraging experimentation with voices, making sounds such as 'wheee!' when riding a scooter or 'whoosh' when pretending to be a rocket and different animal sounds.

- Sometimes varying your own voice when speaking, for example, whispering, growling, squeaking.

- Playing musical instruments with your child and talking about the sounds that different instruments make.

- Making up pairs or strings of words, choosing words that begin with the same sound, for example, happy Harry, delicious doughnuts, big blue ball.

- Singing or chanting rhymes. Clapping, tapping and stamping to rhymes.

- Talking about rhyming words and making up strings, for example, sun, bun, run, fun.

A strong indicator of success as a reader in later life is the child's ability to discriminate between sounds at this early stage.

Figure 4.11 Preparing for phonics

'news' letters. Often children will go home at the end of the session proudly clutching a pile of paintings, drawings, models, etc. This sense of pride is to be fostered and such works of art are usually received with enthusiasm by parents. However, not all learning has a tangible 'end product' and it is important that the value of the learning process, and the conceptual achievements, is also understood by parents.

Although practitioners aim to verbally share information about children's experiences on a daily basis, it can be helpful (particularly to parents who are unable to have daily contact with the setting) sometimes to send a brief written explanation of an activity enjoyed by a child home at the end of the day. This will be especially useful in the absence of an 'end product' to the activity. The production of a photocopiable pro forma (to which individual observations can be added) for use during focus activities reduces the length of time taken to record the information (see Figure 4.13). Where practitioners have access to a photocopier in the

First Steps Nursery
'GROWTH AND LIVING THINGS'

Dear Parents and Carers,

Now that spring is with us, and the children have been showing a keen interest in lambs in the field opposite the nursery we will be looking particularly at 'growth and living things' with the children. We have planned some exciting activities including:

- Observing the life cycle of a butterfly and a frog (caterpillars and frogspawn are due to arrive next week – look out for the 'Living Things' display!)

- A visit to a local farm (parents and carers will be invited to join us – details to follow).

- A search for 'mini-beasts' in the outside play area.

- Growing a range of vegetables and flowers, observing and measuring their growth.

- A visit from a health visitor, talking about keeping healthy.

There are many ways in which you can support your child's interest about 'growth and living things' at home. Here are a few suggestions from us – please let us know about your good ideas so that we can share them with other parents!

- A visit to the park looking at, and talking about, leaves, buds, flowers, insects.

- Making a scrapbook of things found in the park.

- A visit to the local garden centre to look at plants, seedlings, trees, shrubs.

- Digging and planting – there are many plants which will happily grow in pots on a window sill if access to a garden or allotment is difficult. (Cut-off carrot tops in a saucer of water quickly grow shoots and require little attention!)

- Talking about pets – how they have changed as they have grown, and the care they need.

- Talking about their own growth and the food/care they need to be healthy.

- Looking at photographs of themselves (from babyhood to present day).

Thank you for your cooperation – have fun investigating with your child!

The nursery staff

Figure 4.12 Letter to parents: 'Growth and living things'

Today we have read a story called 'Handa's Surprise' in which Handa decides to take a basket full of exotic fruits to her friend as a present.

We have been tasting some of these fruits in nursery.

Daniel

liked _mango and pineapple_

disliked _passion fruit and tangerine_

Figure 4.13 Explanation of 'tasting exotic fruits' activity

setting, written observations of spontaneous activities (intended for inclusion in profiles) could occasionally be photocopied and a copy sent to the parent with a standard explanation note attached. Such information may prove to be a useful prompt for children who, when asked about the day's activities, invariably respond with the easiest answer – 'Nothing', or perhaps, 'I don't know'! Although persistent questioning is unlikely to be the right course of action in such a situation, having some information about a particular activity will enable the parent to more effectively engage in conversation with the child about that activity, asking informed, and focused, questions. It will also help to raise the status of activities with no concrete 'end product' as valuable learning experiences. (See also Chapter 2, page 72, 'Making games' and Chapter 3, page 105, 'Our Goldfish'.)

Figure 4.14 shows how children's learning in the home and the setting is inseparable. This very long message was written by a child at home just as her younger sister was about to start attending the nursery. She was concerned that staff would not know how to look after her sister and, as a prolific emergent writer, recorded the necessary details on paper. She, with her mum and sister, brought in the written instructions the next morning, presented them to the nursery manager and read back her marks. She was then happy to leave her work with the manager, relieved that the important information had been imparted!

Children's 'profiles' should include photographic evidence of learning and are another way in which practitioner and parent can combine information to give a more complete picture of the child's learning achievements. Purposes of, and methods of compiling, profiles will be looked at in Chapter 6.

Producing a letter with a standard format (see Figure 4.15) for recording information about a child's play and learning at home can be useful and some parents will respond to this method. The completed observation can be cut off and immediately stuck into the child's profile creating minimal work for the key person. For others, an informal chat, or a time slot in a meeting with the child's key person,

Figure 4.14 Looking after my sister

will be more appropriate and the key person may then record the information for inclusion in the child's profile. It can help busy practitioners if a stock of paper formats (e.g. speech bubbles, see Figure 4.16) are readily available to scribe parents' comments on, these can then be transferred directly to the child's profile at a more convenient time. An effective practitioner will have a number of strategies for gathering information from home and will tailor his or her approach dependent on what is most comfortable for the parent.

Story sacks containing a book, related props and a list of suggestions as to how parents can extend learning are a useful 'link' resource. Commercially-produced story sacks are available from catalogues but teams often prefer to prepare their own, building up a bank over time. Children will be invited to take a sack home for a few nights and share story experiences with their family. Figure 4.17 shows an example of a supporting leaflet included in a story sack focusing on *The Very Hungry Caterpillar* by Eric Carle.

The provision of information such as play-dough recipes, instructions for how to make a sock puppet and lists of useful resources to include in a 'junk modelling box' at home will be appreciated by many parents. Children may also be asked to

Dear Parents

We are working hard to develop our children's profiles to become useful documents of their learning journeys and celebrations of them as individuals. We use observations of the children as a basis for our planning and would like to include more information about children's interests and learning at home. Please use the format below to record any of the following:

- Experiences or activities that your child has particularly enjoyed recently, times when they have really had fun.
- Personal interests that you have noticed over a period of time.
- Significant learning milestones e.g. putting on own coat, singing favourite nursery rhyme, counting 5 candles on birthday cake.
- Any forthcoming events that will be of importance to your child e.g. a family holiday or celebration, a new baby in the family, grandparents coming to stay, decorating his or her bedroom.

Thank you – please hand your observation to your child's key person. Your contributions will enable us to engage with your child about the things that are interesting them outside of nursery. They will also help us to plan experiences in nursery that motivate and excite them.

OBSERVATION FROM HOME

Child's name:	Date:
Comments:	
Parent's signature:	

Figure 4.15 Letter to parents and format for observations from home

bring resources from home to support learning in the setting such as recycled materials (e.g. cereal boxes, cardboard tubes, yoghurt pots) for model-making in the workshop, items for an 'interest' table (e.g. natural forms), photographs of themselves as babies for a display on 'growing up'.

Children's achievements are often summarised more formally at intervals during and/or at the end of their time in the setting in the form of written 'records of achievement' for parents. These will be looked at in more detail in Chapter 6, but it is worth mentioning here the importance of giving parents opportunities to contribute and respond to, and to discuss, the information included in such reports. Time should be planned for practitioners to talk, undisturbed (as far as possible), with parents about their child's progress.

> Conversations with parents can benefit all parties concerned. It benefits teachers because of their increased knowledge of the child, it benefits parents by making them genuine partners in their child's learning and it benefits children, who see home and school as mutually interested in their education.

> (Fisher 1996)

28.08.12
Today Kayden's mum told us that they had been for a walk at the weekend and he had seen some rabbits running across a field. He had been very excited, asking questions such as 'Where are they going?' and 'Where do they sleep?', then suggested 'I think they sleep under the trees so no rain gets on them'.

29.08.12
We decided to use this interest in rabbits to encourage Kayden to talk as he is shy and still sometimes reluctant to speak at nursery.
We planned to:
• Provide information and story books in nursery about rabbits and read these with him to find out more about rabbits
• Lend books about rabbits to him to share with his family
• Set up a small world 'field' with rabbits, artificial grass, stones, small blocks (for walls)
• Visit the city farm (invite mum).

31.08.12
Mum said that Kayden had really enjoyed the books and was particularly fascinated by the fact that rabbits burrowed and lived in warrens underground.

Through this play theme, we were increasingly able to engage in sustained conversation with Kayden and observed that he also talked more readily to his peers, sharing his knowledge of rabbits proudly. We were now beginning to see in nursery the communication and language skills that he had previously only demonstrated at home.

03.08.12
We put lengths of cardboard tubing in a deep, large sand tray with lots of sand and some small world rabbits. Kayden was really motivated as he made 'warrens' covering the tubes with sand and pushing rabbits through the tunnels. He chatted to me about what he was doing and talked about the rabbits he had seen on his walk, saying 'I think the rabbits in the field went under the soil . . . at night . . . how did they did the tunnels?' I followed his lead and we discussed how rabbits use their front legs to dig.   KD

Figure 4.16 Speech bubbles

STARTING WITH A STORY
The Very Hungry Caterpillar
By Eric Carle

Sharing stories can be a very enjoyable experience for both the adult and the child as well as being crucial to the child's development as a 'reader'. Try to find a slot in the day when you have plenty of time to spend with your child and settle down in a comfortable and quiet place. Here are a few general points to discuss that will help your child to understand how books 'work':

- Ask your child to look at the front of the book cover and to suggest what the book might be about.
- Talk about the author and the illustrator. Think about other books you may have read by the same author. Look for books by the same author in the library or bookshops.
- Encourage your child to find the first page and to turn the pages as you read.
- Talk about the difference between the illustrations and the text. Use words such as 'word', 'letter', 'picture'.
- Encourage your child to look carefully at the illustrations and to talk about what is happening in them. They may be able to tell the story, or make up their own, by 'reading' the pictures.
- Encourage your child to predict what might happen next in the story, or to guess how it might end. Use words such as 'start', 'beginning', 'next', 'after', 'then', 'end'.
- Talk about characters in the story.
- Retell the story together afterwards, sequencing key events in order. Use the illustrations and props as prompts.
- Make up your own stories using the same characters.

Stories can also help to develop children's learning in other areas

Here are a few activity ideas related to the story of *The Very Hungry Caterpillar*. If your child shows interest in particular themes within the story, you may want to try some of them.

- Talking about the life cycle of a butterfly. Looking for caterpillars and butterflies in the garden or park.
- Looking in information books to find out the names of different butterflies, what they eat and where they live.
- Counting pieces of fruit in your fruit bowl. Counting out, for example, four grapes for each person.
- Talking about a healthy diet and the things that help us to grow.
- Looking closely at real apples, pears, plums, strawberries and oranges. Cutting the fruit up and looking at pips and stones.
- Discussing the days of the week and talking about regular weekly activities, for example, 'On Monday we go swimming', 'On Tuesday we go to Grandma's house for tea'. Talking about what you had to eat yesterday and what you would like for tea tomorrow.
- Making butterfly wing pictures by painting a pattern on one side of a piece of paper, folding it over and pressing to produce a mirror image on the other side.
- Using a safety mirror to create symmetrical images of other objects.

Figure 4.17 *The Very Hungry Caterpillar*

The two-way flow of information between practitioner and parent about the child is a vital aspect of the partnership. Children's achievements at home and in the setting should be celebrated as well as concerns voiced, and parents should feel comfortable in approaching staff. If the content of the discussion is of a sensitive nature, it will need to be conducted in privacy and confidentiality respected. It should be the aim of all key adults in a child's life to build an effective network system through which they can communicate information to support the child in making progress in all areas of learning. Sharing the knowledge that each of those adults has about the child is essential in addressing the needs of the 'whole child'.

Planning home and setting 'link activities': introducing Oscar the clown

Working parents, and parents with other demanding commitments, are not always able to enjoy the frequent contact with the setting that they would like, but it is possible to plan activities involving parents and children which take place in the home. The visit of a soft toy character to the setting is a reliable way of engaging children and stimulating their imagination. This approach has already been suggested in the focus activity 'Lion's visit' (Chapter 3, page 92) during which a friendly lion spends time in the setting and challenges children to build him a den. The example used in this chapter is of Oscar, a brightly coloured, well-travelled clown who has visited hundreds of homes in Leeds and has been well cared for in all!

The aim of the 'Oscar project' is to develop children's learning in the areas of personal, social and emotional development, communication and language,

Figure 4.18 Oscar with his suitcase

and literacy, and also to help develop positive links between home and the setting. If introduced at a time when new children are joining the setting, Oscar can also help to ease the settling-in process for children, for example, he could 'befriend' children who are feeling a little unsure; children could take responsibility for looking after Oscar whilst he is 'new' in the setting; they could explain a new activity to him, show him around the setting or merely invite him to watch as they play. The project is an idea which can easily be used in any setting, with little or no adaptation, and which is popular with both children and parents. The following plan is presented in the same format as focus activities cited in other chapters but includes a wider range of possible objectives.

FOCUS ACTIVITY: OSCAR THE CLOWN VISITS CHILDREN IN THEIR OWN HOMES

Focus areas of learning

- Personal, social and emotional development

- Communication and language

- Literacy

Learning objectives

- To develop a sense of responsibility.

- To be aware of the needs of others.

- To take turns.

- To gain confidence in sharing experiences and expressing feelings in a group situation.

- To listen and respond to other children's accounts of their experiences.

- To understand that writing carries meaning.

- To attempt writing to convey meaning.

- To reinforce and develop links with home.

- For parents and children to share in an experience initiated in the setting.

Background information and prior learning

Children may have been introduced to Oscar during a home visit (see 'Home Visit Plan', page 127). Children and staff will have talked about personal hygiene, and in particular the need for washing, brushing teeth and combing hair.

Introduction

The adult will gather together a group of children on the first day of the 'Oscar project'. Oscar will be introduced to the children and they will be shown his suitcase and its contents (see 'Resources'). The leading adult will explain that Oscar has come to spend time in the setting and needs somewhere to sleep at night. Some time for discussion and suggestions will be allowed. The adult will then tell the children that Oscar would like to stay for a night at each of their homes and will read an entry in his diary describing his visit to the home of a member of staff. They will discuss care of Oscar with a focus on personal hygiene and safety.

Main activity

Every day Oscar will go home with a different child. The child will be encouraged to care for Oscar, to share toys and experiences with him and to talk about photographs in his album. Parents will receive a letter of explanation and be asked to participate and, with the child, make an entry in Oscar's diary.

Finishing off and follow-up

In the weekly planning, time will be allocated for daily discussion of Oscar's visits to children's homes. Following each of Oscar's 'home visits', the child concerned will show the group the diary and talk about his or her experiences with the clown. Other children will be encouraged to ask the child questions about Oscar's visit. Photographs, letters to Oscar, diary entries, etc. will be displayed in the setting (on boards or made into books).

Adult role

The adult will:

- Provide resources – check contents of the suitcase after every visit
- Stimulate interest in the activity during the introduction
- Write a letter explaining the activity. Give a copy of the letter, and talk about the activity, to parents when it is their child's turn to take Oscar
- Support and encourage children as they talk about Oscar's visit to their house
- Read entries in Oscar's diary
- Ensure that all children are given the opportunity to take Oscar home.

Key vocabulary and questions

Why do you think Oscar has come to the setting? What do you think he would like to play with? Where will he sleep tonight? Do you think he will be lonely in the setting by himself? Do you think Oscar would like to sleep at your house? How would you look after him? Which of your toys would you show him? What did you and Oscar do yesterday evening? Which other members of your family did Oscar meet? Did he remember to brush his teeth before he went to bed? Did you show him how to comb his hair? What did you and Oscar eat for your tea? Shall we read your entry in Oscar's diary? Would you like to read what you have written? Which part of Oscar's visit did you enjoy the most?

Resources

- Oscar (soft toy clown)
- Oscar's suitcase containing: his diary, photograph album, favourite toy, toothbrush, comb, a pencil and a letter from Oscar[4] addressed to the child
- Letter to parents – a brief explanation of the aims of the project and the required involvement from the parent

Figure 4.19 Snap from Oscar's photograph album

Children will often take Oscar with them to the supermarket, café, park, Grandma's house, the fair – some have even taken him on holiday for the weekend (see Figure 4.22) and come back with very exciting tales to tell about his adventures!

> Monday
>
> Today Oscar came home with Natalia and she was very excited. He sat at the table at lunch time and ate cheese sandwiches with her. After lunch we all went to the post office and Natalia carried Oscar all the way. Oscar helped Natalia to post some letters and then we all came home. Oscar and Natalia played with toys for the rest of the afternoon. We went to Auntie Di's for tea – pasta, Natalia's favourite. At bed time, Natalia helped Oscar to clean his teeth and wash his face. Then they both brushed their hair and went to bed.

Figure 4.20 Natalia's entry in Oscar's diary: Mum and Natalia's writing – Natalia's writing reads 'Oscar came to play at my house'

Figure 4.21 Natalia's drawing – 'Me and Oscar and Mummy'

Figure 4.22 Oscar enjoys a family holiday with Laura and George

KEY POINTS FOR GOOD PRACTICE

- Celebrate diversity and embrace the cultural experiences of children and families. Increase knowledge and understanding within the team of a range of cultures. Support the development of the child's own cultural identity.

- Make sure that you have an effective key person system in place.

- Remember that one strategy for engaging parents will not suit all. Practitioners need to be flexible and creative in their approach.

- Value information from parents and other settings about a child's experiences prior to entering your setting.

  ○ Make sure that the environment you create is welcoming to parents and carers.

- Listen with respect to parents' concerns and respond appropriately, for example giving relevant information, reassurance with reasons, observing the child. Remember that successful partnerships grow when practitioners work *with* parents/carers, rather than doing things *to* them or *for* them.

- Remember that much of children's learning takes place in the home or community. Throughout the Early Years Foundation Stage, take time to find out about children's individual interests and achievements outside the setting.

  ○ Develop systems to ensure that information from home is fed into the planning process. Where possible, involve parents directly in planning to support their child's learning both at home and in the setting.

- Encourage parents to contribute to their child's profile. Emphasise that the profile is a celebration of the child's achievements.

- Involve parents in the planning and reviewing of their child's IEP and in the planning of the next phase (remember the parent's right to be involved in this process).

- Share your observations and assessments of children's learning with their parents on an ongoing basis and in summary reports.
- Be aware of those parents for whom English is an additional language. Where possible offer bilingual support for them during discussions.
- Make sure that systems are in place for communicating with those parents who do not have daily contact with the setting.
- Keep parents fully informed about Early Years Foundation Stage principles and practice.
- Consult with parents during policy making and reviewing.

Nursery education should throughout be an affair of co-operation between the nursery and home and it will only succeed to the full if it carries the parents into partnership.

(Department of Education and Science 1967, para. 32)

Notes

1 From this point, the word 'parents' will be used to refer to all main carers, whatever their relationship to the child.
2 See Chapter 6, 'Observing children's play, assessing learning and keeping useful records' for details of contents and purpose of forms, questionnaires and leaflets.
3 Ibid.
4 These leaflets can also be useful to other adults working in the setting, for example students and new staff.
5 Content will include, for example, a 'thank you' for inviting him to stay, information about his favourite food, activities and toys, a list of items packed in his suitcase and a reminder to take care of him and to return him (with all belongings!) the following day.

CHAPTER 5

Planning display as a teaching and learning tool

A display is, in fact, an extension of the working areas in classrooms. It is a focal point for enquiry, and as such is a vital component in education.

(Lancaster 1990)

The content of this chapter is organised as follows:

- Why is display important? (page 156)
- Planning a display (page 156)
- Display can be interactive (page 158)
- Display can celebrate (page 171)
- Display can be informative (page 177)
- Constructing displays: some practical hints (page 179)
- Key points for good practice (page 182)

Why is display important?

There are a number of reasons why a practitioner may decide to create a display in the setting, including:

- To celebrate children's achievements
- To stimulate children's interest and/or imagination
- To engage children in an activity
- To extend children's knowledge in a particular area
- To share information with adults.

Planning a display

It is not necessary to write a plan for a display but it is important for all adults in the setting to be aware of the aims of the display and its proposed uses. It is a good idea to discuss display plans as a team, and asking questions in order to clarify purpose can be a useful exercise. For example:

- What is the learning focus of the display?
- Who will benefit from the display?
- What will they learn?

Having determined the reasons for constructing the display, the practitioner can then decide on the most appropriate methods of organisation and presentation. There will be a multitude of alternatives and decisions will, again, be influenced to a large extent by practicalities and physical features of the setting. Practitioners may not have access to permanent wall boards, shelving or suitable surfaces and will need to think about how to provide portable displays which can be stored away between sessions. Folding screens can be very useful pieces of equipment in such circumstances, as can wheeled storage units (with a surface at child level), portable frameworks (from which to hang children's work, objects of interest, etc.), free-standing open shelving and sandwich-style boards. Throughout this chapter, examples of displays will be categorised as:

- *Wall*: this will refer to all displays fixed to a vertical surface, for example wall-mounted boards, free-standing boards, screens
- *Table top*: including all horizontal surfaces (e.g. tops of cupboards, large trays or boards)
- *Shelf*: open shelving, fixed or free-standing
- *Suspended*: pieces of work or objects displayed by hanging them from a framework or permanent fixture in the setting.

Whatever the type of display, if intended for children, it should be easily accessible to them visually and (if appropriate) physically. This means making sure that displays are at a comfortable height for children and also that there is ample space around each for children to look at, or work with, displayed items. Ideally, both computer-generated and handwritten labels should be present in the setting. It may also be appropriate to provide labels in a large type or with tactile clues for visually impaired children.

When the intended audience comprises solely of adults, wall displays should be at adult eye level. Where families with English as an additional language attend, labels and leaflets in the appropriate language or script should be included.

The length of time a display stays in the setting is dependent on its purpose. Some displays will be put up spontaneously, perhaps in response to children's immediate interests, and these may only be applicable for a brief period of time. Others are set up to complement work planned around a particular theme. Such displays may need to be added to and remain in the setting long enough for children to observe changes (e.g. tadpoles into frogs, seeds into plants). If a display is intended to engage children in an activity, ample time should be allowed for them to return to the activity, perhaps a number of times, to review or modify work and for reinforcement of concepts. It may be that the display informs children about, for example, the different resources permanently on offer in an area of provision, in which case there would be justification for an extended period of display, as the relevance of that information is 'ongoing'. The practitioner should, however, be aware that display which becomes a 'permanent fixture' in the setting will probably cease to attract children's attention, or hold their interest, and its effectiveness may be significantly reduced after a certain period of time. (This may not be the case if adult time is regularly given to using long-term displays with children.) In any event, displays which are faded, 'tatty' or no longer complete are not going to inspire children to learn and should be dismantled.

In order to look in more depth at the different purposes and aspects of display the next part of the chapter is divided into three sections and explores ways in which display can be interactive, can celebrate work and can be informative. In practice many displays will, and should, include elements from two or all of these categories but examples have been selected according to their dominant purpose.

Display can be interactive

Interactive display can engage children physically and intellectually. It can actively involve children in first-hand learning experiences and challenge them, through questions and provision of appropriate and stimulating resources, to:

- Solve problems
- Design and build or make for a specific purpose (functional or fantasy)
- Find out (specific information or open ended)
- Follow instructions
- Have, and share, opinions
- Develop imaginative ideas
- Record information, observations, findings and imaginative ideas.

The display may target a key area of learning or combine learning in two or three areas through a common theme. There may be a very specific intended outcome, or learning may be more open ended, the emphasis being on experimentation, exploration and investigation through the senses. Interactive display can also encourage collaborative and cooperative work.

Displays of this nature can be regarded rather like a focus activity in that learning goals should be clearly defined and resources carefully selected. The adult role is also an important issue to be discussed by the team. During the period of time that the display is available, children will probably have free access to it and adults will need to intervene and support as appropriate. For this reason, all adults involved in the setting need to be aware of how to effectively support children working at the display from the time of its introduction. The nature of the support will vary from display to display, and child to child. The practitioner may need to focus on supporting the child in using the display independently, or may need to offer more direct learning support. Intervention will often be spontaneous, but there may be occasions when practitioners will want to plan time slots in the weekly planning for adult input, particularly to introduce the display (see 'leaf investigation', page 164) and to develop learning potential.

The following two display plans are offered as examples. The reader will note that, although both displays fall into the category of 'interactive display', each sets different expectations in terms of children's use of resources. The 'shape and colour decision tree' is quite specific in its guidance, offering a series of instructions which will focus children's learning on some specific objectives. In the second example of the 'exploring sound' display, activities are of a more investigative nature and learning intentions more open ended.

INTERACTIVE DISPLAY: SHAPE AND COLOUR DECISION TREE

Date of introduction and expected duration

- 6 January for two weeks

Type of display

- Table top or wall

Key area of learning

- Mathematics

Learning objectives

- To match, recognise and name key colours and shapes.

- To make decisions according to given criteria.

- To develop logical thinking and to follow pathways.

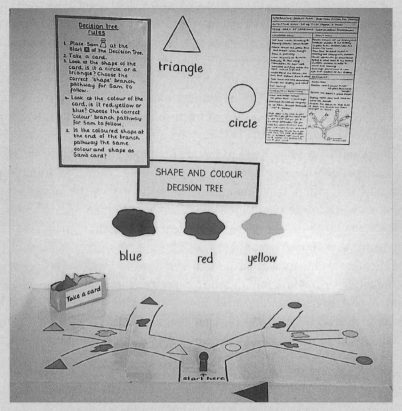

Figure 5.1 Shape and colour decision tree interactive display

Resources

- Horizontal surface and wall space or vertical board
- Decision cards (coloured shapes – red, yellow, blue – circle, triangle) in a box
- Colour and shape labels
- 'Sam' doll
- Decision tree drawn on large sheet of card[1]
- Decision tree instructions for use with or by children
- Copy of display plan (for adult)

Activities

Children will:

- Select a card and look at its shape
- Decide which shape 'branch' to take, circle or triangle
- Follow the branch (with the card or 'Sam' doll) until it divides

- Look at the colour of the card

- Decide which colour 'branch' to take, blue, red or yellow

- Follow the branch to its limit

- Compare the coloured shape at the end of the branch with the one on the card selected – is it the same?

Adult role

Adult will:

- Set up the display and check resources daily

- Introduce the display to children, explaining objectives

- Plan time for adult input (observing, and working with, children)

- Spontaneously support children as appropriate, modelling use of key vocabulary and asking questions.

Key vocabulary and questions

Vocabulary: Colour and shape names: red, blue, yellow, circle, triangle. Positional and directional language: up, down, forwards, backwards, next to, between

Questions: What colour is the circle? What shape is your card? Can you tell me two things about your card (colour and shape)? Have you got the same shape as your friend? Look at the shape of your card – which branch should you choose? Does your card match the coloured shape at the end of your chosen 'route'? Did you make the correct decisions? Did you reach the correct destination? Where do you think you made a mistake? Do you think you would reach the same destination with a different card? Where do you think this card would lead you? Can you explain the 'decision tree' rules to your friend?

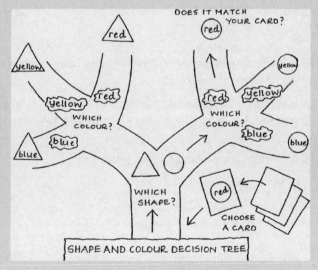

Figure 5.2 Shape and colour decision tree: layout diagram

INTERACTIVE DISPLAY: EXPLORING SOUND

Date of introduction and expected duration

- 10 June for three weeks

Type of display

- Table top or suspended

Key areas of learning

- Communication and language
- Literacy
- Expressive arts and design

Learning objectives

- To listen to, and discriminate between, a variety of sounds.
- To experiment with materials to produce different sounds.
- To represent one sound with another.

Resources

- A range of musical instruments including commercially-produced instruments, instruments made by adults and children in the setting, instruments from other cultures
- Copper piping (cut to different lengths) suspended (to hang at different levels) from a large wire lampshade frame hung from the ceiling. Additional lengths of metal and plastic piping, wooden sticks and fabric-covered sticks provided for use by children to 'play' the hanging pipes
- A range of materials with which children can make their own instruments, for example cardboard boxes, rubber bands, yoghurt pots, margarine pots, cardboard tubes, pieces of fabric, sand, dried peas
- A box of 'animal cards' – photographs of animals to be used as prompts for children when relating sounds to animals, for example lion, mouse, elephant, crocodile, sparrow
- Fiction and non-fiction books about musical instruments
- A board (to be used as a screen)

Activities

Children will:

- Handle commercially-produced, and other, instruments
- Listen to and compare sounds made by different instruments

- Talk about their observations using key vocabulary and descriptive language

- With an adult or friend, play sound matching games (play the instrument behind a screen and ask your friend to guess what is making the sound)

- Experiment with sound using one instrument – looking at the range of sounds that can be produced and how sounds can be changed

- Try different ways of making sounds using the materials provided

- Make an instrument and use it to accompany singing

- Think about the characteristics of an animal and find a sound that expresses the characteristics.

Adult role

Adult will:

- Set up and introduce the display

- Replenish stocks of consumable resources daily

- Plan time to work alongside, and observe, children

- Intervene spontaneously as appropriate, asking questions and modelling use of key vocabulary.

Key vocabulary and questions

Vocabulary: Loud, quiet. Children should also be encouraged to use descriptive language, and make up their own words, related to sounds, for example rattling, banging, twanging, tinkling, pinging, swishing.

Questions: What kind of sound does the instrument make? Does it sound the same as this one? What kind of sound do you think this instrument will make? Can you find an instrument that makes a loud sound? Can you make an instrument that makes a rattling sound? What could you use to make a 'pinging' sound? Which instrument makes a sound like an elephant? What animal does this sound remind you of? Can you guess which instrument is making this sound?

The early years practitioner aims to encourage an independent approach to learning in young children and interactive display has an important role to play in encouraging both independent thought and independent use of resources. Young children's thinking can be challenged, and ideas developed, through stimulation of the imagination, exploration and investigation, and examples of displays included in this chapter illustrate a variety of 'starting points'. The way in which a display is arranged, labelled and used by adults will affect the way in which the child responds to, and interacts with, it. For example, clear instructions, signs and labels which are accompanied by pictures, photographs or symbols will more easily enable a child to complete a task independently. A verbal introduction to the display will alert children to learning opportunities. A written explanation, and questions, focused on the learning objectives can also support adults in helping the child to use the display.

Leaf investigation

Type of display

- Wall or table top

Key areas of learning

- Understanding the world
- Communication and language
- Literacy

Learning objectives

- To observe and compare leaves, looking at shape, pattern and size.
- To talk about observations.
- To understand that non-fiction books can inform and to use non-fiction books as a source of information.

Resources

- Photographs, posters, non-fiction picture books, children's drawings and paintings with a leaf, tree, autumn theme
- A range of autumn leaves
- Magnifying glasses
- Question cards, labels and key vocabulary cards

Suggested content of practitioner's introduction

- Look what we have on our book display today – what do you think the books are about? How do you know?
- Here are some of the leaves we collected in the park yesterday
- Tell us what you already know about these leaves
- Let's see what else we can find out about the leaves
- Look closely at the leaves, what do you notice about them? Are they all the same colour and size? Can you see the patterns that the leaf 'veins' make?
- Look in the books. Look at the pictures, can you match any of our leaves to the pictures? What kind of tree does this leaf come from? What happens to leaves in the autumn?

Following a brief introduction such as this, children are equipped with a purpose and appropriate resources for learning and should (although further adult input at a later stage will be helpful) be encouraged to carry out an independent 'leaf investigation'. Resources should also be made available for them to record their findings (e.g. a camera, mark-making equipment, bookmarks). Of course, as with any learning activity, the practitioner must plan for differentiation and displays should be of interest and use to children at various developmental stages. In the example of the 'leaf investigation', the resources provided will enable learning to take place at all levels from, for example, tactile explorations with no verbal observations, to the accessing of information about specific leaves through reading pictures and key words.

Figure 5.3 shows a display constructed in a setting attended by children throughout the foundation stage. It is a good example of a 'differentiated' display. The examples given of 'possible activities' indicate the wide range of learning experiences that could take place on the 'journey' towards early learning goals, particularly in the areas of knowledge and understanding of the world, and communication, language and literacy. The display enables children to begin the journey at their own starting point – it can challenge all children, but will exclude none.

Come and make a rocket

Type of display

- Wall or table top

Key area of learning

- Expressive arts and design

Resources

- Signs (writing and diagrams): 'Come and make a rocket', 'You will need', 'Can you open the top to let the astronaut in?', 'Sign here when you have made your rocket'

- Components, 'astronaut' dolls, 'launching pad', pen

Possible activities

- Handling, looking at, comparing and talking about the components

- Experimenting with the components, finding ways of fixing them together

- Looking at the joined components and deciding what the 'model' could be, for example, 'It looks like a tower!'

Figure 5.3 Come and make a rocket

- Matching components to those on the 'You will need' sign
- Following the plan to build a rocket using the components[2]
- Exploring different ways of 'hinging' the top of the rocket
- Using the rocket in imaginative play or story-making activities
- Designing and making own rocket, talking about and recording plans or instructions (the child would need access to a range of components)
- Signing name (at own developmental stage of writing) to register engagement in the activity

Children may be required to move around the setting in order to achieve objectives and displays could 'send' children on searches for objects or quests for information, perhaps following arrows or other signs. The following display is an example of this approach.

Billy's Beetle

Although this display offers good opportunities for retelling a favourite story (communication and language and literacy) and also for using everyday language to describe position (mathematics), the practitioners chose technology (understanding the world) as the key area of learning. They had recently purchased some remote-control vehicles but in order for children to be able to control these effectively, they would need to be able to read the arrow symbols on the handset. They used the children's interest in the story *Billy's Beetle* (by Mick Inkpen) to introduce these symbols and to give physically active experiences of responding to them on a larger scale.

Billy's Beetle

Type of display

- Table top (also requires children to move around the setting)

Key area of learning

- Understanding the world

Resources

- A copy of the book *Billy's Beetle*
- An enlarged picture of Billy
- A sign: 'Where is Billy's Beetle?' and 'Follow the arrows', arrow signs (forwards, backwards, left, right – arranged around the setting and leading to the beetles)

- Small boxes

- Information books about beetles

- Plastic beetles will be hidden under a log or in amongst the grass in an area of the outdoor space

Activity

Children look at the story book, talking about characters and events in the story with their friends. They take a box and go to look for the beetle, following the signs until they reach the beetles. They then return the beetle to Billy. At the end of the session or day, the equipment will be replaced and one of the practitioners will move the signs to alter the route for the next day.

The question table

The question table is often offered on a daily basis and can become part of the permanent provision. Children, supported by parents, are required, as part of the beginning of session routine, to register their response to a daily question by placing their name card in a 'yes' or 'no'[3] container. The questions may refer to, for example, interests in the setting, seasonal changes, or may aim to develop concepts.

Children may be asked to:

- Observe

- Reason

- Recall

- Compare

- Predict

- Express opinions and preferences.

Although the name 'question table' implies a 'table top' type of display, this activity could be just as successfully presented on a wall, for example, name cards in the shape of apples, and with hoop and loop fastening tape attached to the back, could be removed from a wall-mounted carpet tile and displayed on either the 'yes' or the 'no' apple tree.

Listed below are some examples of questions:

- Did you pass a shop on your way to nursery today?

- Have the leaves started to fall off the trees yet?

- Are you wearing anything red today?

- Did you enjoy our 'dragon dance' yesterday?

- Is the ball in the box? (provide real objects)

- In our story yesterday, did the fox catch Rosie?

- Do you like to eat apples?

- Do you think it will rain today?

- Have you looked at our 'book of the week'?

- Have you got blue eyes? (provide a mirror)

A variation on the question table idea is the 'question book'. This is usually a large scrapbook covered in 'special' paper. The question is written at the top of the page, and children respond by signing their name in the 'yes' column or the 'no' column. It can be interesting for children to look back at previous pages with an adult, and compare responses to questions.

Figure 5.4 The question table

Other examples of interactive display

'Owl Babies' group behaviour chart

Type of display

- Wall or suspended

Key area of learning

- Personal, social and emotional development

Resources

- Setting's 'rules' sign (e.g. 'Be helpful to other children and look after our toys')

- Large picture of an owl, tree pictures and a picture of three baby owls – pictures to be cut out, laminated and arranged vertically or horizontally: large owl, trees, baby owls

- Sign: 'I want my Mummy!'

- Book: *Owl Babies* by Martin Waddell

Activity

Children will be familiar with, and enjoy, the *Owl Babies* story. They, probably at group time, move the 'mummy' owl towards her babies (one tree at a time) in response to evidence that the rules are being adhered to. When mummy owl reaches her babies, the whole group receives a 'reward', for example another visit from Oscar the clown (see Chapter 4, page 150). This activity will both celebrate the positive behaviour of individuals and promote group responsibility.

Weaving a Christmas tree

Type of display

- Table top

Key areas of learning

- Physical development
- Expressive arts and design

Resources

- A willow twig 'wigwam' or large, triangular piece of plastic webbing (both available from garden centres – intended for training climbing plants)
- Box containing strips of green (a range of shades) fabric, ribbon and cord
- Key vocabulary labels, for example, weave, over, under, in, out

Activity

Children, and parents, select pieces of fabric, etc. to weave into the framework to create a 'woven Christmas tree' over a period of two to three weeks prior to Christmas. The tree can then be adorned with children's made decorations tied onto the framework.

Whose shoes?

Type of display

- Table top

Key area of learning

- Mathematics

Resources

- Five pairs of shoes (soles of various shapes and sizes)
- Templates of the shoes arranged in pairs on the table top
- Key vocabulary labels, for example, big, small

Activity

Children match the shoes to the correct templates looking carefully at size and shape.

Look how we have changed!

Type of display

- Wall

Key area of learning

- Understanding the world

Resources

- Folded cards attached to the wall – one for each child, showing a picture of the child as a baby on the front, and as they are now, inside
- Posters and pictures of 'babyhood'

Activity

Children guess who the baby photographs are, and then lift the flap to find out if they were correct. They talk about how they have changed (e.g. appearance, food, independence).

Where's Spot?

Type of display

- Table top

Key area of learning

- Mathematics

Resources

- Book: *Where's Spot?* by Eric Hill
- 'Spot' soft toy
- Photographs of Spot in different positions around the setting
- Question labels (e.g. Can you hide or find Spot under the table? On the cupboard? In the box? Under the chair?)

Activity

Children work with a friend, hiding and finding Spot, and using key 'positional' vocabulary to describe his location

Five Little Speckled Frogs

Type of display

- Table top or wall

Key area of learning

- Mathematics

Resources

- Rhyme: *Five Little Speckled Frogs*
- Numerals 1–5
- Real log
- Five frog models
- A pond (e.g. small silver foil tray, tissue paper 'pond weed', small stones – children could make these)

Activity

Children sing the rhyme, counting, and putting the frogs into the pool in turn.

Story characters

Type of display

- Table top or suspended

Key area of learning

- Literacy

Resources

Silhouettes of familiar story book characters (e.g. Kipper, the monster from *Not Now Bernard*, Big Bear and Little Bear from *Let's Go Home Little Bear*) cut out of black sugar paper, laminated for durability and hung at different levels from a length of dowel suspended above the table top. All corresponding books displayed on the table top.

Activity

Children recognise and talk about the characters and match silhouettes to pictures in books.

Display can celebrate

Display can be used to celebrate:

- Children's achievements

- Adults' work (e.g. artists)

- Different cultures, languages, beliefs, interests and experiences.

Using display for the purpose of celebration can promote learning in the area of personal, social and emotional development by helping to:

- Raise self-esteem

- Develop in children a respect for their own work and the work of others

- Develop in children respect for, and understanding of, different cultures and beliefs.

Celebration of children's work is a reason for display with which most practitioners feel comfortable. Traditionally the display of children's artwork has been a characteristic feature of the early years setting. Of course it is important to value and celebrate work of this nature, but in doing so practitioners should not exclude work in other areas of the curriculum. Children's achievements in all areas of learning should be in evidence in the setting, and unique qualities and individuality recognised.

In selecting work for display, the practitioner should consider the achievements of the individual, and not judge all work against an inflexible standard in order to display the 'best' items. Although work of a high standard should indeed be displayed, and those children applauded for their achievements, it should not exclude, or undermine, the achievements of those at an earlier stage on the 'learning journey'.

When displaying children's work, the practitioner may choose to exhibit only the finished piece of work or may decide to show the process, or contributory work. A series of photographs of work in progress (e.g. models made in the workshop) is an effective way of showing how the child has arrived at the 'end product'. This type of display will not only serve as a teaching aid to other children, but will also communicate the message to children and adults that the learning process is as important as the end result. The photographic display is also a good way of documenting and celebrating learning achievements that produce no concrete, or permanent, evidence, for example investigating snow in the water tray, mark-making with water and brushes in the outside area (see Figure 1.16) and shadow play (see Figure 1.17).

In the case of observational drawing or painting, it is a good idea, where possible, to display the stimulus alongside children's work. This will encourage further observation and discussion. Activities planned around a theme will often generate some exciting work for display; for example, during a focus on 'hats', activities may be as diverse as trying on different hats and looking at themselves in a mirror, drawing themselves in hats from observation, making up stories about a bejewelled crown, decorating straw hats, and making hats in the workshop to support role-play. A display of children's work showing one aspect of this project could be constructed, or the 'one aspect' could be displayed in the context of all the other related learning.

Following the 'Jungle Play' and 'The Lion's Visit' focus activities described in Chapter 3, a display was constructed which incorporated the following:

- Photographs of 'jungle environments' built by children in the construction area
- Children's paintings of Lion
- Photographs of children constructing dens for Lion in the outside play area and the construction area
- Photographs of the finished den constructions with Lion 'in residence'
- Children's records of materials used to build the dens (picture tick lists, drawings, attempts at written lists)
- Children's letters to Lion
- Photographs of musical instruments made (spontaneously by children in the workshop) for Lion to play in his den
- Children's records of whether their musical instrument produced a 'loud' or 'quiet' sound.

This display also included:

- Lion in his 'jungle box' and letters from Lion (see Figure 3.1 and Figure 3.2) to the children (the stimulus for 'Lion's Visit')
- A list of pertinent early learning goals.

More general celebrations showing the range of activities in which children engage across all areas of provision will generate interest from parents and children, and can be quite enlightening to visitors. Figure 5.5 is an example of such a display. Content includes paintings, writing for different purposes, drawings, three-dimensional work, photographs of children working in areas of provision and brief explanations written by the practitioner.

Children's achievements can also be celebrated on audio tape, and a suitable tape recorder included on a table-top display. 'Sound' poems (e.g. water sounds), word poems, singing, children making music and children talking about holiday experiences or favourite toys can easily be taped and children will enjoy listening.

Areas of provision such as the workshop and construction area should offer permanent display provision for the celebration of children's work and often the most practical type of display is the open shelf. The content of such display may be of a transient nature but it is important that children have a 'safe' place to put their work either as it is in progress or when it is finished. Children will learn to value their own work and that of others, and will enjoy looking at and talking about 'exhibits'. Folded cards and pencils should be supplied in order for children to make a name label to display next to their work.

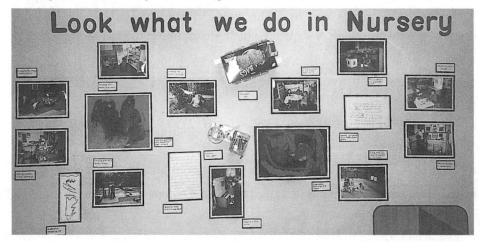

Figure 5.5 Look what we do in nursery

Part of the practitioner's role as an educator is to model skills and it is sometimes appropriate to include the work of adults in a display, preferably alongside the work of the children thereby giving equal status to both. This could be a model made in the setting by a parent, a carving by a local craftsperson, a letter written to the children by a member of staff, a photograph of a parent playing football for the local team or a reproduction of a painting by a famous artist.

An awareness of, and respect for, the beliefs and cultures of others should be part of the very fabric of the curriculum. Display should both reflect the attitude of respect and celebrate cultural diversity. Artefacts used should always be of good quality and authentic, and information accurate. Parents and other members of the community will often be happy to share traditions and help with the writing of dual language signs.

Before moving on to look at more examples of display for celebration, it is worth mentioning the importance of reflecting children's current interests through display. Figure 5.6 shows a display of work around 'superheroes', a play theme that was engaging a number of children at that time. Having recognised this interest, practitioners had supported their play through role-play provision. They had provided cloaks, telephones with contact numbers for a number of 'superheroes' and mark-making equipment for message taking. Photographs of children's imaginative play and their written messages were displayed at child-eye level and a large Spiderman image was attached alongside to draw their attention to the display. Children's comments were scribed and displayed in speech bubbles, for example 'Super action man – he can get lady and make her better'. Staff also included an explanation of children's play for parents and other adults.

Figure 5.6 Save our nursery Spiderman!

Figure 5.7 Displaying children's work in the construction area

Other examples of display for celebration

Meet the authors

Type of display

- Table top or wall

Key area of learning

- Literacy

Content

- Books by familiar authors (e.g. Eric Carle, Mick Inkpen, Pat Hutchins)
- Photographs and brief biographical sketch of each
- Book reviews by children and their parents
- Examples of books of children's work compiled by the practitioner
- Examples of children's story-making and writing attempts with photographs and brief biographical sketches of them

Celebrating

- Children as authors

The magic tree

Type of display

- Table top (workshop)

Key area of learning

- Expressive arts and design

Content

- A branch secured in a pot of sand to look like a tree
- Children's work (e.g. magic jewels, made jewellery, Christmas tree decorations) displayed hanging on the branch

Celebrating

- Children's skills and imaginative ideas

The Gallery[4]

Type of display

- Wall

Key area of learning

- Expressive arts and design

Content

- Children's paintings, prints, drawings and collages displayed alongside the work of established artists from different times and cultures

Celebrating

- Children as artists

The 'action' mobile

Type of display

- Suspended

Key area of learning

- Physical development

Content

- Photographs (pairs stuck together, back to back) of children (climbing, balancing, running, hopping, throwing, catching, kicking balls, crawling through tubes, riding bikes and scooters, sliding down the slide) hanging on thread (at different levels) and suspended from a wire frame, or from branches of a tree in the outside area

Celebrating

- Children's physical achievements (gross motor skills)

Display can be informative

Most aspects of displays have now been covered in this chapter but guidance would not be complete without highlighting the purpose of display to communicate information. This reason for display has already been included as an aspect of other types of display, but there are cases when the main purpose of a display is to inform.

Display can be used to inform:

- Children
- Adults working in the setting
- Parents.

The type of information displayed will vary but, in general terms, can be divided into the following areas:

- Information which directly supports the child in the learning process, either through factual content or instruction
- Information which helps the adult to support the child's learning
- Information which helps the adult to understand curricular aims and the nature of children's learning
- Practical information related to the organisation of the setting.

Direct support can include the provision of books, posters, pictures and photographs to support a learning focus. For example the practitioner may construct a wall display in the water area which informs the child about various uses of water. This could include photographs of children using water in the setting for a variety of purposes, for example drinking, bathing dolls, washing paint brushes, mixing paints, pouring from tea pots during tea parties, washing hands, watering plants. Posters and photographs of water being used outside the setting could also be displayed, for example swimming pools, car washes, agricultural watering systems, narrow boats transporting people on canals, window cleaners. Children's interests can also be supported, and stimulated, by table-top displays offering information in the form of artefacts such as bowls, plates, cups and cutlery made from different materials, and originating from different cultures, connected to a focus on 'food'. Many local authorities have a central stock of artefacts from which practitioners are able to select and borrow. Of course, it is best, where possible, to allow children to handle artefacts but it may be that some of the 'exhibits' are quite fragile and unlikely to stand up to constant handling. In this case they will have to be protected (perhaps in a plastic case) and children taught to look carefully. If practitioners wish the display to be 'interactive', children could be offered the necessary resources and encouraged to draw objects from observation.

Displays can also inform children about, and instruct them how to use, equipment in an area of provision. In, for example, the painting area a display could be constructed to show children the routines, and use of tools and materials, involved in mixing powder paint.

Mixing paint

In order for children to access the information independently, instructions should be illustrated with clear drawings or photographs:

- Put on a red apron.
- Collect a palette, paint pots, water pot, spatula.

- Take your water pot to the tap and fill it with water.

- Choose a piece of paper and a brush.

- Use the spatula to put some powder paint in the palette.

- Use the brush to mix the paint with water.

- Now you are ready to paint.

This sort of information displayed in the setting is also very useful to adults in supporting children. When all adults encourage children to follow the same routines, these routines will become established quickly, and children will soon feel confident in using equipment independently.

Displaying information about curricular aims helps parents and other adults in the setting to understand how and why learning takes place. Such information can be displayed alongside other displays in explanation of activities or learning experiences, or can be sited in an area of provision giving examples, and aims, of cross-curricular learning.

The following hints are of a practical nature and may be useful to practitioners when constructing displays.

Constructing displays: some practical hints

Wall display

- A simple, 'uncluttered' display is usually effective and easy to 'read'. The temptation to cram too much onto the board should be resisted – the result will probably be visual chaos and confusion for the children.

- Coloured work should be mounted carefully. Unless all the work has a common colour theme and can be unified by one colour (e.g. autumn leaves: orange), brightly coloured mounts and backing paper should be avoided as they will detract from, or conflict with, the displayed work. Black-and-white work such as pencil or charcoal drawings can more effectively be mounted on a bright colour.

- The mount should be kept fairly narrow, it is rarely necessary to exceed 1 cm. A slightly wider mount at the bottom will prevent the illusion of the work 'slipping' down.

- Lines should be straight. The composition of a display can be helped by the lining up of verticals and horizontals.

- Arranging items selected for display on the floor before attaching them to the wall is often a useful exercise. It will be easy to move them around until a final decision has been made.

- The composition of a child's work should not be altered by cutting away large amounts.

- To add another dimension to the wall board, a shelf can be attached. This can be used to display items such as books, toys and natural forms. Shelves can easily be made from strong cardboard boxes (see Figure 5.8). They can then be painted or covered with paper or fabric. Once stapled to the wall, the 'box shelves' should provide a firm surface, although it is not advisable to display anything too heavy on them. (Shelves must be visually accessible to children.)

Figure 5.8 Making a shelf for a wall display

Table-top display

- Wooden blocks or upturned boxes under draped fabric are effective in creating surfaces for display at different levels.

- Plywood cuboids (a range of sizes) painted in white emulsion can be used to display natural forms in a simple but eye-catching way.

- Free-standing labels can be made from folded card or signs and labels can be displayed in moulded perspex photograph frames.

- A covering of hessian can be an effective surface on which to display natural forms.

Shelf display

- Open 'grid' shelving units attached to the wall, mounted on unbreakable mirror sheets, make an interesting display. Items will be reflected in the mirror, giving the impression of another dimension, and children will be offered an alternative view of the items.

- Grid shelving units painted with matt black paint show off white objects effectively and create a striking display.

- Shelves attached to adjustable brackets slotted into aluminium strips (all widely available in DIY stores) on the wall make a versatile structure for display. The height of the spaces between shelves can be altered, and shelves removed if necessary.

- Wide shelves (at least 30 cm) are necessary in the workshop area to avoid the frustration of larger models falling off.

- When space is limited, shelves can be hinged and folded flat to the wall when not in use.

Suspended display

- If a number of items are being displayed, they should hang at different levels and not obscure other items or displays from children's vision.

- Hanging items are constantly twisting and turning and may be more effective if double sided. This point is particularly applicable to hanging word labels.

- Practitioners should check that the display is not going to obstruct adults or children (or interfere with 'beamed' security systems!), and should guard against an 'oppressive' feeling in the setting resulting from too much material hanging from low ceilings.

- The effect of transparent or 'sparkly' displays will probably be enhanced if they are situated close to a light source.

Through trial and error, and through the sharing of practice between colleagues, the practitioner will build up a bank of ideas for display which can be adapted and combined to suit the needs of the children and characteristics of the setting. The examples given in this chapter are a small sample but show how display can, with a little imagination and planning, make an exciting contribution to the environment, inspiring children to want to learn and equipping them with the necessary tools and information to support them in their learning.

KEY POINTS FOR GOOD PRACTICE

- Remember that displays are part of the learning environment and should reflect the principles of the Early Years Foundation Stage.
- Think about the purpose of any display that you plan and make sure that it is successful in achieving objectives.
- When displaying children's work, remember that you are celebrating individuality and creativity. Present work with respect and value all stages of development.
- Use photographs to share experiences with no concrete outcome and to celebrate a process.
- Think about how you use display to motivate children. Talk with them about displays around the setting.
- Use display as a way to share information about the curriculum and how children learn with parents.
- Be creative in your use of equipment and space in producing displays.

Curiosity and intrinsic motivation are closely linked and there is no doubt they play an important part in helping children to develop positive attitudes towards learning. One of the main functions of the nursery is to provide a stimulating, enriching environment where children are encouraged to 'learn how to learn'.

(Curtis 1998)

Notes

1 It is helpful to include a diagram of the layout of the decision tree at this point – see Figure 5.2.
2 The display photographed in Figure 5.3 offered a limited range of components (i.e. only those needed to build the rocket). Practitioners may decide to offer a wider range of components, requiring children to make the necessary selection when following the plan.
3 This does not always have to be the case – children could be offered a number of alternative answers, for example 'What is your favourite colour?' Children are required to put their name card in the red, blue or yellow bowl (labelled with colour names). Practitioners should take care not to confuse children by frequently changing the 'answering system'.
4 The 'gallery' idea can also be used to display three-dimensional work.

Observing children's play, assessing learning and keeping useful records

Assessment plays an important part in helping parents, carers and practitioners to recognise children's progress, understand their needs, and to plan activities and support.

(Department for Education 2012)

The content of this chapter is organised as follows:

The assessment and planning cycle

Observation, assessment and planning are all vital aspects of the educator's role and part of an ongoing cycle of identifying and providing for children's learning needs. Figure 6.1 explains this cycle and shows clearly how one stage informs the next.

'Some planning will be short term – for a week or a day and will show how you support each child's learning and development.

This planning always follows the same pattern – observe, analyse, and use what you have found out about the children in your group so that you can plan for the next steps in their learning.'

Principles into Practice card 3.1. Enabling Environments: Observation, Assessment and Planning

(DfES Publications 2007)

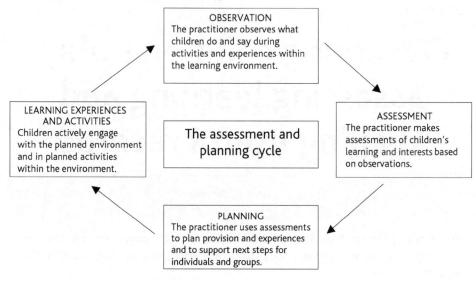

Figure 6.1 The assessment and planning cycle

Collecting information during the 'first contact' period

Neither the learning process nor the 'assessment cycle' begin as the child enters the setting – parents have already spent three years with their child, observing and supporting her or his diverse learning, and will have assimilated a wealth of useful information. A child's learning will be continued, and built upon, in the setting. Prior experiences and achievements will influence the way in which a child approaches a new learning situation, and will impact on the learning that takes place. Practitioners should encourage parents to share information about their child on entry, and throughout their time at the setting.

In Chapter 4, ways in which useful information can be communicated between practitioner and parent are suggested. Ideas include the use of forms and questionnaires (during the 'first contact' period) on which to record personal details and also information about the child's previous experiences. The practitioner may complete the form during discussion with the parent or, alternatively, parents may be asked to complete it at their own convenience. Recorded information could include:

- Full name, date of birth, address and telephone number
- Names of main carers and siblings
- Home language
- Religion
- Contact names, addresses and telephone numbers

- Health – details of any contact with specialists or other agencies
- Previous pre-school experience (response re: settling in, relationships with other children, activities enjoyed)
- Significant experiences or family circumstances such as a new baby in the family, loss of a family member, house move
- Particular interests, preferences and dislikes
- Information from the parent about the child's stage of development
- Any anxieties or behaviour issues.

Many practitioners also produce an 'About Me' booklet which parent and child are encouraged to complete together at home. The child is often asked to bring the booklet back to the setting in order for the practitioner to talk with him or her about the content. It can then be included in the child's records. The 'About Me' booklet will probably require the adult and child to respond to statements such as the following:

- This is me. My name is _____
- I am _____ years old
- I live with _____
- My pets are _____
- My friends are _____
- My favourite book is _____
- My favourite toy is _____
- My favourite food is _____
- I am happy when _____
- When I come to pre-school, I will play with _____

Ample space should be available in each section for the child's own mark-making. Some of the information collected at this early stage will be mainly of practical use to staff and some will be more directly useful in planning learning experiences for the child. A composite of all the information will help to give practitioners an understanding of where the child is on the 'learning journey' and what motivates him or her. It will provide a bank of knowledge which will enable the adult to interact more productively with the child. During the period of first contact, information about the child can be acquired through observation of his responses during, for example, the home visit, as this practitioner's account illustrates:

> As we arrived at the house for the home visit, Alistair flung open the door and shouted excitedly to his Gran – 'My teachers are here!' He was eager to look at the nursery photograph album and asked questions about the activities, particularly those taking

place in the outside area. When asked if he liked to play outside, he responded 'Yes – I like to ride my bike – I want to go on that bike' (pointing to the nursery tandem bike in the photograph). Alistair showed us his train track with pride and explained how he had fixed it together – Gran says that he spends a lot of time playing with his train, looking in his train books and watching his train video. As I talked with Gran, Stella [other member of staff] joined in the 'train play'. After a short while, Alistair's cousin [present during the whole visit] approached and asked to play. The two children became quite engrossed for about ten minutes, taking turns in pushing the train around the track to the shops, park, etc. At the end of the visit, I explained to Alistair that I had to go back to nursery and would see him again when he next came to nursery, and he replied 'Can I come back with you now?'

The account tells staff the following information, which can then be used, in conjunction with other information when planning Alistair's 'settling-in' programme:

- He uses spoken language readily.
- He is interested in what happens in nursery.
- He is eager to come to nursery.
- He is keen to play outside.
- He likes to ride bikes.
- He is interested in trains.
- He is able to maintain concentration at a self-chosen activity.
- He is able to share and take turns with another child.
- He approaches adults with confidence in familiar surroundings.

Observation and assessment in the setting

Victoria Hurst and Margaret Lally comment that:

> Children tell us about themselves through their behaviour, and there are clues to how we can best teach them to be found in their play and social interactions, in their conversations and the things they bring to school, in the way they use opportunities to explore new areas of learning and in the way they create stories, pictures, models and music.
>
> (Hurst and Lally 1992)

Observing children's play is the key to understanding their interests and learning needs and is a salient feature of the 'teaching' role. Practitioners will need to allow time for observation of children at play in the setting. Such 'observation time' may be pre-planned, with a definite focus, or may be incidental. Staff teams will find the most effective way of ensuring that each practitioner has enough time to observe the children in their setting. Some teams plan for each practitioner to have, for example, half a day a week when they are able to take the role of 'observer'. Others, having difficulty in finding time to observe, may evaluate their practice and decide to cut down on the number of planned, adult-led activities and involve themselves more in child-initiated play in areas of provision, allowing themselves greater opportunity to stand back and take note. Observations can be written down, or noted verbally, but however they are reported, practitioners should have an effective system for sharing observations. A brief, daily meeting when staff talk about their observations of children can be a successful way of 'pooling' information, as can regular entries in, and discussion of, children's profiles (see page 196).

The broad aim of observation is:

- To gather information that will enable the practitioner to assess children's learning and consequently plan an appropriate curriculum, providing for the full range of needs within the setting.

More particularly, practitioners may decide to make focused observations with the ultimate aim of:

- Identifying what is interesting and motivating individuals or groups of children at the current time in order to plan exciting contexts for learning in the future
- Assessing individuals in terms of areas of their learning and development, using a number of observations in a range of contexts to inform the planning of next steps
- Finding out more about *how* children learn and in what contexts they demonstrate the characteristics of effective learning
- Evaluating and improving areas of provision in terms of learning opportunities for all children
- Raising the profile of an area of learning and ensuring that learning in this area is taking place for all children and throughout the setting.

Observing and assessing individuals

Practitioners observe children in order to find out:

- What they are able to do (skills)
- What they know and understand (knowledge and concepts)
- How they approach learning (attitudes).

When observing individuals, the practitioner may 'track' a child over a period of time perhaps looking specifically at an area of development – this can be a particularly useful approach when there are concerns about a child's development. Alternatively, the child may be observed in a particular area of provision or during a focus. Sometimes a child is 'targeted' by the team, and all practitioners make observations as they come into contact with her or him over the course of a session, or a few sessions. Although it is essential to plan observations such as those just described, the necessity for practitioners to be constantly 'tuned in' to children's learning should be stressed. Opportunities to observe, and assess, should be taken as they arise. Quite often unplanned observations are made in response to a significant behaviour or activity, and these can provide just as useful information as the 'scheduled' observations. Young children should not be put in a 'test' situation. Assessment should always take place in an appropriate context and when a practitioner decides to plan an activity with a specific learning focus in the hope that he or she will be able to assess certain aspects of a child's learning, that activity must be purposeful and interesting to the child. The most reliable information about children's learning is likely to be derived from times of deep involvement at a self-chosen activity.

When making structured observations, it can be useful to refer to lists of statements or questions; these prompts will help the practitioner to focus observations and to make clear assessments. For example, a practitioner may plan, in the weekly planning, to observe new children during the settling-in period, and start with the questions:

- *Who* do I want to observe?
- *What* do I want to find out about the child?
- *How* will I find out that information?
- *How* will I use the information?

It may be that the practitioner is concerned specifically with learning more about the child's social and emotional development at this stage. Of course, what the practitioner learns about a child during the periods of focused observation will not have been restricted to the key area targeted. Other information will have been gleaned and its contribution to the whole picture of a child's learning and development should not be disregarded. When making focused observations, the skill is in registering the 'additional' information, without being distracted from the focus of the observation.

Making assessments of individuals from a number of observations (focused or incidental) over a period of time, rather than from one isolated observation, will give a more accurate picture of a child's stage of development, revealing strands and patterns across a range of situations. Sometimes patterns of repeated behaviours (often referred to as 'schemas') become apparent and form the basis of planning for individuals (or groups of children preoccupied by similar schemas).

> The early schemas of babies form the basis of the patterns of behaviour which children show between the ages of 2 and 5 years, and these in turn become established foundations for learning.
>
> (Nutbrown 2006)

For example, a child might be observed joining paper clips together with treasury tags, playing with interlocking jigsaws, connecting components from a construction set, and taping together cardboard tubes. Such observations would indicate to the practitioner that the child may be fascinated by 'connection' and may prompt her or him to offer the child a range of materials and equipment through which to explore this schema further. Many practitioners will recognise the scenario of a child gathering up armfuls of plastic play food from the home corner and depositing it all in the book area. Exasperating as this behaviour may prove to be at tidy-up time, it may be an indication of, not necessarily a role-play interest in picnics, but perhaps a preoccupation with 'transporting'. Of course, an isolated observation should never be taken as firm evidence of a child's schematic learning and, following initial observations, the practitioner would need to be alert to other possible indications in alternative contexts (including information from home where possible) and emerging patterns before jumping to hasty conclusions. It may turn out that the first observation, although interesting, was not significant in terms of schema and was a 'one-off' action. In the case of 'transporting', further evidence could include taking all the cushions from one room at home to another, taking sand across the nursery to the dough area and carrying all the bricks from the indoor construction area to the outdoor area. The study of schemas is a complex and fascinating area and we should be cautious about oversimplification. However, practitioners equipped with some basic knowledge of schemas will have an increased awareness that all may not be as it first seems, and that further observation may reveal more information about what it is that is driving the child, and intrinsically motivating him, to act in a particular way. This understanding may lead them to look at the appropriateness of their expectations of children's behaviour. It may also help them to extend provision and plan engaging experiences, offering children opportunities to further explore their schemas, in order to meet the learning needs of individuals. Certainly, an introduction to schemas can offer the practitioner an additional perspective on learning and development and a viewpoint for analysis that is likely to lead to a deeper insight into a child's world.

> 'New connections help to transform our understanding but this can often be a long process.'
>
> Principles into Practice card 4.3. Learning and Development: Creativity and Critical Thinking
>
> (DfES Publications 2007)

The importance of matching the curriculum to the child has already been highlighted a number of times in previous chapters on planning but cannot be overemphasised. It is as a result of observing and assessing individuals that the practitioner is able to define and address their needs. With sound assessment procedures in place, staff will be able to identify any special educational needs at an early stage, and produce effective Individual Education Plans (IEPs) to support children in making progress. Careful record keeping is crucial in providing information to facilitate planning for current needs but also in providing evidence of difficulties in the early stages which may impact on the provision of support later on.[1] (See also Chapters 1 and 4.)

In order to plan appropriately for the child's next steps, the practitioner needs to be aware of the stages that a child passes through on the journey towards, and beyond, the early learning goals. Some practitioners will have studied children's development in areas of learning during their initial training and perhaps through subsequent training, others may feel less confident in this area. The DfE guidance material (*Development Matters in the EYFS*) for practitioners in early years settings offers examples of children working at different stages and breaks down learning (in each of the seven areas) into developmental stages. Practitioners will find the guidance in the learning and development grids a helpful tool in understanding children's learning and in planning to support their next steps but it is important to remember that the grids are offered as a guide only and should never be used as a checklist. Children will not necessarily move sequentially through the stages (highlighted in the 'A Unique Child' column) towards the early learning goals and may take more time to embed some elements of learning than others. Stages overlap in recognition that children's developmental pathways and time scales will vary.

As the practitioner observes children, it may become apparent that a few have reached a similar stage in their development and are ready for certain next steps at the same time, or that two or three children have a shared interest. It may then be appropriate to plan an activity (or series of activities) for this group.

Evaluating and improving the provision

In aiming to offer all children rich learning opportunities in areas of provision, practitioners will have produced long-term plans detailing key areas of learning, resources, organisation, anticipated learning experiences and activities, adult role and key questions and vocabulary (see Chapter 1). Regular observation of children's play in each area will provide teams with the necessary information to evaluate the success of the area in terms of children's learning, to review long-term plans and to make the necessary changes to improve provision.

Before spending time observing in an area of provision, it will probably be a good idea to read through the long-term plan for that area. Asking the following questions whilst observing in an area is also likely to be helpful:

- Which children are choosing to work in the area?
- Are all needs being met? (Taking into consideration: gender, special educational needs, disabilities, more able children, ethnic groups and religious, social and cultural backgrounds)
- Which resources are being used? (Frequently? Regularly? Occasionally? Never?)

- How are children using the resources?

- How are all areas of learning developed through the provision? Which are the dominant areas?

- What kind of activities and learning experiences are taking place?

- What have the children learnt?

Figure 6.2 illustrates how observations of children in the water area have been used by the practitioner, or team of practitioners, to:

- Plan possible follow-up activities and next steps for individuals

- Assess provision in the water area.[2]

In order to check that there is breadth and balance in the curriculum, practitioners will need to study assessments of provision and this is one of the reasons for keeping clear records (see below, 'Recording and reporting'). As identified in the long-term plans, each area of provision will promote 'key' areas of learning (although learning will not be exclusive to these areas). An overview of assessment records for each area of provision will inform the practitioner as to how successfully the long-term aims are being met in practice. Discussion of these records by the team should then lead to any necessary changes being made.

Assessing how areas of learning are being developed in the setting

Practitioners can assess how a particular area of learning, or aspect of an area, is being developed throughout the setting using a similar procedure to that used in evaluating provision. Children will be observed in all areas of provision and with a focus on, for example, writing. The practitioner will look at the purposes for, and opportunities to, write that children are offered, and also at the provision of mark-making equipment and how this is used. The data collected from observations will then be collated and used to inform long-term planning.

Engagement and motivation

> The ways in which the child engages with other people and their environment – playing and exploring, active learning and creating and thinking critically – underpin learning and development across all areas and support the child to remain an effective and motivated learner.
>
> (Department for Education 2012)

The dispositions and attitudes that are laid down in the early stages of children's learning are crucial to their success later on. In order to engage them fully in the learning process, we need to look at what is motivating them, at the experiences that they are driven to seek out and at the contexts that are most conducive to deep concentration and commitment.

DATE: 10, 14 June		TIME AND DURATION: 9.30 am for 15 minutes each day
CHILD	ACTIVITY	POSSIBLE NEXT STEPS FOR THE CHILD/FOLLOW-UP ACTIVITIES
Tamara	Lining up plastic bottles on the side of the tray, randomly selected from the shelf. Picking up bottles, one at a time, putting them down again. Pointing to each bottle in turn.	Counting experience and familiarity with number language, particularly number names one–five. Plan opportunities for counting in a 'real' context.
	Filling plastic bottles with water (using jugs) and then emptying them.	More 'filling and emptying' activities using various containers, perhaps in dry sand or home corner (tea parties). Understanding and using vocabulary: full and empty.
Shelley and Patrick	Playing with boats. Filling boats with water and watching them sink.	Finding out how many plastic pots full of water can be poured into the boat before it sinks. Further investigation: floating and sinking using a range of materials and objects. Making own boats. Understanding and using key vocabulary: float, sink.
	'Story-making' about boats in a shark-infested sea.	Opportunities for developing story ideas and sharing them with other children.
Sean	Using water poured from plastic bottles to make the water wheel work.	Making water wheels using, for example, plastic spoons. Looking at other ways of moving objects using water.
Kelly-Marie, Holly, Jordan	Using plastic containers, first child fills up a container, passes it to the next child who passes it to the third child who empties it into a transparent plastic bottle. Holly asked 'Is it full – put some more in?' and when it was full, said 'Now make it empty'. The other children responded appropriately.	Counting how many containers full of water it takes to fill a jug, bowl, bucket, etc. Comparing containers re. capacity. Vocabulary: Kelly-Marie, Jordan: Confident use of full and empty, understand and begin to use comparative vocabulary, for example, more, less, fuller Holly: use increased range of comparative vocabulary with confidence. Develop 'chain gang' cooperative work, for example, can you pass the cup of water along a chain of five children without spilling any? – negotiation of roles.
	Making ice creams using yoghurt pots. 'Selling' ice creams.	Hot and cold, freezing and melting investigations in the water tray. Ice cream van role-play.
Tim	Watching Kelly-Marie, Holly and Jordan's play.	Encouragement to join in play with other children and to become physically involved with resources in exploration and investigation.

GENERAL OBSERVATIONS:

- Children tend to leave equipment in the water tray when they move away from the area. This is inhibiting other children's play and discouraging some from entering the area.
- Most verbal interaction took place during imaginative play.
- Little attention was paid to pictures and photographs displayed in the area.

Figure 6.2 Observation and assessment: the water area

OBSERVED LEARNING IN THE SEVEN AREAS OF LEARNING:	
COMMUNICATION AND LANGUAGE	MATHEMATICS
Giving verbal instructions to another child. Asking questions. Listening and taking turns in conversation. Use of descriptive language ('It's making a clapping noise like a waterfall'). Use of mathematical language, for example, full, empty, more. Some reference to resources by name.	Investigating capacity – filling and emptying. Early counting, and one-to-one counting of four children to four aprons. Use of mathematical language such as more, full, number names. Matching resources to templates looking at shape and height. Matching numbers on resources to numbers on templates.
LITERACY	
'Story-making' – discussion of characters and events. Signing name on 'register' on leaving the area.	
PERSONAL, SOCIAL AND EMOTIONAL DEVELOPMENT	UNDERSTANDING THE WORLD
Working together – one child holding a container whilst another pours water into it; 'chain gang' approach to passing resources. Child showing interest whilst observing others. Involvement in an activity. Concentration during an investigation. Independent selection and use of resources.	Investigating 'water power' (water wheels), floating and sinking. Discussion of hot and cold in relation to ice creams. Understanding that the water can make materials wet, and can 'spread' on a flat, non-absorbent surface (water spilt on clothing and floor).
EXPRESSIVE ARTS AND DESIGN	PHYSICAL DEVELOPMENT
Story-making – using imagination and expressing ideas (boat and sharks story). Role-play – making and selling ice creams.	Coordination – pouring from one container to another, holding a container in one hand and pouring water into it from a container in the other hand, passing containers to the next child in the line.

TEAM DISCUSSION: IMPLICATIONS FOR THE FUTURE AND ACTION TO BE TAKEN:

- All staff to encourage children to replace resources before leaving the area. To ensure that provision is also supporting children in doing this, CP will renew templates, replace storage boxes for tubes, shells, stones, yoghurt pots, etc. with shallow baskets and label these clearly with pictures and words.
- Remember that, for some children, 'next steps' will mean 'more of the same' to allow for consolidation and application of knowledge and skills.
- Plan 'link' activities between areas, for example, making water wheels in the workshop for use in the water tray; set up role-play area around the outside water tray (e.g. cafe – pouring cups of tea; ice cream van – selling lollies and ice cream made from crushed, coloured ice).
- Use coloured water to enable children to see water levels in containers more easily.
- Plan regular adult input with a focus on encouraging talk and use of key vocabulary during investigations, and supporting individuals and groups of children in moving forward in identified areas.
- Make display more interactive encouraging children to read picture and signs, answer questions and respond to challenges. Change display more frequently. Link displays to children's current interests and investigations.
- Order the following resources: set of graded (tall, narrow) measuring cylinders, small-world people and sea creatures, plastic lolly moulds, shallow storage baskets for permanent and additional resources. Organise and catalogue additional resources according to concept development.

Further points for discussion by foundation stage staff:

- What can children learn from observing other children's play?
- How can resources encourage problem-solving?

Figure 6.2 (continued) Observation and assessment: the water area

Ferre Laevers (a researcher at Leuven University, Belgium) has developed a tool for assessing involvement which can be very useful in finding out times at which children are intrinsically motivated and working at the very limits of their capability. He has devised a scale from 1 to 5, 1 being little or no involvement and 5 being sustained and intense activity and has also identified a number of signs or signals of involvement (e.g. persistence, concentration, energy), many of which will be evident during periods of high involvement. Many of these indicators of involvement are included in the 'Characteristics of Effective Learning' (Active Learning, motivation) in 'Development Matters in the in the Early Years Foundation Stage (EYFS)' (2012), for example:

- Maintaining focus on their activity for a period of time
- Showing high levels of energy, fascination
- Not easily distracted
- Paying attention to details
- Persisting with an activity when challenges occur
- Showing satisfaction in meeting their own goals

(DfE Development Matters in the EYFS 2012)

This approach to assessment can offer an exciting perspective on children's learning and has far-reaching implications. Where children are deeply involved in their play and learning, the practitioner will see them demonstrating competencies and applying their learning in a context which is important and meaningful to them. Such contexts would be likely to generate reliable information about a child's knowledge and understanding. Observations over time may reveal that children quickly reach high levels of involvement during particular activities or experiences and offer the practitioner more information about, or evidence towards, current individual or group interests.

Levels may be seen to dip for some or all children at certain times during the day and this may lead to an audit of routines and a closer look at how the rhythm of the day is tailored to meet the needs of all children. A number of things can impact on a child's ability to become deeply involved in their learning; it may be that children are hungry and an additional snack is made available, or that children are unable to sustain involvement due to too many interruptions in which case the team would take steps to ensure that longer periods of uninterrupted play are facilitated. However, it is important to emphasise at this point that children would not be expected to demonstrate high levels of involvement at all times. All children, especially those in full day care, need times for relaxation and reflection when they are not over-stimulated or challenged.

The involvement signs and levels may also be used as an effective tool when evaluating areas of provision. When observing in, for example, the indoor construction area, a practitioner may note that very few children who enter the area reach high levels of involvement and many leave the area without having experienced any satisfying or sustained play. This observation would alert the practitioner to the fact that the provision is in some way failing to meet the needs of the children. There may be many reasons why this is the case. It could be that the area is positioned in a thoroughfare and models are frequently knocked down by children passing through, or it may be that resources are not presented in an attractive or inviting way, perhaps there is not enough equipment in each set or key pieces are missing, or maybe provision in the area simply does not reflect the interests of children at that time and does not enable them to engage in play themes that are motivating to them.

> Interest and involvement frequently occur at the same time (although one can have interest without involvement), and creative problem-solving is frequently (but not always) a common factor in both involvement and the tackling of difficulty.
>
> (Carr 2001)

Recording and reporting

> Careful assessment and record keeping underpin all good educational practice. They are essential elements in securing effective continuity and progression.
>
> (Department of Education and Science 1990)

Before making any decisions about record-keeping systems, practitioners should first consider the following questions:

- *Why* are we keeping records?
- *How* will the records be used?
- *Who* will contribute to and use the records?
- *What* will be included?
- *Which* is the most useful way of presenting and storing recorded information?

In answer to the first question, there are usually a number of reasons why practitioners keep records and these will probably include:

- To make sure that information is available to, and easily shared with, all concerned parties
- To enable practitioners to monitor, or plot, the progress of individuals or groups of children
- To ensure continuity for the child
- To enable practitioners to check that breadth and balance across the areas of learning are being maintained
- In order to be accountable to, for example, the LA, school management, Ofsted.

Records are used:

- As a 'central point' for the ongoing collection of information and/or evidence
- As a source of reference when planning for individuals or the curriculum
- As evidence to support assessments or referrals
- To communicate information to parents
- To communicate information to other professionals
- To inform summative reporting.

Some records will be in daily use and need to be readily available at all times. Others will be accessed less frequently but all concerned parties should know where they are kept. There will be times when the content of records is of a sensitive nature, or is strictly confidential, and such information must be stored carefully to ensure that it is only available to its intended audience.

The obvious contributors to the records are the staff themselves, but practitioners should also consider how to include information from:

- Parents and carers
- Outside agencies (e.g. health visitors, speech therapists, GPs).

The suitability of record-keeping systems for use in early years settings will depend on the purpose of the record, and its audience and contributors. Systems should be efficient and support, not hinder, the practitioner in their role as an educator. Time is a limited resource and a balance must be sought between recording observations and interacting with the children. Practitioners should set themselves realistic goals and only record what is useful. The next part of the chapter looks at some methods of recording and reporting information.

Individual profiles of children's work

The profiling system is in operation in many settings and can be a very successful way of combining observations and assessments made in the setting and in the home. The profile is started on the child's entry to the setting (often with a 'home visit' entry) and is an ongoing and formative record of a child's achievements. The profile will be used by the practitioner in assessing and addressing individual learning needs and, as well as being informative and attractive to the child and parent, should be effective in informing the planning and reporting process and in supporting continuity for the child during times of transition. Information should be presented in a logical way, and should be easily accessible and useful.

Compiling a profile

There are a variety of ways in which information can be organised in a profile. Some practitioners favour the diary format, making entries (including observations from home) in chronological order regardless of the curricular content of the learning. This system enables practitioners to identify any patterns in play, repeated behaviours or interests that are revisited from a glance through the last few weeks' entries. It recognises the holistic nature of young children's learning in that longer observations covering a number of areas or aspects of learning can be included. Friendship groups and preferred areas of provision are also usually clear in a diary profile. This type of profile can be used effectively to monitor children's progress and cross-referencing grids are often used to draw together information about children's learning and development 'pulled out' from significant observations with summary assessments being made at key points. In recognition of the continuum of learning, diary format profiles are often referred to by titles such as 'Anna's Learning Journey', 'Anna's Story' or 'Anna's Learning Journal'.

Others prefer to organise information according to curricular focus. In the latter type of profile, there will be a section for each of the seven areas of learning and possibly a page for each aspect within the seven areas. Entries will be made in chronological order within each section – this system does show clearly a child's progress in a particular area of learning and immediately highlights gaps in assessments; however, patterns are not always as evident. When producing a profile such as this, observations will be short and focused. It is probable that watching a child involved in one activity or experience will generate a number of observations to be filed under different areas. In such cases, some rewriting of material may be inevitable even though each observation has a different perspective. It may also be necessary to cross-reference some evidence; for example, the observation shown in Figure 6.6 focuses on 'Understanding the world' but could also provide useful information about the child's physical development (using tools and materials) and personal, social and emotional development.

Whether teams select diary, or area of learning, format for their children's profiles, the document should be a celebration of each child as an individual. It should capture the essence or 'magic' of that child and should reflect fun times, times of reflection and relaxation, factors that contribute towards well-being and times of deep involvement as well as providing information about a child's journey towards the early learning goals.

In practical terms, the profile should be durable enough to withstand frequent handling over a considerable period of time. Entries can be made on sheets of paper which are then inserted into transparent plastic pockets and filed in a plastic-covered ring binder. Alternatively, a scrapbook could be used for entries and kept in an envelope file or plastic cover for protection. Practitioners will probably want to peruse the numerous stationery catalogues on the market before making a decision!

Again, effective systems need to be in place to ensure that members of staff do not become overloaded with paperwork and administration. For example, key workers responsible for entering observations (written by all staff) into children's profiles within their key group could request that observations are collected in plastic pockets on the wall in the office. These pockets would display the name of the key person and the names of all children within the group. At the end of the session, staff would file their observations in the appropriate pocket. Key workers would then remove their pocket from the wall when planning to update profiles.

The content of the profile will include:

- Written observations
- Pieces of the child's work (e.g. mark-making, paintings)
- Photographs of children's work – for example, these should be used to capture significant moments, learning with no concrete outcome, work in progress (e.g. the stages in building a model), a physical activity (such as riding a bike) and work too large or transient to be kept or taken home (e.g. an outdoor construction or a snow sculpture)
- Contributions from parents or their comments scribed by the practitioner.

(For examples of contents, see Figures 6.4, 6.11.)

When making entries in the profiles, practitioners should adhere to the following guidance:

- The emphasis should be on what the child *can* do – the profile is a record of the child's *achievements.*
- Entries should be written objectively.
- All entries must be dated.
- Children's work and photographs should be annotated including information on context (e.g. area of provision in which the learning took place, time span, adult or peer support received, working independently/with or alongside other children).
- When photographs or pieces of work relate to other written observations, there should be clear referencing.
- In the event of an extended period of absence, this should be recorded in the child's profile.
- Where possible, children should be involved in making entries (particularly own work and photographs).
- Practitioners should keep abreast of entries from home and add their own notes to these as appropriate.

Recording observations and assessments for profiles

Written observations can be recorded straight away in the profile, or can be written on large, white adhesive labels to be added to the profile later. It can be helpful to keep a stock of labels or pieces of paper, and a pen, in each area of provision – it is very frustrating, having anticipated a milestone achievement, to miss the 'magic moment' whilst in search of tools and equipment with which to record it! Some practitioners prefer to write in a personal notebook and transfer information to the profile – these written observations are sometimes cut out of the book and glued into the profile.

There are also times when observations will be recorded on a standard format. There are three clear purposes for using a framework within which to record observations and assessments:

- To support the practitioner in focusing observations and assessments
- To support the practitioner in organising the written content
- To enable the reader to more easily understand and use information.

When observing children in the setting, it can be physically difficult, and probably not necessary, to write down everything that is witnessed. Having access to a few carefully chosen headings on a sheet of paper will support the practitioner in selecting information to record. Information recorded on standard formats is easily accessed by colleagues who are also familiar with the format, and this shared understanding of the system will impact positively on the efficiency of team assessment and planning discussions.

Sometimes teams produce a simple pro forma on which to record observations during a planned activity. These can help practitioners to adhere to a specific observation focus and can, when completed, be stuck straight into the profile (see Figure 6.11). Practitioners will almost certainly find a standard annotation format useful, as illustrated in Figure 6.7. In the process of transferring jottings to such a framework, information will be organised in a more readable and logical form.

It will not, however, always be appropriate to use a pro forma for the recording of observations and sometimes a separate list of 'prompts' or a clear focus in the practitioner's mind can be just as capable of effecting a coherent and useful record. Although the reorganisation of some written material will be necessary (perhaps onto an annotation form), copying out long observations into profiles is an unproductive use of time and should be avoided where possible. Although children's work should always be presented in a respectful fashion, and entries neat and orderly, the profile is a working document and presentation should not take priority over content.

As mentioned earlier in this chapter, young children should not be placed in a 'test' situation which is likely to result in distorted assessments. It is possible to observe and assess children's learning in a range of curricular areas through a single experience or activity in an area of provision (see the example in Figure 6.3). Practitioners must take opportunities to watch children as they become deeply

Observations across the curriculum

Observing a child working in an area of provision can provide us with information about their learning across many areas of the curriculum as the following example shows:

NAME: Michael (aged 3 years, 11 months)

DATE: 17 October 2012

TIME: 10.05–10.20 am

CONTEXT:

Playing in the water area alone at first and then joined by two other children. Adult observing in the area giving occasional support as appropriate (e.g. asking questions, discussion, playing alongside). Equipment available: jugs, beakers, funnels, tea set, water wheels, buckets.

Area of learning	Observation
Mathematics *(shape, space and measures)*	Playing in the water tray, using a plastic beaker to fill a jug with water, Michael said 'It's getting full now'. When he tipped the water out, he said 'Empty'.
Personal, social and emotional development *(self confidence and self awareness)*	Handling a plastic jug, Michael turned to another child saying 'My mummy has got a jug like that – I think she puts milk in it. My orange juice is in a jug too ... In the fridge. Do you want a jug?' Michael offered a jug to the child.
Expressive arts and design *(Being imaginative)*	Playing in the water tray with another child, Michael filled up the teapot with water and poured some into a jug which he offered to his friend saying 'Want a drink? It's dinner time!'
Communication, language and literacy *(language for thinking)*	In the water tray — pouring water into the spout of a teapot through a funnel, Michael said 'Water's going in... then it [the lid] pops up... now it's full... It's going up to the top... press down the top [lid]... Now it's coming through the hole! [steam hole in the lid] Put more water in and make the top pop off!'
Personal, social and emotional development *(making relationships)*	Playing in the water tray with Liam, Michael rolled up his own sleeves and then helped Liam to roll up his. Later he included Liam in his investigation saying 'You hold this down and I'll pour the water in'. He also reminded Liam 'Don't throw water or the floor will get wet'.
Physical development *(moving and handling)*	Playing in the water area, Michael showed good control and coordination as he carefully directed the end of the funnel with one hand and poured water into it from a jug with his other hand.
Understanding the world *(moving and handling)*	Michael selected a water wheel from the shelf whilst working in the water area. He made the wheel go round with his hand and then lifted up the wheel on its frame, looking from underneath to find out more about how it moved. He turned the wheel around again with his hand, but very slowly this time and looking closely. He was excited when he made it go very fast by pouring a whole jug full of water through its funnel!

Characteristics of effective learning: Michael approached the water area with enthusiasm and explored the equipment with interest. He was delighted to see the water wheel go round as he poured water through the funnel and laughed as the water splashed onto his hand.

Figure 6.3 Observations across the curriculum

involved in a challenging, self-initiated activity – they can then be sure that they are seeing a true picture of what children know and can do. Sometimes a direct link with language from 'Development Matters' can be made if appropriate (see example in Figure 6.7) and a reference from the 'A Unique Child' guidance will help practitioners towards an assessment of a child's developmental stage in many cases. Reference to the sections 'Positive Relationships' and 'Enabling Environments' will help staff in supporting children's next steps. However, it is important to note that, for the purpose of explaining a process, reference to specific developmental stages has been made on some observations (e.g. 6.7, 6.11) in this chapter but that, in practice, the team may decide that such information should be stored more discreetly, perhaps in an assessment file. It is also worth reiterating that one observation does not provide enough evidence for an assessment in a particular aspect of learning but merely contributes some information towards a summary based on a number of observations across a range of contexts.

It is important that observations not only inform practitioners about *what* children learn, but also about *how* they learn. Such indications can either be included in the main text of the observation or can be added in a discrete section. The DfE guidance around the 'Characteristics of Effective Learning' (Development Matters in the Early Years Foundation Stage, 2012) offers practitioners a tool to identify and describe the ways in which children learn.

When a pattern or interest has been identified, annotated photographs can be used to tell the 'story' of the child's learning over time. Figure 6.4 shows how Kamisha's interest in baking and her fascination with mixing materials together developed and was supported through the provision. A baking session was on offer weekly at the Centre and Kamisha was always first in line to offer her services! She also took her baking theme to other areas (such as sand, water), often engaging in imaginative role-play and representing her 'real' baking experiences through her pretend play. However, sometimes her self-chosen experiences were more concerned with the handling and manipulating of materials and the sheer enjoyment of the sensory exploration. As Kamisha's gravitation towards particular activities or resources became clearly apparent, practitioners began to offer her additional experiences that they thought might engage her, for example mixing oats, flour and water or providing baking equipment in the outdoor water area. Her enthusiastic response to such provision reassured the practitioners that they were 'on the right track' and they continued to support her through planning additional activities and enhancements to areas. Kamisha's interest continued for a number of weeks and her 'baking' experiences (real and role-play) provided a very sound context for observation towards assessment of her learning and development. She displayed high levels of involvement and a mental, and physical, energy that indicated that she was challenging herself to the limits.

Figure 6.4a Baking 'for real'!

Figure 6.4b Stirring sand and water in a mixing bowl

Figure 6.4c Mixing flour and water with her hands

Figure 6.4d Pretend baking with salt and miniature utensils

Photographs of Kamisha's continuing interest were stored in a folder on the computer and added to over the weeks. A book about 'Kamisha's Baking' was produced using key photographs (annotated) and given to Kamisha to take home. A series of photographs was also displayed in the centre at children's eye level. Both the book and display offered Kamisha an opportunity to revisit her experiences and to reflect on her interest and learning. The book particularly served as a prop for Kamisha in sharing her experiences in the centre with her family, and her key person discussed with Mum ideas for supporting the 'baking' interest at home.

Figure 6.5 demonstrates again the effective use of a series of photographs to document a child's learning, this time using images taken at key points during a period of about 20 minutes. Once this experience was over, there was no concrete outcome to show although the learning that had taken place was very meaningful. The photographs tell us about the process that Grace went through during her investigation but also capture her concentration and involvement, shown clearly through facial expression and body language. It also shows how a child's scribed talk can provide additional information about her learning, and what it is that is particularly interesting her about the experience. The observer has highlighted links to areas and aspects of learning using only initials in order to keep the reference as discreet as possible.

Profiles as 'shared records'

Young children's profiles are an ongoing record of their achievements (from entering to leaving the setting) in all areas of learning and are often referred to as their 'special books'. Children should be encouraged to look at, and talk about, the contents and the learning it represents with friends, practitioners, parents and carers. For this reason, profiles should be made accessible (perhaps in book racks on the wall or open boxes), and should be easy to handle. They should be clearly named and ideally display a photograph of the child on the front so as to be instantly recognisable. When children feel 'ownership' of their profile, and a pride in their achievements, they will probably ask to make their own entries, sharing experiences from home as well as in the setting.

Although practitioners will have talked with parents about profiles (purpose and content) during the first contact period, it is a good idea to display a notice of explanation and encouragement, similar to the example shown in Figure 6.6, close to where the profiles are kept (see Children's profiles, below).

Children's profiles

The children's profiles are a celebration of their achievements and contain examples and photographs of work, and observations by nursery staff. They are

| **NAME:** Grace | **DATE:** 17th June 2008, 10.15 am |

OBSERVATION:

Playing in the outside sand provision, Grace leaned over the tray and dug her hands into the wet sand, enjoying manipulating and squeezing it and saying 'Wet . . . wet . . . wet sand . . . pat, pat, pat'. She then continued to chant rhythmically, 'Pat, pat . . . pat, pat . . . pat, pat', as she patted the sand with the palm of her hand.

Then she dropped a few handfuls of the wet sand into the top of the sand wheel and pressed it until some dropped through onto the first wheel causing it to move slightly. Grace continued to use this strategy for a few minutes but soon realised that it wasn't very effective in making the wheel turn continuously and she started to push it around with her fingers as lumps of sand dropped through. Then she tipped out the sand from the top and tried dropping in the wet sand in very small amounts from between her index finger and thumb – this proved to be more effective in making the wheel turn as the hole didn't become obstructed with sand as quickly but it still wasn't flowing freely. Grace noticed some dry sand on the ground and said to herself, 'That better – dry'. She scooped up some dry sand between her hands and poured it into the top of the sand wheel – she watched as it flowed quickly through the wheels and said again, 'That better'.

At this point, Emily arrived and helped Grace to collect more dry sand from the paving stones. Grace held out her hands and enjoyed feeling the dry sand trickling from Emily's fingers onto her palms. She then picked up a handful of wet sand and pressed it against her plastic apron – saying 'On my apron . . . stick . . . ooo . . . stick on my apron'. When most of the sand fell off her apron onto the floor, she picked it up and tried again to stick it to the plastic, pressing even harder this time.

PHOTOGRAPHS:

(Continued)

Figure 6.5 Sand observation

LINKS TO AREAS/ASPECTS OF LEARNING AND DEVELOPMENT:

PD: UEM
LC: U, S
L: R
KW: TW

LINKS TO CHARACTERISTICS OF EFFECTIVE LEARNING:

Engagement: Finding out and exploring
Motivation: Being involved and concentrating, keeping trying
Thinking: Having their own ideas

Figure 6.5 Continued

intended to show learning across the seven areas (see Profiles as 'shared records', page 204):

- Personal, social and emotional development
- Physical development
- Communication and language

- Literacy
- Mathematics
- Understanding the world
- Expressive Arts and Design.

Expressive arts and design (exploring and using media and materials)

<u>12th February</u>
Today Sarah chose to work in the workshop and told Sandeep that she was going to make a kite. She selected the following materials: tissue paper, two lolly sticks, string, glue, sellotape and scissors. Sarah cut the paper with the scissors and fastened it to the stick with sellotape (having tried and rejected the glue because it was 'too wet'). As Sandeep held the kite, she fastened the string to it with sellotape. They took the finished kite outside and, pulling it behind her as she ran, Sarah shouted 'Look! It's flying! The wind's blowing it!'

Figure 6.6 Adhesive label entry: 'Kite observation'

Children learn in many different situations and places, and much of their learning takes place at home. You should use the profile to record significant home learning experiences, and 'landmark' achievements. This will help to give a fuller picture of your child's learning, and will enable staff to share achievements. The profiles are always available and you are welcome to look through them at any time – your children will probably be only too happy to share theirs with you! The nursery staff regularly spend time looking at, and talking about, children's own profiles with them and are happy to discuss these records with you.

A brief explanation of each area of learning can also be included in the profiles. Practitioners often use short paragraphs quoted from the *Statutory Framework for the Early Years Foundation Stage* for this purpose. See also Chapter 4 (page 133) for sharing information through discussions about a video compilation or a series of photographs.

Class and group files

There will be some information which will need to be accessible to staff but which should not be readily available to all adults in the setting. A ring binder divided into sections, one for each child, will be useful for the storage of information such as personal details collected during first contact period, and will be less cumbersome than individual files. Record card index boxes are compact and can provide

NAME Elizabeth	DATE 4 May

OTHER CONTEXTUAL INFORMATION

Talking with an adult in a one-to-one situation. Selecting mark-making equipment independently.

AREA OF PROVISION

Accessing equipment from the office area to use on the table where the gerbils are kept.

OBSERVATION

After caring for the nursery gerbils at home for the weekend, Elizabeth was keen to share her experiences with adults and other children. She suggested that a member of staff should look after the gerbils for a night and wrote a list of care instructions for her. She divided the paper in half with a line and used 'bullet points' every time she started a new line of marks. She said each word carefully as she made marks to represent her speech. When her list was completed, she gave it to the practitioner and said, 'This is how you look after the gerbils – now you can take them to your house'.

KEY AREA AND ASPECT OF LEARNING

Literacy: writing.

ASSESSMENT

There is clear evidence towards the early learning goals for writing:

● Gives meaning to marks they make as they draw.
● Begin to break the flow of speech into words (*A Unique Child*: 40–60+ months).

Elizabeth knows that information can be communicated through writing and is beginning to make marks in an attempt to record thoughts and ideas. She shows an understanding of some features of lists and is exploring these in her emergent writing.

NEXT STEPS

What does the practitioner need to do?

● Provide further activities during which Elizabeth will experiment with writing. Include opportunities for writing during play.
● Act as a scribe for Elizabeth. Say each word as you write.

Figure 6.7 Care instructions for the gerbil and observation format

HOW TO LOOK AFTER THE GERBILS

- The gerbils are called Fizz and Bella.
- The fat one bites.
- They have very sharp teeth and when they are hungry sometimes they eat the paint on their bars – tell them not to do that.
- They need water every day – you have to fill up the bottle and they suck the water out when the blobs come.
- You have to fill the food bowl up to the top.
- They have to have tissues and paper for their bed – they tear it up.
- Don't put hay in because it pokes their eyes.
- They have to have sawdust on the floor.
- They have to live inside – they can't go outside.
- When you take them home, don't put them on the back seat because the sun gets in their eyes and makes them poorly. Put them in the boot.
- If they get stuck on the high floor, don't worry because they can jump.
- Check that the door is closed so they can't escape.
- If they do a poo on the bridge, put a glove on and throw it in the bin.

Figure 6.8b Care instructions for the gerbil-Adults scribings of child's comments as she made the marks

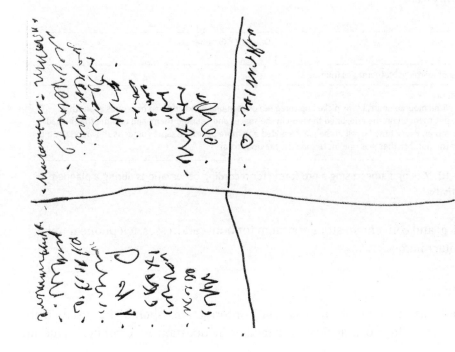

Figure 6.8a Writing care instructions for the gerbil

<u>17 September (construction area)</u>

Isaac spent 20 minutes building a jungle with a group of children. He contributed lots of ideas during discussions about plans and use of materials. He suggested making a waterfall using blue cellophane and white crepe paper and when it was finished he commented, 'It looks splashy'.

Isaac continued to play with the jungle for 10 minutes after the other children had left the area – he built a 'sand mountain' (using a toy lorry and orange tissue paper) and a bridge so that the animals could 'go and have their babies there'. Isaac was keen to talk to Mrs R. about the jungle and introduced the animal characters to her before explaining where they all lived. He then went on to tell her about the small elephant's adventure (using the toy elephant to demonstrate actions):

'He was running, he lost his mummy. He went up the rocks and he fell down the waterfall. It was like a slide. Then he saw his mummy and he was happy.'

<u>Expressive arts and design (being imaginative):</u>

Isaac used one object to represent another (e.g. tissue as sand). He introduced a story line into his play and entered into dialogue about his creation.

Figure 6.9 Jungle play in the construction area: observation (see Chapter 3, page 90 for 'Jungle Play' activity plan)

Name: Lewis	Date: 23rd October 2012
Key area of learning: Mathematics (numbers)	

Observation:
Playing with coloured bears, Lewis picked up three red ones in one hand and two blue ones in another. He then put them all on the grid, lined them up in the spaces and counted them, and told me that he had five altogether. Every time he rolled the die, he added one more bear (the same colour as shown on the die) and said the number that was one more than the previous total.

Figure 6.10 Making games: using a pro forma for recording observations during a planned focus activity

a practical and convenient storage system for home addresses, telephone numbers and contact names.

Tick lists

Tick lists as a method of recording information should be used with caution. A tick in a box against a statement or question is of limited value in communicating information about a child – children's learning rarely progresses in 'boxed' stages.

If this method is used, it should always be supported by observations which offer an explanation of context and a more accurate assessment of learning. Sometimes it can be useful to transfer certain information from a number of observations onto one 'check list' record sheet to give an overview of, for example, how many children observed playing in the home corner used the mark-making equipment in that area. This could help practitioners in assessing how provision is being used. It can be useful to keep a tick list record of profile entries so that practitioners can see at a glance whether or not a child has been observed recently in a particular area of provision or learning. It may also be necessary to provide summary information for whole groups or classes for another setting and this may be presented on an overview grid (see 'Summative reporting').

Another circumstance in which the use of a tick list might be justified is when children are required to register their presence in an area – this is often done by making a mark, or tick, next to their name. This type of record will only tell the practitioner that the child has been in the area, not what she or he has done or learnt.

Tracking progress and summative reporting

Each child's learning should be reviewed at key points during the year. During such reviews, practitioners will make written records, although it would be a daunting task to commit to paper all that they know about the child! Information and evidence collected in profiles and through other assessments should be used to inform practitioners and support them in producing an accurate summary. Parents should be involved in the process of reviewing the child's learning and progress, and in planning next steps. These periodic reviews may be kept in the child's profile or learning journey showing very clearly the link between assessment and planning.

Many settings implement a policy of summarising what they know about children after the first few weeks following entry. This then provides a baseline from which practitioners are able to plan for children's learning, plot their progress and identify areas for further support. It is important, considering the variation in starting points for children, that these areas are carefully assessed using observational evidence gathered during the first weeks in the setting, relevant information from home and any available information from previous settings. It is unlikely, if there is no previous information available, that practitioners will have collected useful information on a very young child (e.g. a three-year-old entering nursery provision for the first time) in all aspects of learning within, for example, a six-week period, and teams will probably prioritise areas such as personal, social and emotional development, communication skills and physical development in the first summary. Indeed, undue pressure to collect information across a wide number of areas in a short space of time may lead to inappropriate practice. However, where information is available from a previous setting, this should be taken into account when making initial assessments. For example, reception staff making on entry assessments of children who had attended the school nursery class, would be equipped with a more sound knowledge of the child's capabilities following consultation with each child's previous key person and having read any written records that were passed on at the time of transfer. In cases where children appear to have regressed, staff can then consider influencing factors and take steps to support the child appropriately. It may be that the child's well-being has dipped and that they are not able to demonstrate competences until they feel more secure and confident, or it may be that the new provision does not offer contexts in which the child has opportunities to show what they really know and understand.

Summaries at key points throughout the child's time in the setting may include information on personal interests (at home as well as in the setting) and emotional well-being. Where teams are using involvement signs and scales, this information may also be included (see also page 194). Such summaries should be shared with

MONTHLY SUMMARY		
Child's name: Kada	**Key person:** Emma	**Date:** 30 November 2012

What has been significant in Kada's learning and development this month?

Kada has been enjoying the rhyme books in the book corner and joining in enthusiastically with action rhymes at group time. Mum says she teaches the rhymes she has learnt at nursery to her at home. Mum has taught her a couple from her own childhood too. Recently Kada has begun to notice when two words rhyme. She is showing an interest in counting in her play and can usually count four objects saying one number name for each. She is very proud of herself that she can now climb up to, and jump off, the second log in the outdoor area without any help!

How will we respond to extend her learning?

We will extend Kada's learning at nursery and at home by playing rhyme games with her, encouraging her to change rhymes' endings and continue rhyming strings. Mum will buy Kada a rhyme book from Santa at Christmas. Emma will provide interesting things for Kada to count (e.g. buttons, shells) and will spend time playing with her using the language of number. At home, Mum will take opportunities to count with Kada, e.g. when shopping, counting steps going up the stairs, chimes of the clock. We will continue to encourage her, and build her confidence, as she challenges herself physically.

Figure 6.11 Example of an individual monthly summary

parents, perhaps at meetings with the child's key person, and will be used to inform planning for the child's play and learning over the next few weeks.

> Children's progress should not be viewed as a 'race to the goals'. The extent of children's progress relates mainly to the quality of teaching and the impact this has on children's progress.
>
> (Ofsted 2012a)

In order to create a clear picture of children's progress over time, a system will need to be embedded that requires the key person to make judgements about a child's stage of development against aspects of learning at key points, for example every term (or half-term if this is manageable within the setting). These summative assessments will be informed by ongoing assessments including written observations and practitioner and parent knowledge. For children over three, it is reasonable to expect information about all 17 aspects across the seven areas of learning unless the child has recently entered the setting and there is not enough information available in which case the three prime areas should be prioritised. Teams, or local authorities, may agree ways in which to identify smaller progress steps within the developmental bands although these decisions need careful consideration and a 'best fit' approach to judgements should be implemented rather than a 'check list' approach.

> The development statements and their order should not be taken as necessary steps for individual children. They should not be used as checklists.
>
> (DfE, Development Matters in the Early Years Foundation Stage, 2012)

An individual child's progress tracking record need not be a lengthy document and a simple table on an A4 sheet of paper should suffice. If it includes an entry (or 'base line') assessment and then a judgement for each aspect each term, the key person will easily be able to view progress from starting points and, over time, identify gaps in learning and highlight areas in which the child may need more support or challenge. It is important that the key person is aware of the child's chronological age in months and asks the question 'Is the child meeting age-related expectations?' once the summative assessments have been made. Where a child is falling below age-related expectations, the setting will want to see rapid progress in order to offer the child the best opportunities for the future and planning should reflect strategies to support such progress. Of course, the setting will aim to see all children making good or outstanding progress and a clear, manageable tracking system is a key component in keeping a sharp focus on progress.

Information from individual tracking sheets can then be collated onto a group tracker and with children organised, for example, in school cohorts. These will show, at a glance, patterns or trends across a group, and perhaps the whole setting. This data should be analysed looking at the attainment and progress of particular groups within the larger group (such as boys, girls, summer-born children, children with

English as an additional language) and at attainment within each strand of learning. Group trackers can also show shifts in a group, for example the percentage of children meeting or exceeding age-related expectations at the beginning of the year compared with the percentage at the end of the year. Findings will support teams in improving provision, focusing planning and identifying staff training needs.

In reporting upon children's progress to parents, the emphasis should be on informal discussion, and the two-way *sharing* of information, at regular intervals throughout the child's time in the setting. Written, summative reports to parents are produced in most settings as a child moves onto to the next room or class or setting but should be in addition to the before-mentioned discussions.

Reports should be always be written in a positive way, with the emphasis on the child's achievements and interests. The way in which content is organised in the report will vary between settings. There is likely to be information about the child's interests and a summary of achievements and progress within some or all areas of learning. There may also be space allowed for an example of the child's work, comments from the child and parents, and for identifying 'next steps'. It will be necessary, as pointed out in Chapter 4, to make time for discussion of the content of the report between parent and practitioner. Where there are concerns about a child's learning and development, the written report is not the place to introduce these to parents. The key person should be talking to parents frequently and any concerns will have been raised and discussed before the report is written.

It is good practice, in the interests of continuity, to make communication links between settings, and practitioners should give careful consideration to what, and how, information is passed between professionals. A copy of the written summative report will usually be sent on to the next setting, often supported by samples from the child's profile. This system of reporting will be strengthened and supported if a more interactive approach to the 'passing on' of information is also in operation. Discussions between practitioners prior to the child's transition, and the sharing of profiles, can be very productive and illuminating. Teams should be aspiring to build positive and professional relationships with all settings from whom they receive children, and to whom they pass on children. There should be opportunities for children to visit their new settings and for practitioners (preferably including the child's new key person) to visit the child in his current setting. Other activities planned to support children through the transition process can help them to understand and make sense of changing situations. Books containing photographs of school buildings, classroom provision and staff enable children to revisit experiences following visits to schools and are a talking point for children and adults. The provision of 'school equipment' in a nursery setting prior to starting school (such as book bags, uniform and school dinner trays at meal times) can help to take away some of the anxiety around the unfamiliar. The nature of any follow-up support after transfer to a new setting will vary. A telephone call from the previous key person to the new key person may establish that all is well and no further action is needed. Whatever the situation, it is crucial that channels of communication are always kept open and that all practitioners recognise the importance of working together with a seamless approach to ensuring children's emotional well-being. Particularly where children have been in full day care and made very close attachments to key people in that setting, the transition can be difficult. Transition policies should genuinely address the needs and take into account the circumstance of the children concerned and not merely be about the passing on of written records on transfer.

Guidelines for writing summative reports

Consider these points when summarising a child's achievements and reporting on their progress:

- Remember the audiences you are writing for – information should be accessible and useful to both parents and practitioners.

- Summarise what you know about children in positive terms following discussions with key workers and other members of the team.

- Summaries should relate to the EYFS curriculum but should also be individual to the child. Use the language from the Development Matters grids where appropriate and illustrate some points with examples of what the child has actually done or said (probably quoted from profiles).

Make sure that reports reflect the individual interests and preferences of the child:

- To differentiate your statements further, tag on words and phrases such as 'occasionally', 'often', 'confidently', 'with support'.

- Include relevant information about learning at home and ask for parents' comments.

- When you have completed a report, ask a colleague who knows the child well to read it through and make any suggestions as to how the statements could give a more accurate or individual summary.

When passing on information between settings within the EYFS, particularly when children transfer from a nursery setting to the reception class, it can be useful to provide a group summary overview of where you assess individuals in terms of learning and development. Obviously such summaries should be backed by observation-based evidence.

The Early Years Foundation Stage Profile

Practitioners should build their knowledge of what each child knows and can do over the course of the year, so that they can make an accurate end of year judgement.

(Standards and Testing Agency 2013)

There is a statutory requirement to make summary assessments of children's learning and development at two key points during the EYFS. The first of these is the progress check between the age of two and three and the second is the assessment that takes place in the final term of the year in which the child reaches age five, the Early Years Foundation Stage Profile (see Early Years Foundation Stage Profile 2013 for exceptions and exemptions).

The EYFS Profile includes a summary of a child's attainment in all 17 aspects of the prime and specific areas of learning and a description of the ways in which a child learns based on the characteristics of effective learning (playing and exploring, active learning and creating and thinking critically). In areas of learning, judgements are made against the early learning goals and levels of development described as 'emerging', 'expected' or 'exceeding'.

Throughout the EYFS framework, there is an emphasis on continuity and smooth transitions. The principle of starting with what the child already knows and understands when planning to support his next steps is clearly evident and observation continues to be the key to successful assessment for learning. A main aim of the EYFS profile is to provide information that will support Year 1 teachers in planning an appropriate curriculum that will match the children's individual needs and stage of learning and development. Year 1 teachers must be given a copy of the Profile with the summary of how the child demonstrates the three characteristics of effective learning.

The general principles of good assessment practice apply just as directly to the EYFS Profile as they do throughout the earlier stages of the EYFS and beyond it. Good provision and practice, informed by a sound pedagogy, should provide the basis for all assessment as discussed earlier in this chapter. If a summary assessment is to give an accurate picture of a child's learning and development at a particular point in time, it should take into account information from a number of perspectives (including that of the child and the parents) and contexts. Of course, written observations are important and will form part of the picture but practitioners, and other adults close to the child, will know so much more than what is written down. It is the bringing together of all this knowledge about the child that will lead to reliable judgements. Contexts for assessment should be sympathetic to the child's stage of development and interests, and judgements should reflect embedded learning.

> Practitioners should reflect on their observations and ensure that the provision enables all children, regardless of their stage of development or interests, needs and inclinations, to demonstrate attainment in ways that are motivating to them.
>
> (Early Years Foundation Stage Profile Handbook 2013)

In order to ensure that summary information is accurate and credible, systems for moderating assessments should be in place. As with any assessment procedures, practitioners within settings and across settings need time to discuss sample observations and agree judgements. Only when a shared understanding of what is sound evidence towards each early learning goal has been developed, will the data generated be reliable. Providers have an obligation to reports EYFS Profile results to local authorities on request. The local authority has a responsibility to review EYFS Profile data produced by settings and to be part of an effective moderation process checking that teachers are able to make accurate judgements through training and cycles of visits.

To recap, observation and assessment are extremely important aspects of the early years practitioner's role but they are not an end in themselves. In fact, they are only the start. They are tools to be used by the practitioner to make sure that the environment, the planning of activities and experiences, and the adult guidance are all tailored to meet the needs of children and successfully support their learning and progress.

> Simply gathering information about a child is not enough. It is how the information is used to affect children's opportunities and experiences which makes a difference to their learning and development.
>
> (Department for Children, Schools and Families 2009)

KEY POINTS FOR GOOD PRACTICE

- Recognise the importance of observation as part of the teaching role and plan time to observe children.

- Assess children's learning based on observations made in a meaningful and purposeful context for the child. It is when children are deeply involved in their learning that you will find out what they really know and understand.

- Observe children in a number of different contexts before making final assessments to be sure that learning is firmly embedded.

- When recording observations of children's learning, be concise but include relevant information about context. To make assessments easier, and if appropriate, use language from the 'A Unique Child' in Development Matters for aspects of learning.

- Think about how children's learning over time, and repeated actions or interests are documented.

- Gather information about 'how' children learn (the characteristics of effective learning) as well as 'what' they learn.

- Remember the importance of viewing a child's learning and development holistically when making assessments.

- Use assessments to inform your planning of children's next steps. Sometimes, 'next steps' will mean moving forward perhaps into the next developmental stage. However, children often need more learning experiences with a similar objective in a range of different contexts to ensure that their understanding is embedded. They may also need to revisit the same activity or experience to consolidate what they have learnt and to develop ideas.

- Make time for moderation discussions to ensure consistency and accuracy. Compile a portfolio of evidence using observations of children in the setting.

- Make sure you are aware of children's 'starting points' before being in a position to comment on their progress.

- Recognise the importance of using information from previous settings when planning support for new children.

- Remember that children's learning takes place wherever they are – at home, school, in the supermarket, on a walk to the park. Never underestimate the importance of listening and talking to children, parents and carers in order to build up a whole picture of children's achievements and needs.

- Value the contribution of the child's parents and the child in the planning and reviewing of IEPs. Remember the parent's right to be involved in this process.

- Remember that for children diagnosed with special educational needs and disability (SEND) the family may have an Early Support file. This may provide very useful information for the practitioner about the child's condition so it is a good idea to ask about it.

- Set up effective systems for collecting and collating evidence that work for the whole team.

- Share summary information about your assessments of children's achievements and progress with parents and next settings.

In concluding this chapter, the following extract from Mary Jane Drummond's book *Assessing Children's Learning* is offered as a summary of the purpose and role of assessment in the foundation stage:

> In assessment, we can appreciate and understand what children learn; we can recognise their achievements, and their individuality, the differences between them. We can use our assessments to shape and enrich our curriculum, our interactions, our provision as a whole; we can use our assessments as a way of identifying what children will be able to learn next, so that we can support and extend that learning. Assessment is part of our daily practice in striving for quality.
>
> (Drummond 1993)

Notes

1 See SEN Code of Practice (DfES 2001) for categories of special educational needs.
2 Other observations of children's use of water provision (made over a period of four weeks) were also considered as the team discussed implications for the future – it is advisable to make a series of observations when assessing provision in order to be sure that the full picture is reflected.

CHAPTER 7

Looking forward

A quality learning experience for children requires a quality workforce.... Providers should regularly consider the training and development needs of all staff members to ensure they offer a quality experience for children that continually improves.

(Department for Education 2012)

Having looked in depth at the role of practitioners in early years rooms, it only remains to highlight the importance of effective leadership and management in supporting this good practice.

The content of this chapter is organised as follows:

- Leadership for learning (page 219)
- Moving forward with colleagues (page 220)
- Development planning (page 222)
- Action planning (page 223)
- Post-inspection action plans (page 224)

Leadership for learning

Excellent pedagogical leadership is vital in improving the quality of provision.

(Nutbrown, 2012)

All practitioners in a setting have a crucial part to play in offering high-quality provision, experiences and opportunities to the children in their care. Indeed, the relationship between key person and child, and the teamwork between practitioners, are integral to children's positive experiences in they early years but, unless the setting is led with vision, passion and a commitment to quality, there is a limit to the impact individuals can have on long-term developments in practice. It is the responsibility of leadership and management teams to ensure that all statutory requirements are understood and met, and that effective programmes for learning are promoted within a safe context where children's welfare and well-being are of paramount importance. The most successful settings are those which benefit from the combination of inspirational leaders and effective managers working with capable teams for a common purpose.

Leaders and managers have the overview of practice across the setting and it is they who can, and should, ensure that a consistent and principled approach is adhered to by all. They are responsible for knowing that policies and procedures support good practice and for promoting effective partnerships with parents and external agencies.

Of course, all staff should be part of change processes and feel ownership of developments; their contributions of new ideas should be encouraged and respected and they should feel valued as professionals. Effective leadership is not about dictating (although there will be expectations that are non-negotiable); it is about motivating, coaching and leading by example. There will be management issues that impact significantly on the smooth running of the setting and also on the capacity of the setting to maintain quality in terms of children's learning and to sustain improvements; for example shift patterns should, where possible, ensure that a child's key person or significant second is available at dropping off and picking up times, systems for staff supervisions should be effective in supporting training.

The most effective leaders and managers have ambition for their setting. They strive for outstanding provision. They do not settle for mediocre, or even good, but reach for the quality that will enable every child, and practitioner, to achieve their potential. They have high expectations of themselves, their staff and the children in their care and they are accountable for the practice within their setting. They continuously reflect and review, monitoring and evaluating to find even more successful ways of ensuring that children make good progress and are offered the best possible opportunities for life.

Moving forward with colleagues

Good teamwork is essential if a setting is to provide a rich and secure environment for young children, and to make positive steps forward. All staff should be purposefully involved in discussions and decision-making about curricular and organisational issues, and about long-term developments. Such involvement will encourage attitudes of commitment and self-confidence, and will ensure a firm understanding of the aims of the setting by all staff, irrespective of background or current responsibilities.

There is much to be gained from the sharing of knowledge and ideas between colleagues. The strengths, skills, training and experience of all individuals should be valued and used to enrich and fortify the team as a whole. Roles should be complementary, not conflicting, and teams built on a foundation of:

- Communication
- Cooperation
- Respect
- Support.

> 'If you value and respect yourself, you will do the same to others.
>
> Professional relationships focus on respecting and valuing the strengths, skills and knowledge of the people you work with and recognising the contribution made by everyone in your setting.
>
> There should be open communication to ensure that everyone's views are listened to and considered fairly, always keeping the needs of the children firmly in mind.'
>
> Principles into Practice card 2.1. Positive Relationships: Respecting Each Other
>
> (DfES Publications 2007)

Communication between practitioners need not be restricted to the immediate team within which individuals work on a day-to-day basis. Indeed there are many childminders who spend much of their working time as the only adult with a group of children. The wider 'network' of practitioners offers a rich source of professional support. Inter-setting meetings, or visits to other settings during the working day, can prove to be both informative and stimulating. Meetings may be used as a forum for the sharing of good practice or the discussion of new initiatives, legislation and policies; practitioners can decide their own agenda, addressing issues of interest or concern to them in their situation.

> The daily experiences of children in early years settings and the overall quality of provision depends on all practitioners having appropriate qualifications, training, skills and knowledge and a clear understanding of their roles and responsibilities.
>
> (DfE 2012)

In order to build a 'balanced' team with expertise and knowledge across a range of areas, a programme of professional development for staff will need to be planned. This programme should allow scope for individual professional interests to be developed as well as addressing the needs of the whole team and setting. This is an area which should be considered in the long term so that all needs are coordinated and met over a period of time. Professional development can take a number of forms and practitioners will make judgements regarding suitability according to the content of the learning, the prior training and experience of the individual or individuals involved, the convenience of the timings (e.g. organisation of staff release time or cover) and cost. However, it should be said that, if a team has a serious commitment to staff development, and a clear view of the way forward, every effort will be made to find appropriate routes for development. It is a good idea to 'appoint' a member of the team as the person responsible for collating and presenting information about professional development opportunities. It may be that the local education authority offers courses or workshops tailored to the identified needs of the team, or that arranged visits to, for example, other agencies to learn about services offered, may be more useful.

Working in genuine partnership with other professionals should be an aspiration, if not a reality, for all settings. Children's Centres particularly are focused very clearly on multi-agency working and teams may include family outreach workers, health visitors and social care professionals. Effective communication between professionals, and an integrated approach from all those involved, not only impact positively on experiences and outcomes for children and families, but also create a rich and fertile context for professional development.

It is also useful to consider the value of delegation in supporting professional development within the team. Delegating tasks and roles should not be undertaken in a random or impulsive way but should be planned carefully. Busy managers sometimes need to hand over responsibilities to enable them to perform their own specific management duties efficiently and effectively. They should resist the temptation to 'cling on' to too many tasks themselves in order to 'get the job done properly' or to maintain unnecessary control. Taking on a delegated responsibility can be a great opportunity for a practitioner to develop their own learning, experience and confidence but it has to be the right responsibility, and the right time, for that practitioner. It is the manager's job to ensure that the practitioner is clear about new responsibilities, supported in their new learning and enabled to be successful in the role.

Development planning

Practitioners should be constantly evaluating the service that is offered to children and parents, looking for ways to develop the setting. It is never possible to sit back and think that the job of planning for young children's learning is complete; a 'static' setting is inevitably a stale environment, unlikely to inspire children or adults.

Development is about:

- Evolving
- Growing
- Advancing.

Some decisions regarding improvements will be made from day to day, and others as immediate needs arise, but, in order to organise and integrate needs and successfully effect improvements, practitioners will need to agree a longer-term plan for development. This plan will identify where the setting is at the starting point, and where practitioners intend it to be at the end of, for example, three years. It will broadly outline steps to be taken, and changes to be made, during that period. Development planning can be used to address issues such as curriculum development, staff development, organisation of staffing, building maintenance and alteration, and is about having a 'vision' for the future of the setting.

There will probably be many potential areas for development and prioritising can be difficult. Some will be obviously urgent and take priority; others will have to be 'put on hold' or scheduled for a later date. Sometimes a weakness will have been identified and the relevant area targeted for improvement; in other cases, practitioners will plan to build on successes. It is important to be realistic and guard against trying to tackle too much in a short space of time; targets should be manageable and organised in a time sequence.

When making decisions, practitioners should take into account factors such as the following:

- Financial constraints
- Expertise available
- Introduction of, for example, new government requirements
- Communication systems
- Time constraints
- Other responsibilities and commitments.

Although plans will span a period of up to five years, they should be viewed as working documents and reviewed and amended in progress. For example, at the end of year one in a three-year plan, practitioners should evaluate success, revising the plan as necessary for years two and three, and perhaps adding targets for an additional year.

Action planning

Through the process of development planning, practitioners make decisions about *what* needs to be done in order to move the setting forward. Action planning is the process by which they clarify *how* improvements will be realised in practice. For example, practitioners may take an area targeted for development and draw up a programme for the forthcoming year. In their plan they will define:

- Key issue
- Objectives
- Action to be taken
- Roles and responsibilities

- Resource implications
- Criteria for success
- Monitoring success: responsibilities and methods
- Time scales.

If a plan is to be implemented smoothly, all involved adults will need to be part of the planning process throughout and should fully understand their responsibilities. A commitment from all parties is necessary in order to effect a successful outcome within the allotted period of time.

Post-inspection action plans

Post-inspection action plans are about making improvements in areas where weaknesses have been identified during an Ofsted inspection. It may be that some of the issues for concern have already been recognised by the practitioner, or team of practitioners, and steps taken to address them but a 'post-inspection action plan' is a statement of how the practitioner intends to address the key issues identified during the inspection. It will probably include short-, medium- and long-term intentions and should aim to have successfully achieved all targets within a year.

Although the core principles of good early years practice remain constant, Early Years Foundation Stage practitioners find themselves in a period of policy change and revised frameworks, and it is to their credit that they embrace initiatives with commitment and an open mind. The workforce is widening to include new roles and responsibilities and the introduction of new positions may change the dynamics within teams. The need for respect between professionals is greater than ever and often the demands on individuals are manageable only when support from colleagues is strong. In striving to keep abreast of developments in local and national policy, and to be practising in accordance with current thinking, it is easy to lose direction or cohesion as a team. Practitioners should give priority to developing a shared ethos and moving forward together. Above all they need to invest in time for talking and listening to each other. Only when effective team and interagency work is established, and with strong leadership and management, can settings hope to offer children and families the service they deserve and move towards achieving the best outcomes for all children.

> Working as a team is a process not a technique. It is rooted in an ideology of empowerment, encouraging adults (whether parents or staff) to take control of their own lives and giving children permission to do the same.
>
> (Whalley in Pugh 1996)

Bibliography

Abbot, L. and Nutbrown, C. (eds) (2001) *Experiencing Reggio Emilia*, Buckingham: Open University Press.

Abbot, L. and Rodger, R. (eds) (1994) *Quality Education in the Early Years*, Buckingham: Open University Press.

Anning, A. (ed.) (1994) *The First Years at School*, Buckingham: Open University Press.

Anning, A. (1999) *Promoting Children's Learning from Birth to Five: Developing the New Early Years Professional*, Buckingham: Open University Press.

Athey, C. (1990) *Extending Thought in Young Children: A Parent Teacher Partnership*, London: Paul Chapman Publishing.

Bennet, N., Wood, L. and Rogers, S. (1997) *Teaching Through Play: Teachers' Thinking and Classroom Practice*, Buckingham: Open University Press.

Blenkin, G. M. and Kelly, A. V. (eds) (1992) *Assessment in Early Childhood Education*, London: Paul Chapman Publishing.

Blenkin, G. M. and Kelly, A. V. (eds) (1996) *Early Childhood Education: A Developmental Curriculum*, 2nd edn, London: Paul Chapman Publishing.

Bruce, T. (1987) *Early Childhood Education*, Kent: Hodder & Stoughton.

Bruce, T. (1997) *Early Childhood Education*, 2nd edn, London: Hodder & Stoughton.

Bruce, T. (2001) *Learning Through Play*, Kent: Hodder & Stoughton.

Carr, M. (2001) *Assessment in Early Childhood Settings*, London: Paul Chapman Publishing.

Chapman, L. (1978) *Approaches to Art in Education*, New York: Harcourt Brace Jovanovich.

Cullingford, C. (1997) *Assessment Versus Evaluation*, London: Cassell.

Curtis, A. (1998) *A Curriculum for the Pre-School Child*, 2nd edn, London: Routledge.

Children's Workforce and Development Council (2007) *Guidance to the Standards for the Award of Early Years Professional Status*.

David, T. (1990) *Under Five – Under Educated?*, Buckingham: Open University Press.

Bibliography

Department for Children, Schools and Families (2007) *The Early Years Foundation Stage*, London: DCSF.

Department for Children, Schools and Families (2008a) *Early Years Quality Improvement Support Programme (EYQISP)*, London: DCSF.

Department for Children, Schools and Families (2008b) *The Impact of Parental Involvement on Children's Education*, London: DCSF.

Department for Children, Schools and Families (2009) *Progress Matters*, London: DCSF.

Department of Education and Science (1967) *Children and Their Primary Schools: A Report of the Central Advisory Council for Education (England)*, London: HMSO (The Plowden Report).

Department of Education and Science (1990) *Starting with Quality: The Report of the Committee of Inquiry into the Quality of Educational Experience Offered to 3 and 4 year Olds*, London: HMSO (The Rumbold Report).

DfES (1999) *Early Learning Goals*, London: Qualifications and Curriculum Authority. London: DfES.

DfES (2000) *Curriculum Guidance for the Foundation Stage*, London: Qualifications and Curriculum Authority.

DfES (2001) *Special Educational Needs Code of Practice*, London: Qualifications and Curriculum Authority.

DfES (2007) *Letters and Sounds: Principles and Practice of High Quality Phonics*, London: DfES.

DfES (2007) The Early Years Foundation Stage: *Practice Guidance for the Early Years Foundation Stage.*

DfES (2007) The Early Years Foundation Stage: *Statutory Framework for the Early Years Foundation Stage.*

Department for Education (DfE) (2012) *Statutory Framework for the Early Years Foundation Stage,* London: DfE.

Drake, J. (2003) *Organising Play in the Early Years*, London: David Fulton Publishers.

Drifte, C. (2002) *Early Learning Goals for Children with Special Needs*, London: David Fulton Publishers.

Drummond, M. J. (1993) *Assessing Children's Learning*, London: David Fulton Publishers.

Duffy, B. (1998) *Supporting Creativity and Imagination in the Early Years*, Buckingham: Open University Press.

Early Education: The British Association for Early Childhood Education (2012) *Development Matters in the Early Years Foundation Stage* (EYFS).

Edgington, M. (1998) *The Nursery Teacher in Action*, London: Paul Chapman Publishing.

Field, F. (2010) *The Foundation Years: Preventing Poor Children Becoming Poor Adults*, London: H.M. Government.

Fisher, J. (1996) *Starting from the Child?*, Buckingham: Open University Press.

Fisher, R. (1990) *Teaching Children to Think*, first published by Basil Blackwell, reprinted (1995), Cheltenham: Stanley Thornes.

Foster, J. (1991) *Twinkle, Twinkle Chocolate Bar*, Oxford: Oxford University Press.

Hall, N. (1987) *The Emergence of Literacy*, London: Hodder & Stoughton.

Hurst, V. (1991) *Planning for Early Learning: Education in the First Five Years*, London: Paul Chapman Publishing.

Hurst, V. and Lally, M. (1992) 'Assessment and the nursery curriculum' in Blenkin, G. M. and Kelly, A. V. (eds) *Assessment in Early Childhood Education*, Ch. 3, London: Paul Chapman Publishing.

Isaacs, S. (1929) *The Nursery Years: The Mind of the Child from Birth to 6 Years*, London: Routledge & Kegan Paul.

Kress, G. (1997) *Before Writing – Rethinking the Paths to Literacy*, London: Routledge.

Lancaster, J. (1990) *Art in the Primary School*, London: Routledge.

Laevers, F. (1994) *The Leuven Involvement Scale for Young Children*, Leuven, Belgium: Centre for Experiential Education.

Laevers, F. (1997) *A Process-oriented Child Monitoring System for Young Children*, Belgium: Leuven University.

Leeds Early Years Partnership Advisory Team (2004) *Exploring Outdoor Learning*, Leeds: Leeds City Council.

Lindon, J. (1997) *Working with Young Children*, 3rd edn, London: Hodder & Stoughton.

Lindsay, G. and Desforges, M. (1998) *Baseline Assessment: Practice, Problems and Possibilities*, London: David Fulton Publishers.

Macintyre, C. (2002) *Play for Children with Special Needs*, London: David Fulton Publishers.

Miller, L., Drury, R. and Campbell, R. (2002) *Exploring Early Years Education and Care*, London: David Fulton Publishers.

Moyles, J. R. (1989) *Just Playing*, Buckingham: Open University Press.

Moyles, J. R. (1994) *The Excellence of Play*, Buckingham: Open University Press.

National Society for Education in Art and Design (NSEAD), Lancaster, J. (ed.) (1987) *Art, Craft and Design in the Primary School*, 2nd edn Corsham: NSEAD.

Nutbrown, C. (1999) *Threads of Thinking*, 2nd edn, London: Paul Chapman Publishing.

Nutbrown, C. (2006) *Threads of Thinking*, 3rd edn, London: Sage Publications.

Nutbrown, C. (2012) *Foundations for Quality*, London: DfE.

Nutbrown, C. and Page, J. (2008) *Working with Babies and Children from Birth to Three*, London: Sage Publications.

Bibliography

Office for Standards in Education (1999) *Handbook for Inspecting Primary and Nursery Schools with Guidance on Self-evaluation,* London: HMSO.

Office for Standards in Education (2000a) *Are You Ready for Inspection? A Guide for Nursery Education Providers in the Private, Voluntary and Independent Sectors,* London: Ofsted, HMSO.

Office for Standards in Education (2000b) *Handbook for Inspecting Nursery Education in the Private, Voluntary and Independent Sectors including the Inspection Framework,* London: Ofsted, HMSO.

Office for Standards in Education (2012a) *Conducting Early Years Inspections,* London: Ofsted.

Office for Standards in Education (2012b) *Evaluation Schedule for Inspections of Registered Early Years Provision,* London: Ofsted.

Ouvry, M. (2000) *Exercising Muscles and Minds,* London: The National Early Years Network, reprinted by National Children's Bureau, 2003.

Perry, R. (1997) *Teaching Practice – A Guide for Early Childhood Students,* London: Routledge.

Piaget, J. (1962) *Play Dreams and Imitation in Childhood,* London: Routledge & Kegan Paul.

Pugh, G. (ed.) (1996) *Contemporary Issues in the Early Years: Working Collaboratively for Children,* London: Paul Chapman Publishing.

Rosen, M. and Steele, S. (1993) *Inky Pinky Ponky.* London: Picture Lions.

Standards and Testing Agency (2013) *Early Years Foundation Stage Profile Handbook,* London: Standards and Testing Agency.

Stewart, N. (2011) *How Children Learn: The Characteristics of Effective Learning,* London: British Association for Early Childhood Education.

Sylva, K., Melhuish, E. C., Sammons, P., Siraj-Blatchford, I. and Taggart, B. (2004) *The Effective Provision of Pre-school Education EPPE Project: Technical Paper 12 – The Final Report: Effective Pre-School Education,* London: DfES.

Teaching Agency (2012) *Early Years Professional Status Standards,* London: Teaching Agency.

Tickell, C. (2011) *The Early Years: Foundations for Life, Health and Learning,* London: DfE.

Whitebread, D. (ed.) (1996) *Teaching and Learning in the Early Years,* London: Routledge.

Index

Note: references in **bold** refer to illustrations and tables.

Index

creative development *see* expressive arts and design

cultural diversity 105–6, 172, 174, 178, 190

Curtis, A. 182

Dear Zoo 11

decision trees 159–61

den play 3–4, 10, 14–15, 46, 93–4, 173

Department for Children, Schools and Families 2009 217

Department of Education and Science xv, xvii; *see also* Principles into Practice cards

Development Matters in the Early Years Foundation Stage (*EYFS*), 2012 xvi, 6, 190, 194, 201, 213, 215, 217

development planning 222–3

displays for teaching and learning 156–82, **174, 177, 178**; celebratory displays 171–7; informative displays 9, 81, 87, 101–2, 133, 141, 177–9; interactive displays 58, 158–71; making displays 179–82; planning 156–8

displays of children's work 11, 17, 24, 40, 50n3, 62, 112

diversity 105–6

Dodd, Lynley 113

Dr. Seuss 113

Dragon Poems 113

Drummond, Mary Jane 218

Duffy, B. xviii

Each Peach Pear Plum 113

EAL (English as Additional Language) 104, 125, 157

early learning goals xvi, 97, 190, 206–7, 216–17; *see also* communication and language; expressive arts and design; literacy; mathematics; physical development; PSED (personal, social and emotional development); understanding the world; individual focus activities; individual provision areas

Early Years Foundation Stage (EYFS) xi, xii, xv, xvi, 140, 215–17

Emergence of Literacy, The 12

enabling environments xvi, 4, 41, 183, 201

engagement and motivation xvii, 104, 166, 183, 191, 194–5

Escher, M.C. (*Belvedere*) 114

exploring and using media and materials **48, 117**; focus activities for 75, 90, 92, 98, 107, 114, 119

expressive arts and design xvi, 97, 162, 169, 176, 177; displays 162, 165, 169, 173, 176;

focus activities for 75, 78, 90, 92, 97, 107, 114, 118; provision areas for 25, 36, 39; *see also* being imaginative; exploring and using media and materials

EYFS (Early Years Foundation Stage) *see* Early Years Foundation Stage (EYFS)

festivals 105–6

Field, F. 124

first contact 124–6, 184–6

Fisher, J. xvii, 147

Fisher, R. 123

Five Little Speckled Frogs 171

focus activities, examples: art-based 113–16; autumnal topics 57–8; bear hunt 82–4; *Belvedere* (Escher) 113–16; *Billy Goats Gruff* 107, 110; boat-making 73, 75–6; bridge building 107, 110; budding engineer 95–7, **96**; circle sessions 79–82; DIY enthusiasts 97–8, **98**; game-making 71–3, **74, 210**; goldfish poem 105; hats 172; house building 62; Jasper's birthday 69–71; jungle play 90–1, **210**; King Lanzarote 100–5, **100, 102, 103**; lion's visit 92–5; music-based 116, **117**; obstacle courses 82–4; Oscar the clown 150–3; Post Office 118–20; rhymes 111–13; snow 116, 120–2; spiders 59–60; story-based 107–11; story-making 76–9, **77**, 114–16, **115**; tadpoles 67; *Three Little Pigs* 62

focus activities: planning 51–68

Foster, John 112, 113

games 11, 45, 71–3

gross motor skills 42, 177

group development tracking 213–14

growing plants 10, 45–6

Hairy Maclary 113

Hall, Nigel 12

Handa's Surprise **108**

handwriting 12–13, 18; *see also* writing (literacy)

health & self-care **48**

Hill, Eric 170

home corners 10, 11, 14, **17**, 21, 34–8, 63, **63, 64**, 70–1

home: positive links with 124–55; first contact 124–6; good practice 154–5; link activities 150–4; settling-in 128–31; supporting and extending learning 133–50; *see also* parents/carers

Humpty Dumpty **111**, 112

Index

painting areas 38–41, **39**, 58, 98, 178–9

parents/carers: first contact 124–6, 184–6; home visits 126–8; information sharing 5, 9, 104, **137–8**, **139**, 140–5, **142–3**, **144–5**, **147**, **148**, 214, 218; involvement in focus activities 69, 70, 72, 81, 95–8, 102, 105, 211, 212–13; link activities 150–4; within the setting 129, 131–3, 141; supporting and extending learning 133–50

party celebrations 69–71, 101–2, 106

people and communities **48**, **117**

personal interest plans 56–7, 59–60

personal, social and emotional development (PSED) 79, **193**, 206, 211; displays 168, 172; focus activities for 59, 80–2, 90, **117**, 150–1; making relationships **48**, 49, 80, 90, **200**; managing feelings and behaviour **48**, 80, **117**; provision areas for 36, 46; self-confidence and self-awareness **48**

phonics 18, 32, **143**

physical development: displays 169, 177; focus activities for 70, 82, 97; health & self-care **48**; moving and handling 18, **48**, 59, 70, 82, 97, **117**, 197, **200**; provision areas for 32, 39, 42

planning xviii; action plans 223–4; for development 222–5; for displays 156–8; long-term planning 8–9, 21–41, **48**, 50, 72, 190–1; a responsive approach 55, 87–9, 98, **99**, 104–5, 122–3

Planning for Early Learning 186

play: importance of xv, xvii, xviii, 2, 8; *see also* observing children's play

playing and exploring xvii, 191, 216

Plowden Committee, 1967 xv

Principles into Practice cards xvii; enabling environments 4, 41, 183; learning and development 2, 189; positive relationships 52, 130, 134, 221; a unique child 7, 106, 131

profiles 104, 128, 131, 135, 144–6, 187, 196–207, 211, 215

provision areas: evaluating 190–1, 194–5, 211, 212, 214, 216, 218

provision areas: planning 1–50; adult roles in 4–6, 19; good practice 49–50; inside areas 9–21; for literacy and numeracy 12–19; long-term planning 21–41; for mathematical learning 19–21; outside areas 7, 41–9; for rest and relaxation 3–4; *see also* individual provision areas

PSED (personal, social and emotional development) *see* personal, social and emotional development (PSED)

question tables 167–8

rain play **99**

reading (literacy) 18–19, **117**; focus activities for 70, 112, 114, 119; provision areas for 16, 31, 32–4, 36, 44–5

reception classes 129, 130, 135, 212, 215

recording observations on play 195–215

relaxation times 3–4

resources: from home 146–7; for inside areas 9–21, 23; for outside areas 10, 12, 46–7; *see also* individual focus activities; individual provision areas

responsive planning 55, 87–9, 98, **99**, 104–5, 122–3

rest times 3–4

rhymes **108**, 111–13

risk assessments 49, 95

role-play 11, 14, 42, 46, 95; focus activities for 66, 69–71, 95–8, **109**, 114, 118–20, 201; *see also* home corner

Rosen and Steele 112

Rosen, M. 82–4

Rosie's Walk **108**

Round and Round the Garden 113

routines, auditing 5, 7, 49, 194

Rumbold Committee (1990) xvii

safety 49

sand play 2, 3, 9–10, 11, 13, **13**, **47**, **48**, 58, **99**, **205–6**

schemas 188–9

school readiness xvi–xvii; *see also* reception classes

self-confidence and self-awareness (PSED) **48**, 80

self-initiated learning *see* child-initiated learning

SEN (special educational needs) 2, 134, 189, 190, 218

Sendak, Maurice 46, **47**, 73, 75, **108**

settling-in 128–31, 188, 211

shadow play 46, **47**, 172

shape, space and measures (mathematics) 9–10, 19–20, 25, 29, 45–6, **48**, 57–9, 61, 72, **99**, 107, **142**, **200**

shared thinking 6, 60, 97

shelf displays 157, 181

snack times 6, 7

snow investigation 121–2

Snowman, The 116

speaking (communication and language) 18–19, **48**; focus activities for 90, 114, 121